My
iPad®
for Seniors

Gary Rosenzweig
Gary Jones

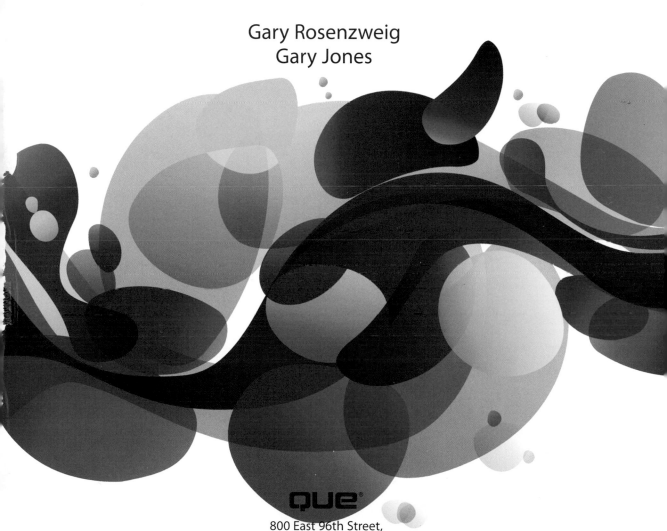

que®

800 East 96th Street,
Indianapolis, Indiana 46240 USA

My iPad® for Seniors

ISBN-13: 978-0-7897-5182-9

ISBN-10: 0-7897-5182-8

Library of Congress Control Number: 2013940575

Printed in the United States of America

Third Printing: February 2014

Trademarks

All terms mentioned in this book that are known to be trademarks or service marks have been appropriately capitalized. Que Publishing cannot attest to the accuracy of this information. Use of a term in this book should not be regarded as affecting the validity of any trademark or service mark.

Warning and Disclaimer

Every effort has been made to make this book as complete and as accurate as possible, but no warranty or fitness is implied. The information provided is on an "as is" basis. The author(s) and the publisher shall have neither liability nor responsibility to any person or entity with respect to any loss or damages arising from the information contained in this book.

Special Sales

For information about buying this title in bulk quantities, or for special sales opportunities (which may include electronic versions; custom cover designs; and content particular to your business, training goals, marketing focus, or branding interests), please contact our corporate sales department at corpsales@pearsoned.com or (800) 382-3419.

For government sales inquiries, please contact governmentsales@pearsoned.com.

For questions about sales outside the U.S., please contact international@pearsoned.com.

Editor-in-chief
Greg Wiegand

Senior Acquisitions Editor and Development Editor
Laura Norman

Managing Editor
Kristy Hart

Project Editor
Lori Lyons

Proofreader
Kathy Ruiz

Indexer
Erika Millen

Editorial Assistant
Cindy Teeters

Cover Designer
Mark Shirar

Compositor
Bronkella Publishing

Technical Editor
James Floyd Kelly

Graphics Technician
Tammy Graham

Contents at a Glance

Bonus Chapter, "Writing with Pages," available online.

Register your book at quepublishing.com/register for access to the bonus chapter.

Find this bonus chapter and other helpful information on this book's website at quepublishing.com/title/9780789751690.

Table of Contents

11   Enhancing Your Next Meal with Your iPad   271

12   Communicating with Your Loved Ones Using Your iPad   293

13   Finding and Using Apps for Entertainment   329

14 Keeping Informed Using News and Weather Apps   365

15 Using Apps That Help You Stay Healthy and Fit   389

About the Authors

Gary Rosenzweig is an Internet entrepreneur, software developer, and technology writer. He runs CleverMedia, Inc., which produces websites, computer games, apps, and podcasts. CleverMedia's largest site, MacMost.com, features video tutorials for Apple enthusiasts. It includes many videos on using Macs, iPhones, and iPads.

Gary has written numerous computer books, including *ActionScript 3.0 Game Programming University, MacMost.com Guide to Switching to the Mac, Special Edition Using Director MX,* and *My Pages (for Mac).*

Gary lives in Denver, Colorado, with his wife, Debby, and daughter, Luna. He has a computer science degree from Drexel University and a master's degree in journalism from the University of North Carolina at Chapel Hill.

Website: http://garyrosenzweig.com

Twitter: http://twitter.com/rosenz

More iPad Tutorials and Book Updates: http://macmost.com/ipadguide/

Gary Jones is a retired school administrator. In retirement he has become an avid traveler, foodie, rare book seller, and an individual who uses his iPad in most of his ventures. He runs Juniper Point Books, an online rare and used book business, travels the world attempting to live, shop, and eat like a local, occasionally provides educational consulting services, and works hard at retirement. Gary has degrees in English, philosophy, and a master's degree in school administration.

He lives in Round Lake, NY with his wife Susan, has two children, Karianne and Katelyn, and a dog Bubba.

Acknowledgments

Thanks, as always, to my wife, Debby, and my daughter, Luna. Also thanks to the rest of my family: Jacqueline Rosenzweig, Jerry Rosenzweig, Larry Rosenzweig, Tara Rosenzweig, Rebecca Jacob, Barbara Shifrin, Richard Shifrin, Barbara H. Shifrin, Tage Thomsen, Anne Thomsen, Andrea Thomsen, and Sami Balestri.

Thanks to all the people who watch the show and participate at the MacMost website.

—Gary Rosenzweig

Thanks to my wife Susan, for being on my team with all that we do.

—Gary Jones

Thanks to everyone at Pearson Education who worked on this book: Laura Norman, Lori Lyons, Tricia Bronkella, Kathy Ruiz, Kristy Hart, Cindy Teeters, Mark Shirar, and Greg Wiegand.

We Want to Hear from You!

As the reader of this book, *you* are our most important critic and commentator. We value your opinion and want to know what we're doing right, what we could do better, what areas you'd like to see us publish in, and any other words of wisdom you're willing to pass our way.

We welcome your comments. You can email or write to let us know what you did or didn't like about this book—as well as what we can do to make our books better.

Please note that we cannot help you with technical problems related to the topic of this book.

When you write, please be sure to include this book's title and author as well as your name, email address, and phone number. We will carefully review your comments and share them with the author and editors who worked on the book.

Email: feedback@quepublishing.com

Mail: Que Publishing
           ATTN: Reader Feedback
           800 East 96th Street
           Indianapolis, IN 46240 USA

Reader Services

Visit our website and register this book at quepublishing.com/register for convenient access to any updates, downloads, or errata that might be available for this book.

Learn to tap, swipe, flick, and pinch your way through the iPad's interface.

Learn to use the iPad's physical switches.

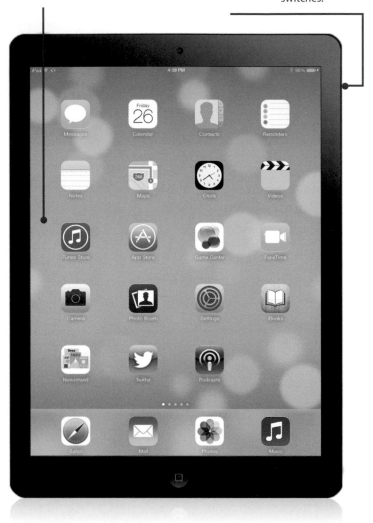

In this chapter, you learn how to perform specific tasks on your iPad to become familiar with the interface.

→ Generations of iPads

→ The iPad Buttons and Switches

→ Screen Gestures

→ iPad Screens

→ Interacting with Your iPad

→ Using Siri

→ Using Notifications Center

→ Using Control Center

Getting Started

Before you learn how to perform specific tasks on your iPad, you should become familiar with the interface. If you have used an iPhone or iPod touch, you already know the basics. But if the iPad is your first touch-screen device, you need to take time to become accustomed to interacting with it.

Generations of iPads

The first thing you may want to do is identify which iPad you have and what features are available to you. There have been many versions of the iPad: the iPad, the iPad 2, the 3rd and 4th generation iPads, the iPad Air (5th generation iPad) and two generations of the iPad mini.

Identifying Your iPad

The following table shows the major differences between these iPads:

iPad Comparison Chart

Model	Released	Display Size	Screen Resolution
iPad	April 2010	9.7-inch	768x1024
iPad 2	March 2011	9.7-inch	768x1024
3rd Generation	March 2012	9.7-inch	1536x2048 Retina
4th Generation	November 2012	9.7-inch	1536x2048 Retina
iPad mini 1st Generation	November 2012	7.9-inch	768x1024
iPad Air	November 2013	9.7-inch	1536x2048 Retina
iPad mini 2nd Generation	November 2013	7.9-inch	1536x2048 Retina

Model	Front Camera	Rear Camera	Processor	Connector
iPad	None	None	A4	30-pin
iPad 2	0.3MP/VGA	0.7MP/720p HD	A5	30-pin
3rd Generation	0.3MP/VGA	5MP/1080p HD	A5X	30-pin
4th Generation	1.2MP/720p HD	5MP/1080p HD	A6X	Lightning
iPad mini 1st Generation	1.2MP/720p HD	5MP/1080p HD	A5	Lightning
iPad Air	1.2MP/720p HD	5MP/1080p HD	A7	Lightning
iPad mini 2nd Generation	1.2MP/720p HD	5MP/1080p HD	A7	Lightning

After you know which iPad you are using, you should also know that they differ in what iOS features they can use. The original iPad cannot use iOS 7 at all, or even iOS 6 for that matter. If you have one, the best you can do is iOS 5. Even some of the iPads that can use iOS 7 do not have the ability to access certain features like Siri or AirDrop. We look at Siri at the end of this chapter and AirDrop at the end of Chapter 3.

iPad Capabilities Chart

Model	iOS 7-Compatible	Siri-Compatible	AirDrop
iPad	No	No	No
iPad 2	Yes	No	No
3rd Generation	Yes	Yes	No
4th Generation	Yes	Yes	Yes
iPad mini 1st Generation	Yes	Yes	Yes
iPad Air	Yes	Yes	Yes
iPad mini 2nd Generation	Yes	Yes	Yes

The 3rd and 4th generation iPads, the iPad Air and the 2nd generation iPad mini use a very different display than the previous versions. They are the same size, but a higher resolution. Instead of 768 pixels across and 1024 vertically, they contain 1536 and 2048, giving you four times as many pixels. This means photographs and text are crisper and clearer. In fact, you can't even distinguish the individual pixels with your eye unless you hold the iPad very close.

Another difference between iPads is the cameras. The original iPad had no camera at all. The 2nd and 3rd generations had cameras, but the more recent iPads have a rear-facing camera that is capable of much higher resolution for both still photos and video.

Each iPad has also become a little more powerful with a faster processor at its heart. The latest iPad has the 64-bit A7 processor, which gives it the capability to handle voice dictation and render beautiful graphics for games.

iOS 7

The primary piece of software on the iPad is the operating system, known as iOS. This is what you see when you flip through the screens of icons on your iPad and access the various default apps such as Mail, Safari, Photos, and iTunes.

This book covers iOS 7, the version released in September 2013. There have been seven generations of the software that runs iPhones and iPads. The original iPhone OS was developed for the first iPhone. The third version, iOS 3, worked on iPhones and the iPad. This latest version, iOS 7, works on the iPad 2 and newer. If you have an original iPad, you can only use up to iOS 5. Many of the features and tasks in this book work the same in iOS 5 and iOS 6, but you will not be able to use the latest features such as the new Maps app or Siri. To find out which version you are using and to learn how to update, see "Keeping Your iPad Up-To-Date" in Chapter 3.

The iPad Buttons and Switches

The iPad features a Home button, a Wake/Sleep button, a volume control, and side switch.

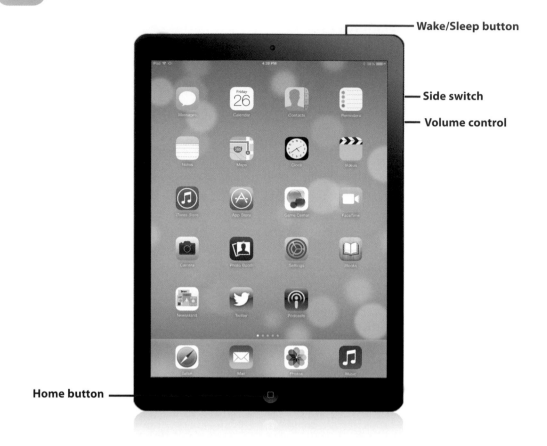

Wake/Sleep button

Side switch

Volume control

Home button

The Home Button

The Home button is probably the most important physical control on the iPad and the one that you will use the most often. Pressing the Home button returns you to the Home screen of the iPad when you are inside an application, such as Safari or Mail, and you want to get back to your Home screen to launch another app. You can also double press the Home button to jump to the app switching screen.

Where's the Quit Button?

Few, if any, apps on the iPad have a way to quit. Instead, think of the Home button as the Quit button. It hides the current app and returns you to your Home screen. The app is actually still running, but hidden, in the background.

The Wake/Sleep Button

The primary function of the Wake/Sleep button (sometimes called the On/Off button) at the top of your iPad is to quickly put it to sleep. Sleeping is different than shutting down. When your iPad is in sleep mode, you can instantly wake it to use it. You can wake up from sleep by pressing the Wake/Sleep button again or pressing the Home button.

Peek a Boo!

If you are using the Apple iPad Smart Cover, your iPad will go to sleep when you close it and wake up when you open it, as long as you use the default settings.

The Wake/Sleep button can also be used to shut down your iPad, which you might want to do if you leave your iPad for a long time and want to preserve the battery life. Press and hold the Wake/Sleep button for a few seconds, and the iPad begins to shut down and turn off. Confirm your decision to shut down your iPad using the Slide to Power Off button on the screen.

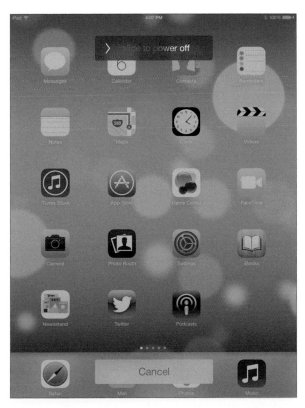

To start up your iPad, press and hold the Wake/Sleep button for a few seconds until you see the Apple logo appear on the screen.

When Should I Turn Off My iPad?

It is normal to never turn off your iPad. In sleep mode, with the screen off, it uses little power. If you plug it in to power at night or during longer periods when you aren't carrying it with you, you don't need to ever shut it down.

The Volume Control

The volume control on the side of your iPad is actually two buttons: one to turn the volume up, and the other to turn it down.

Your iPad keeps two separate volume settings in memory: one for headphones and one for the internal speakers. If you turn down the volume when using headphones and then unplug the headphones, the volume changes to reflect the last settings used when the headphones were not plugged in and vice versa. A bell icon and a series of rectangles display on the screen to indicate the level of volume.

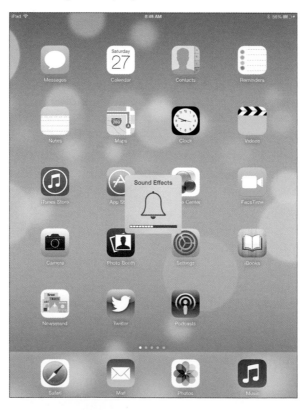

The Side Switch

The switch on the side of your iPad can do one of two things: It can be set as a mute switch or an orientation lock. You can decide which function this button performs in your iPad's settings. See "Setting Side Switch Functionality" in Chapter 2.

If you choose to use this switch as a mute switch, it will mute all sound if switched to the off position. You will see a speaker icon appear briefly in the middle of the screen when you do this. A line through the icon means you just muted the sound; otherwise, you just unmuted your iPad. By default, the iPad comes with the switch configured to mute.

If you choose to use this switch as an orientation lock, it will do something else entirely. Your iPad has two primary screen modes: vertical and horizontal. You can use almost every default app in either orientation. For example, if you find that a web page is too wide to fit on the screen in vertical orientation, you can turn the iPad sideways and the view changes to a horizontal orientation.

When you don't want your iPad to react to its orientation, slide the iPad side switch so that you can see the orange dot, which prevents the orientation from changing. When you need to unlock it, just slide the lock off.

This comes in handy in many situations. For instance, if you are reading an ebook in bed or on a sofa while lying on your side, then you may want vertical orientation even though the iPad is lying sideways.

Orientation and Movement

I know I said there were only four physical switches on your iPad, but there is another one: the entire iPad.

Your iPad knows which way it is oriented, and it knows if it is being moved. The simplest indication of this is that it knows whether you hold it vertically with the Home button at the bottom or horizontally with the Home button to one of the sides. Some apps, especially games, use the screen orientation of the iPad to guide screen elements and views.

Shake It Up!

One interesting physical gesture you might perform is the "shake." Because your iPad can sense movement, it can sense when you shake it. Many apps take advantage of this feature and use it to set off an action, such as shuffling songs in the Music app, erasing a drawing canvas or as an "undo" function.

Screen Gestures

Who knew just a few years ago that we'd be controlling computing devices with taps, pinches, and flicks rather than drags, key presses, and clicks? Multitouch devices such as the iPhone, iPod Touch, and the iPad have added a new vocabulary to human-computer interaction.

Tapping and Touching

Since there is no mouse, a touch screen has no cursor. When your finger is not on the screen, there is no arrow pointing to anything.

A single, quick touch on the screen is usually called a "tap" or a "touch." You usually tap an object on the screen to perform an action.

Occasionally you need to double-tap—two quick taps in the same location. For instance, double-tapping an image on a web page zooms in to the image. Another double-tap zooms back out.

Pinching

The screen on the iPad is a multitouch screen, which means it can detect more than one touch at the same time. This capability is used with the pinch gesture.

A pinch (or a pinch in) is when you touch the screen with both your thumb and index finger and move them toward each other in a pinching motion. You can also pinch in reverse, which is sometimes called an "unpinch" or "pinch out."

An example of when you would use a pinch would be to zoom in and out on a web page or photograph.

Dragging and Flicking

If you touch the screen and hold your finger down, you can drag it in any direction along the screen. This action often has the effect of moving the content on the screen.

For instance, if you are viewing a long web page and drag up or down, the page will scroll. Sometimes an app will let you drag content left and right as well.

What if you have a long web page or a list of items inside an app? Instead of dragging the length of the screen, lifting your finger up, and moving it to the bottom to drag again, you can "flick." Flicking is like dragging, but you move quickly and lift your finger off the screen at the last moment so that the content continues to scroll after you have lifted your finger. You can wait for it to stop scrolling or touch the screen to make it stop.

Pull Down and Release to Update

A common gesture is to tap in a list of items, drag down, and release. For instance, you would do this in Mail to get new messages. You would also do this in Twitter to get new tweets. Many Apple and third-party apps use this gesture to let you signal that you want to update the list of items. So if you don't see an obvious "update now" button, try this gesture.

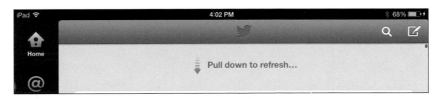

Four-Finger Gestures

You can perform one of three special functions by using four or five fingers at a time on the screen. If you put four or five fingers on the screen and pinch them all together, you will be taken out of your current app and back to the Home screen, similar to just pressing the Home button.

You can swipe left or right using four or more fingers to quickly page between running apps without going to the Home screen first. Swiping up with four fingers will bring you to the multitask switcher.

iPad Screens

When using a desktop computer, you can usually see multiple windows on the screen that represent different applications, documents, and controls. The iPad doesn't use a window metaphor like this, but instead usually displays a full screen dedicated to a single purpose.

The Lock Screen

The default state of your iPad when you are not using it is the lock screen. This is just your background wallpaper with the time at the top and the words Slide to Unlock at the bottom. You can see the date under the time. The battery status is at the top right, and you can also see it under the time, alternating with the date, if the iPad is currently charging. There is also a small button at the bottom right for quick access to the camera app. The top and bottom of the screen show short bars to allow you to access the Notifications Center at the top and the Control Center at the bottom.

We look at customizing what appears on the lock screen in Chapter 2, as well as the Control Center and the Notifications Center later in this chapter.

By default, you see the lock screen when you wake up your iPad. Sliding your finger from left to right near the words Slide to Unlock takes you to the Home screen or to whichever app you were using when you put the iPad to sleep.

The Home Screen

Think of the Home screen as a single screen but with multiple pages that each features different app icons. At the bottom of the Home screen are app icons that do not change from page to page. The area resembles the Mac OS X Dock.

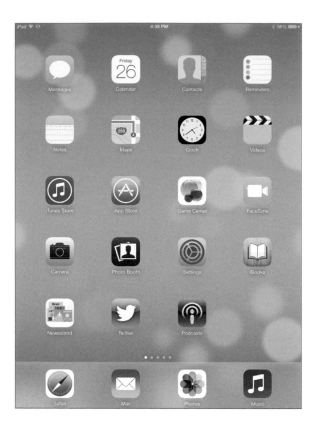

The number of pages on your Home screen depends on how many apps you have. The number of pages you have is indicated by the white dots near the bottom of the screen, just above the bottom icons. The brightest dot represents the page you are currently viewing. You can move between pages on your Home screen by dragging or flicking left or right.

An App Screen

When you tap on an app icon on the Home screen, you run that app just like you would run an application on your computer. The app takes over the entire screen.

At this point, your screen can look like anything. If you run Safari, for instance, a web page displays. If you run Mail, you see a list of your new email or a single incoming email message.

Home Screen Searching

If you are on your Home screen looking at page one of your app icons, you can drag from the center of the screen downward to bring up a Search iPad field at the top and a keyboard at the bottom. This allows you to search your iPad for apps, contacts, events, and other information.

You can type in anything to search for a contact, app, email message, photo, and so on. You don't have to define what type of thing you want to search for.

1. From the Home screen, tap in the center of the screen and drag down. Don't start at the very top of the screen, as that will bring up Notifications Center instead.

2. Type a search term using the on-screen keyboard.

3 You see a list of items on your iPad that match the search term. Tap the Search button on the keyboard to dismiss the keyboard and complete the search.

4 Tap the X in the search field to clear the search and start again.

5 Tap any of the items to go to the appropriate app and view the content.

The Settings Screen

One of the apps that you have on your iPad by default is the Settings app. With the Settings app, you can control several basic preferences for your iPad. (See Chapter 2 for more on customizing settings.)

This is really just another app screen, but it is worth singling out as you'll need it to customize most aspects of your iPad.

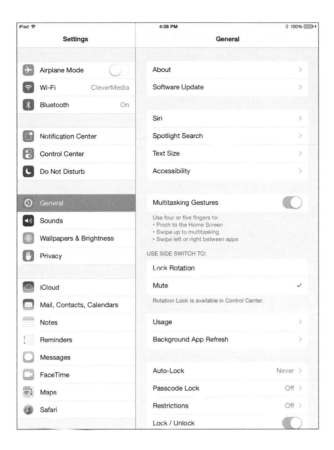

Interacting with Your iPad

Now let's examine the different types of on-screen interface elements, the on-screen keyboard and how to use it, and specialized interactions such as text editing and copy and paste.

Common Interface Elements

Several interface elements are more complex than a simple button. In typical Apple style, these elements are often self-explanatory, but if you have never used an iPhone or iPod touch before, you might find some that give you pause.

Switches

A switch is like a simple button, but you need to tap only the switch to activate it. A switch gives you feedback about which state it is in.

For example, two switches indicate whether the Sound Check and Group By Album Artist features of the Music app are on or off. Tapping on either switch changes the position of the switch.

Toolbars

Some apps have a set of buttons in a toolbar at the top of the screen that are general controls. Each button is nothing more than a word or two that you can tap on to trigger an action. The toolbar might disappear or the buttons might vary depending on the mode of the app. An example of a toolbar is in the Videos app, which lets you switch between Movies, TV Shows, and Music Videos at the top. There is also a button to return to the main Store screen. But this toolbar can change. For instance, if you add some of your own video clips to your iPad, a new Home Movies item will be added to this toolbar.

Menus

Often tapping a single button in a toolbar brings up more buttons or a list of choices, which are like menus on your Mac or PC. The choices in the list are usually related. For example, a button in Safari gives you many different ways to share a web page.

Tab Bars

Sometimes you see a row of buttons at the bottom of the screen that function similarly to toolbars, but each button represents a different mode for the app. For instance, at the bottom of the App Store app, you see a Tab bar that you use to switch between various lists of apps: Featured, Top Charts, Near Me, Purchased, and Updates.

Using the On-Screen Keyboard

The interface element you might interact with the most is the on-screen keyboard. It pops up from the bottom of the screen automatically whenever you need to enter some text.

The default keyboard has only letters and the most basic punctuation available. There are two shift keys that enable you to enter uppercase letters. You also have a Backspace key and a Return key.

Is There a Quicker Way to Capitalize?

So to capitalize a word, you tap the Shift key and then type the letter, right? You can. But a faster way is to tap the Shift key; then, without letting your finger off the screen, drag it to the letter and release in a single tap, slide, release action.

You can do the same with numbers and punctuation by tapping the .?123 key and sliding and releasing over the key you want.

To enter numbers and some other punctuation, tap the .?123 key to switch your keyboard into a second mode for numbers and punctuation.

To return to the letters, just tap the ABC key, or tap the #+= key to go to a third keyboard that includes less frequently used punctuation and symbols.

There are other keyboard variations. For instance, if you type in a location that needs a web address, a keyboard that doesn't have a spacebar appears that instead has commonly used symbols such as colons, slashes, underscores, and even a .com button. Instead of a Return key, you might see an action word like "Search" written on that key—tapping it will perform an action like searching the web. All keyboards include a button at the bottom right that enables you to hide the keyboard if you want to dismiss it.

You can also split the keyboard and/or move it up away from the bottom of the screen. Just tap and hold the keyboard button at the bottom-right corner of the keyboard. It has a little keyboard icon on it. Then select Undock or Split. The first will simply move the keyboard to the middle of the screen. The second will do that as well, but will also split the keyboard into two halves. You can then drag the keyboard up and down by tapping, holding, and dragging on that same keyboard button. Drag it all the way back down to the bottom to dock it to the bottom again. You can also split the keyboard by placing two fingers on the keyboard and dragging them apart, and then rejoin it by dragging the fingers together.

Dictating Text

If you have a 3rd generation iPad or newer, or an iPad mini, you can also dictate text using your voice rather than typing on the keyboard. Almost any time you see a keyboard you should also see a small microphone button to the left of the spacebar. Tap that and you will be prompted to speak to your iPad. You will need to be connected to the Internet through a Wi-Fi or cellular connection for this to work.

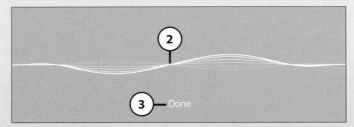

1. Any time you see the default keyboard, you will see the microphone button to the left of the spacebar. Tap it to begin dictating.

2. The keyboard is replaced with a waveform line that vibrates as you speak. Speak a few words or a sentence or two.

3. Tap Done when you are finished speaking. After a few seconds your spoken words will be translated into text and inserted as if you had typed them.

Speak somewhat slowly and clearly, and in segments about the length of a sentence for best results. Of course this feature isn't perfect. Pay careful attention to what is transcribed and correct any mistakes using the keyboard. Over time you will get better at speaking in a way that minimizes mistakes.

>>>Go Further

DICTATION TIPS

The dictation button will appear any time a standard keyboard is present in any app. You can use it in Notes, Pages, or any writing app. You can use it in search fields and text entry fields on the web. But you cannot use it when there are specialty keyboards like the ones used to enter in email addresses, web URLs, telephone numbers, and so on. So, for instance, you can use it in the Contacts app to speak a name or address, but not to enter an email address.

You need to be connected to the Internet for dictation to work. Your iPad sends the audio to Apple's servers, which handle the transcription and send the text back to your iPad. If you are not connected, it won't work.

Dictation works according to your language set in Settings, General, International. Not all languages are supported, but Apple is adding more all the time.

You can indicate the end of a sentence by saying "period" or "question mark." You can also speak other punctuation like "comma" or "quote."

You can also speak commands like "new line" or "cap" to capitalize the next word. There is no official list of what the dictation feature supports, and since the transcription takes place on Apple's servers they can change how it handles commands at any time.

Editing Text

Editing text has its challenges on a touch-screen device. Even though you can just touch any portion of your text on screen, your finger tip is too large for the level of precision you usually get with a computer mouse and cursor. To compensate, Apple developed an editing technique using a magnifying glass area of the screen that you get when you touch and hold over a piece of text.

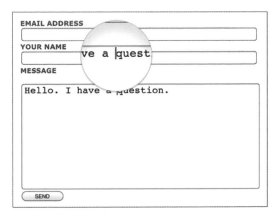

For example, if you want to enter some text into a field in Safari, touch and hold on the field. A circle of magnification appears with a cursor placed at the exact location you selected.

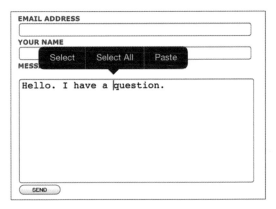

When you find the exact location that you want to indicate, release your finger from the screen. Then a variety of options display, depending on what kind of text you selected, such as Select, Select All, and Paste. You can ignore the options presented and start typing again to insert text at this location.

Copy and Paste

You can copy and paste text inside an app, and between apps, on your iPad. Here's how you might copy a piece of text from one document to another in the Notes app.

1. Launch Notes. If you don't have any notes yet, create one by typing some sample text.

2. Touch and hold over a word in your note. The Select/Select All pop-up menu appears.

3. Choose Select.

4. Some text appears highlighted surrounded by dots connected to lines. Tap and drag the dots so the highlighted area is exactly what you want.

5. Tap Copy.

6. Tap the new note button to create a new note.

7. Tap the empty document area once to bring up a pop-up menu with the Paste command.

8. Tap Paste to insert the copied text.

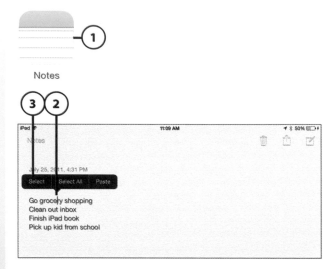

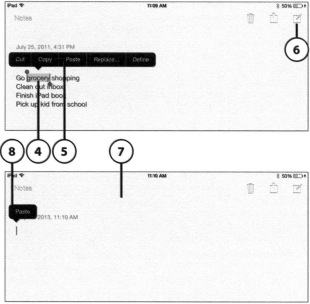

Using Siri

Siri is a voice-activated assistant that was first introduced in 2011 on the iPhone 4S. You can use your voice and speak commands to your iPhone and Siri will respond. It will either give you information or take action using one of the apps on the iPhone.

To use Siri on your iPad, you need to make sure you have Siri turned on in the Settings app under General settings. Then, you use the Home button to activate Siri.

1 In your Settings app, tap the General settings.

2 Make sure Siri is turned on.

3 Press the Home button to exit Settings.

4 Press and hold the Home button for about a second. The Siri interface will pop up, showing a waveform line at the bottom of the screen that reacts to the sound of your voice.

5 The help button brings up a list of examples of things you can ask Siri.

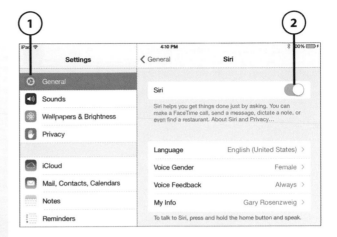

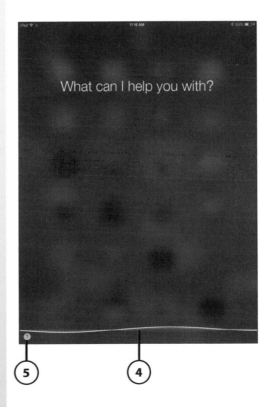

(6) Speak clearly at a normal pace and say "What's the weather like today?" After a short delay, the words you spoke will appear and Siri will attempt to perform an action based on those words.

(7) In this case, a short weather forecast will appear.

(8) Siri also responds with a statement and will speak it audibly. The text of the response will typically appear above the response.

(8) You can ask Siri another question by tapping the microphone button at the bottom of the screen.

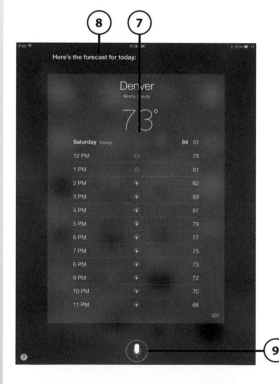

SIRI TIPS

To use Siri, you must have a connection to the Internet. It can be a Wi-Fi connection or a mobile connection. When you speak text, the audio is transmitted to Apple's servers to convert it to text and interpret the command. The results are sent back to your iPad.

It is best to speak clearly and to limit background noise. Using Siri in a quiet room works better than in a crowded outdoor space or in a car with the radio on, for instance.

Because Apple's servers control Siri, they can update Siri's capabilities at any time. For example, originally Siri did not understand a request for local sports scores, but after an update this functionality was added.

You can use Siri to perform many tasks on your iPad without typing. For example, you can search the Web, set reminders, send messages, and play music. Throughout the rest of this book, look for the Siri icon for tips on how to use Siri to perform a task related to that section of the book.

Using Notifications Center

To move between pages on your Home screen, you swipe left and right. But you can also pull down and pull up two special screens from any Home screen, or just about any screen at all, even if you are in an app.

Swiping from the very top of your screen downward pulls down the Notifications Center.

(1) Swipe down from the top of the screen to pull down the Notifications Center. If you are having trouble, try placing your finger above the screen, outside of the actual screen area, and moving your finger down onto the screen, continuing all the way down.

(2) In large type at the top of the screen, you will see today's date.

(3) Under that, you may see a summary of today's weather, depending on your settings for the Notifications Center.

(4) More information about today are summarized under the weather.

(5) A preview of your calendar events for the day are shown. You can tap on an event to open the Calendar app and go right to it.

(6) If you have any items set for today in the Reminders app, you will see them here. You can tap them to open the Reminders app.

(7) If you have more information than can fit on the screen, you can swipe up to see it. This screen shows information about tomorrow as well as today.

8 Tap All to see other notifications, such as incoming email,
Messages, and App Store
updates.

9 Tap Missed to see events and
other information from earlier in
the day.

10 Tap the flat arrow at the bottom of the screen and drag up
to the top of the screen to close
the Notifications Center. You can
also just press the Home button
at the bottom of your iPad.

You can customize the Notifications
Center in the Settings app, deciding
exactly what appears in it. We look at
that in Chapter 2.

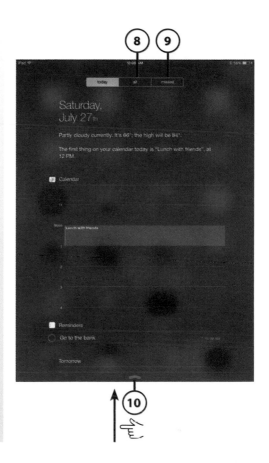

Using Control Center

The Notifications Center comes down from the top of your iPad's screen, but the
Control Center comes up from the bottom.

1 To bring up the Control Center, swipe up from the very bottom of the screen. If you are having trouble, try starting below the screen and swiping up onto the screen area all the way to the top.

2 The upper-left corner of the Control Center is a complete set of music playback controls. You see the name of the song playing and can pause or resume the song, and move the white line to jump around inside the song. You can also skip to the next or go back to the previous song.

3 Below the playback controls is a volume slider.

4 The first in a set of buttons in the middle of the Control Center is a switch that lets you quickly turn on Airplane mode. This shuts off all Wi-Fi, Bluetooth, and cellular data connections.

5 The next button lets you toggle on and off the Wi-Fi connection.

6 Likewise, you can toggle on and off the Bluetooth connection that you may be using with wireless headphones, a keyboard, or to connect to a wireless audio speaker.

7 You can quickly switch to Do Not Disturb mode, which silences all notifications such as incoming messages.

8 This switch locks the iPad's orientation to the current state—horizontal or vertical. In Chapter 2, you learn how to use the iPad's side switch for this, which then changes this Control Center button to a mute switch instead.

9 This button is a shortcut to take you to the Clock app.

10 This is a shortcut to take you to the Camera app.

11 If you have an iPad that supports AirDrop, this button lets you turn AirDrop on or off. We'll look at AirDrop in Chapter 3.

12 The AirPlay button lets you choose a device to stream audio or video to, assuming you have such a device connected to your network.

13 The bottom-right corner of Control Center lets you adjust the brightness of the iPad's screen.

14 To dismiss Control Center, you can tap the flat arrow at the top and drag down. You can also tap the screen above Control Center or simply press the Home button.

There's not much that Control Center does that cannot be done in the Settings app or the Home screen. Control Center simply provides quick access to a variety of functions.

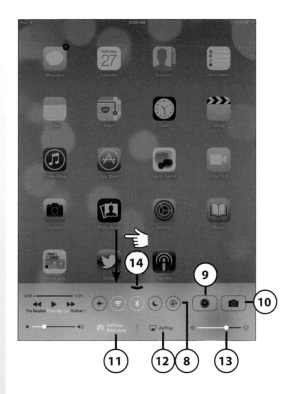

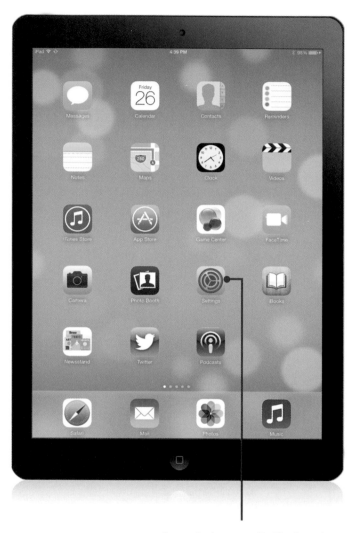

Customize how your iPad looks and
works through the Settings app.

In this chapter, you learn how to change some of the settings on your iPad such as your background images, sounds, passcode, and how some apps behave.

Customizing Your iPad

Like with any relationship, you fall in love with your iPad for what it is. And then, almost immediately, you try to change it.

It's easier, though, to customize your iPad than it is your significant other because you can modify various settings and controls in the Settings app. You can also move icons around on the Home screen and even change how the Home button works.

Changing Your Wallpaper

The wallpaper is the image behind the icons on the Home screen and on the lock screen, so make sure it's something you like.

1. Tap the Settings icon on your Home screen.

Settings

2. Choose Wallpapers & Brightness from the Settings on the left side of the screen.

3. Tap the Large Wallpaper button that shows previews of your lock and home screens.

4. If you want to use one of Apple's dynamic wallpapers, tap here. Dynamic wallpapers are patterns that slowly animate.

5. If you want to select an image from your photo library—either of a photo you took with your iPad or one you synced from your computer—tap one of the groups of photos listed.

6. If you want to use one of Apple's default wallpaper images, tap here.

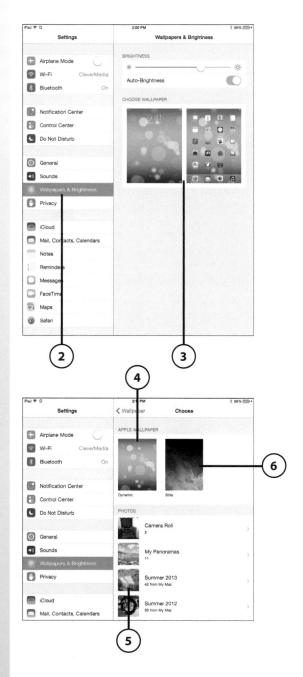

7) Choose an image from the category you selected in step 4, 5, or 6.

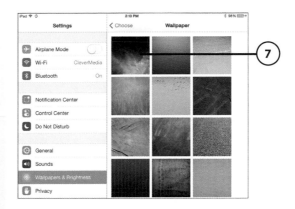

8) You'll see the full image in a preview covering the entire screen.

9) Choose Set Lock Screen to set this image as the background of your lock screen.

10) Choose Set Home Screen to set this image as the background for your Home screen.

11) Choose Set Both to make the image the background for both screens.

12) Tap Cancel at the bottom-left corner of the screen to go back to the wallpaper icons.

Adjusting the Wallpaper Image

You can touch and drag in a photo to move to other areas of the image so you can choose the part of the image you want as your wallpaper. You can also pinch to zoom in and out on your photographs.

Getting Details About Your iPad

One of the many things in the Settings app on the iPad is an About section, from which you can learn details about your iPad.

(1) Tap the Settings icon on your Home screen.

(2) Tap General from the list of settings on the left.

(3) Tap About, the first item at the top of the list of General settings.

Settings

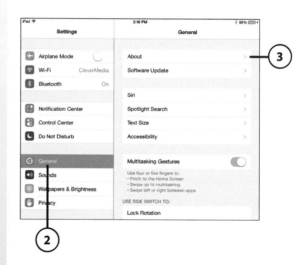

4 Tap Name to change the name of your iPad as it is seen in iTunes and iPhoto when you sync with your computer and various other instances.

5 See how many songs, videos, photos, and apps you have.

6 See the total capacity of your iPad and the amount of space available.

7 The version number tells you which version of the iPad operating system you are running. Check this to make sure you are running the latest version of iOS.

8 The model number tells you exactly which iPad you own if you happen to get it serviced or perhaps to report a bug to a third-party app developer.

9 The serial number, Wi-Fi address, and Bluetooth address are unique to your iPad. Apple may ask for your serial number if you are sending your iPad in for repairs. The Wi-Fi number is what you need if you are asked for a "MAC address" or "Ethernet address" for your iPad.

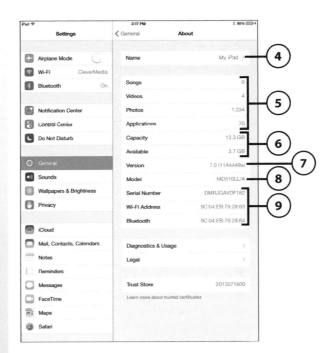

Why Am I Missing Space?

Notice in the example here that the capacity of the iPad is shown as 13.3GB. However, that particular model is advertised as a "16GB" model. The discrepancy between the two is because of space used by the operating system and other system files.

Another Model Number?

If you tap the Legal button and then the Regulatory button on the About screen, you are taken to another screen that lists another model number for your iPad. For the 4th generation iPad, Wi-Fi only model, this is A1458. The models A1459 and A1460 represent the AT&T and Verizon 3G models. When you are buying third-party accessories for your iPad, the specifications for those accessories may say "compatible with model X." In that case, X may represent either model number.

Setting Alert Sounds

Your iPad can be a noisy device with various events that trigger alert sounds. Just typing on the on-screen keyboard can produce a series of clicks.

Here's how to adjust your iPad's alert sounds.

(**1**) Tap the Settings icon on the Home screen.

(**2**) Tap Sounds from the list of settings on the left.

(**3**) Adjust the volume of system sounds, like FaceTime ringtones and notification alerts. This does not affect the volume of music or video.

4) When this is turned on, the volume in step 3 can change by using the buttons on the side of the iPad. If you turn this off, you can still use the buttons to adjust the volume of music and video when those are playing, but otherwise the side volume controls won't affect the system sound volume.

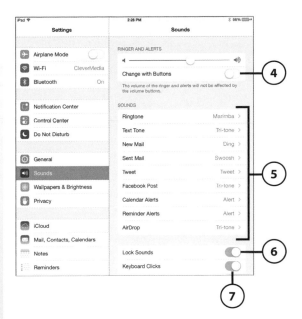

5) Tap any of these settings to set the sound that plays when an event occurs. You can choose ringtones, alert tones, or custom tones for any of the events. Ringtone refers to FaceTime calls and Text Tone refers to the Messages app.

6) Switch the Lock Sounds on or off. When this setting is on, a sound plays when you unlock the Lock screen.

7) Switch Keyboard Clicks on or off.

How About Custom Sounds?

Any sound event can play a ringtone rather than a plain alert sound. You will see a list of "Alert Tones" that are built into iOS, as well as a list of ringtones, which include the built-in ringtones and any custom ringtones. You can add your own custom ringtones in iTunes on your Mac or PC and then sync them with your iPad. After the sync, you will see them listed when selecting an alert sound. See "Syncing Music," in Chapter 3. By obtaining or creating your own custom ringtones, you can set your alert sounds to anything you want.

Password Protecting Your iPad

Password protecting your iPad is a great way to make sure that someone else can't access your information or use your iPad.

(1) Tap the Settings icon on the Home screen.

Settings

(2) Tap General from the list of settings on the left.

(3) Tap Passcode Lock.

Even More Security

To lock your iPad automatically when you aren't using it, choose Auto-Lock from the General Settings and set your iPad to automatically lock at 2, 5, 10, or 15 minutes. You can also choose to never have it auto-lock. Of course, you can manually lock your iPad at any time by pressing the Wake/Sleep button at the top.

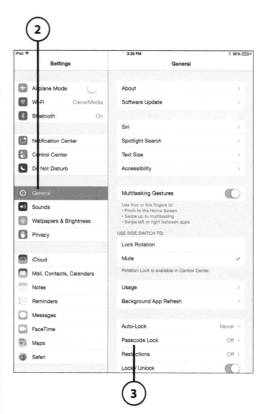

4 Tap Turn Passcode On to activate this feature. You then are prompted to enter a passcode.

5 Type in a four-digit passcode that you can easily remember. Write it down and store it in a safe place—you can run into a lot of trouble if you forget it, most likely needing to erase your iPad and restore it from your last backup.

6 You will be asked to re-enter your passcode.

7 Tap the Require Passcode button and choose the delay before a passcode is required. If you choose anything other than Immediately, someone else using your iPad can work on it for that period of time before needing to enter the code.

8 Tap Simple Passcode to switch from using a 4-digit number to a longer password that can include both letters and numbers, if you want additional security; otherwise, your password will consist of 4 digits. Tap Turn Passcode On.

9 Turn off Siri to disable the ability to use Siri from the Lock screen.

10 Turn on Erase Data if you want to erase the iPad data after 10 failed passcode attempts.

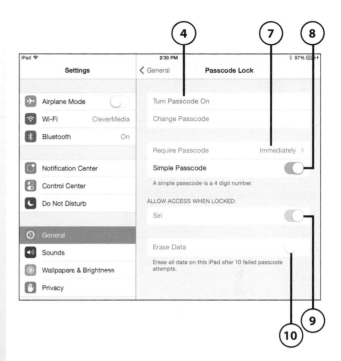

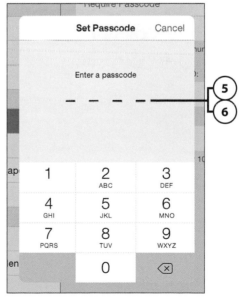

(11) Press the Wake/Sleep button to confirm your new settings work. Then press the Home button and Slide to Unlock. The Enter Passcode screen displays.

You Forgot Your Passcode?
Well, it wouldn't be secure if there were a way to get around the passcode, so you're out of luck until you can connect your iPad to your Mac or PC and use iTunes to restore it. Hopefully, this never happens to you.

Setting Parental Restrictions

If you plan to let your kids play with your iPad, you might want to set some restrictions on what they can do.

(1) Tap the Settings icon on the Home screen.

Settings

(**2**) Tap General.

(**3**) Tap Restrictions.

(**4**) Tap Enable Restrictions to turn restrictions on.

(**5**) Type in a four-digit code and then re-enter the code when prompted. Remember this code, or you can't turn off or change restrictions later.

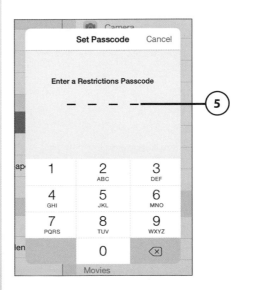

6 To remove the Safari, Camera, FaceTime, iTunes and iBooks Store apps from your Home screen, turn the switches to off. The user of the iPad will not be able to access these apps.

7 The Installing Apps switch prevents new apps from being installed.

8 Turn Deleting Apps on to prevent the user from removing apps.

9 Another way to access information on the Internet is to ask Siri. Turn this switch off to prevent that.

10 Turn AirDrop off to prevent the use of AirDrop for transferring photos and other data to or from this iPad.

11 The Allowed Content settings enable you to restrict access to various content based on ratings systems and filters. Each works slightly differently depending on the type of content and the way that content is rated. But you can also turn off each of these completely.

12 You can choose to turn off the In-App Purchases switch completely, or require a password for each purchase, or require the password once every 15 minutes. These settings help parents by preventing kids from making purchases from within an app, such as a game, using their iTunes account.

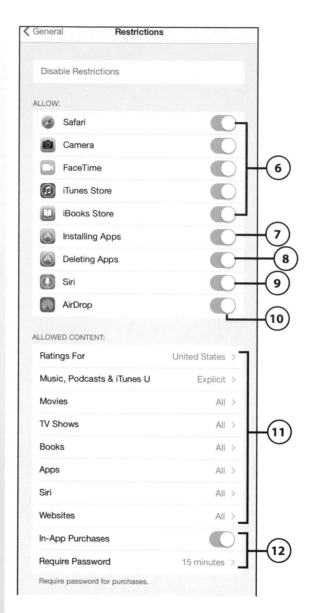

(13) Tap Location Services to enable or disable location-based functions of all apps, including Find My Phone.

(14) All of the Privacy settings control the use and editing of stored information. For instance, you can set it so Contacts can be accessed fully, allowing changes, or accessed without allowing changes. Each subcategory gives you a list of apps that use the information, and you can turn each app's access to that information on or off. For instance, you can allow Pages and Keynote to access your photos, but not the Facebook app.

(15) Tap Accounts to disallow adding or changing Internet accounts, such as email, contacts, and calendar events.

(16) Turn Background App Refresh off to stop apps from updating in the background.

(17) The Volume Limit settings allow for a maximum volume limit to be set and adjusted.

(18) Select options in the Game Center functions you want to allow. This will only affect games that use Game Center to communicate with other players. Some apps use their own system of communication or other systems, like Facebook.

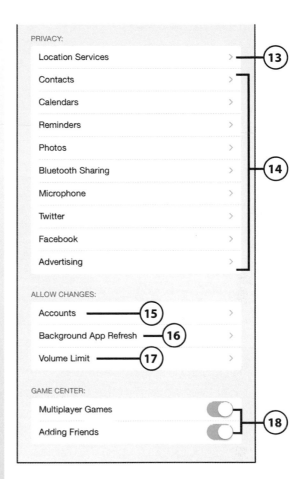

Privacy Settings

The permission settings in step 14 are also available outside of parental controls. You can select Privacy on the left side of the Settings app and then view all the apps that have requested access to contacts, events, reminders, photos, and your location. You can review and deny access to these apps. See "Privacy Settings" later in this chapter.

It's Not All Good

Settings Not Remembered

It would be nice if you could just switch Restrictions on and off, so you could hand off your iPad to Junior after quickly turning them on, but the settings are reset each time. So you need to set the switches each time after turning Restrictions back on.

Setting Side Switch Functionality

The switch on the side of your iPad can be used for one of two things: muting the sound or locking the screen orientation. Whichever one you choose for the switch, the other will then appear in the Control Center as a button. See "Using Control Center" in Chapter 1. So either way, you have fairly quick access to both functions.

(1) Tap the Settings icon on the Home screen.

Settings

(2) Tap General.

(3) Tap Lock Rotation if you want
your side switch to be an orientation lock switch.

(4) Tap Mute if you want the side
switch to mute the volume on
the speakers and earphones.

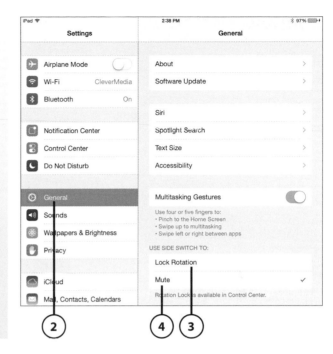

Setting Your Date and Time

You can set the date, time and time zone for your iPad and even choose whether
to display the time in 12- or 24-hour mode.

(1) Tap the Settings icon on the
Home screen.

Settings

(2) Tap General.

(3) Scroll down to the bottom of the General Settings list and tap Date & Time.

(4) Turn the 24-Hour Time switch on to show the time in 24-hour format (military time). Turn it off to revert to 12-hour format.

(5) Turning Set Automatically on syncs the date and time with the Wi-Fi network or cellular network that the iPad is connected to.

(6) Tap the Time Zone button and then enter the name of your city, or a nearby city, to set the zone.

(7) To manually set the time, tap the date and time shown to bring up a set of controls underneath.

(8) The controls are four "wheels" that you can spin by dragging up and down. You can set the day, hour, minute, and AM or PM.

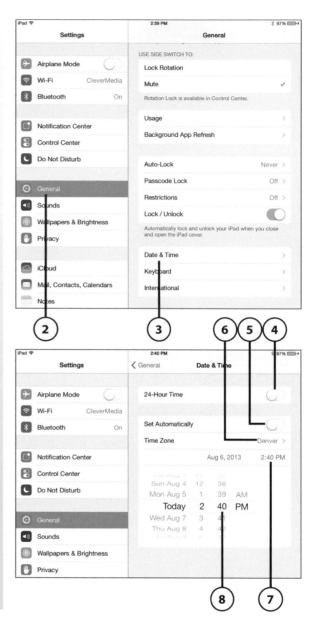

Modifying Keyboard Settings

If you use your iPad for email or word processing, you will use the on-screen keyboard a lot. The keyboard does several things to make it easier for you to type, but some of these might get in the way of your typing style. Use the following steps to modify the keyboard settings to your preferences.

1. Tap the Settings icon on the Home screen.

2. Tap General.

3. Scroll down to the bottom of the General Settings list and tap Keyboard.

4. Turn Auto-Capitalization on to automatically make the first character of a name or a sentence a capital letter.

5. Turn Auto-Correction on to have mistyped words automatically corrected.

6. Turn Check Spelling on or off to control whether possible misspellings are indicated.

7. Turn Enable Caps Lock on or off. By default, this is off. When Caps Lock is enabled, you can double-tap the shift key to lock it.

8. Turn on the "." Shortcut if you want a double-tap of the space-bar to insert a period followed by a space.

9. Use the Keyboards button to choose a different keyboard layout. In addition to keyboards commonly used in other countries, you can switch to a Dvorak keyboard or one of several other alternatives to the traditional QWERTY keyboard.

Settings

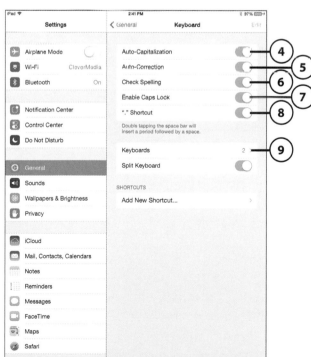

(10) If you want to lock the keyboard so it can never be split and moved up vertically, then switch this to off. See, "Using the On-Screen Keyboard," in Chapter 1.

(11) You can add your own short-cuts. For instance, you can set it so when you type "omw," it will instantly expand to "On my way!" Add your own shortcuts for things you commonly type.

(12) After you add a second keyboard in step 9, you now see a special key that lets you switch between keyboards. So, you can have both an American English keyboard and a Dvorak keyboard selected in Settings, and tap here to switch between them.

SMILE!

When you look at the list of special keyboards, you'll mostly see ones for various languages. But there is one special keyboard called Emoji that is something different. If you add that one, you can switch to a keyboard that features smiling faces and other little graphics you commonly see in text messages. You can actually use these little pieces of clipart in many apps, although some, like Pages, do not support them.

Do Not Disturb Settings

Your iPad is trying to get your attention. It beeps and rings with notifications, FaceTime calls, messages, and event alarms. In fact, it might be hard to have it nearby when trying to sleep or enjoying some time "offline."

Do Not Disturb is a mode where your iPad quiets down. Most audible alerts are silenced. You can set your iPad to enter this mode manually with the Do Not Disturb settings, or set a predefined block of time each day.

(1) Tap the Settings icon on the Home screen.

Settings

(2) Tap Do Not Disturb on the left.

(3) You can turn on Do Not Disturb mode manually with this switch.

(4) Tap Scheduled for Do Not Disturb mode to automatically start and end at a specific time. For instance, you can set it to start at 10 p.m. and end at 7 a.m. so you aren't disturbed while sleeping.

(5) Tap here to use time and date controls to set the start and end times.

(6) Tap Allow Calls From to allow FaceTime calls and messages from specific people by selecting a group in your contacts list.

(7) Turn on Repeated Calls so that someone can reach you in an emergency by calling twice within three minutes.

(8) Do Not Disturb can work at all times, or only when you have your iPad locked. Tap the desired setting so that a blue checkmark appears next to it.

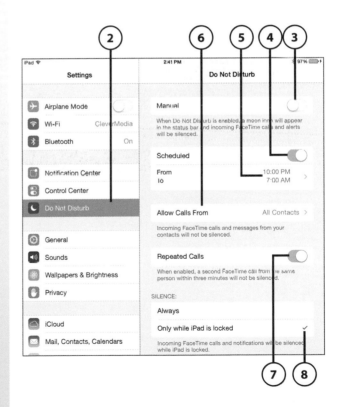

Privacy Settings

Information on your iPad can flow between apps. For instance, your Mail app will use email addresses from your Contacts app to allow you to easily address messages.

You may not want all apps to have access to all your information. Sure, sharing email addresses between Contacts and Mail makes sense, but does that game you just downloaded really need access to your contacts, or photos, or calendar events? Privacy settings allow you to see which apps have access to what and to turn off those connections, if you like.

(**1**) Tap the Settings icon on the Home screen.

(**2**) Tap Privacy on the left.

(**3**) The list includes different sources of information, such as your contacts, location, reminders, and even your Twitter and Facebook accounts. Select any one to see which apps have access to that information.

Settings

4 After you select an app, you see the list of apps that have permission to use the data.

5 Tap the switch to turn access on or off for each app.

Notification Center Settings

Apps communicate with you through the Notifications Center. See "Using Notifications Center" in Chapter 1. There you receive alerts telling you all sorts of things: incoming email, new messages, game events, news items, and so on.

The Notification Center settings is where you decide how important each type of notification is, and how it should be displayed, if at all.

1 Tap the Notifications Center category in Settings.

2 Use these switches to configure whether notifications and the summary of today's events should be shown in Notifications Center while you are on the lock screen. This information would be available to anyone holding your iPad, even if they have not entered your passcode to get past the lock screen.

3 Use these switches to configure what information should be available in the Today View portion of the Notifications Center screen.

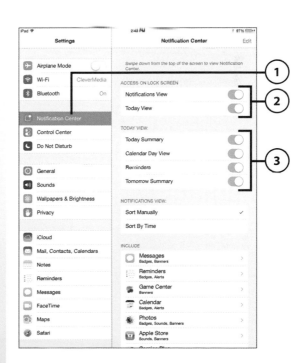

4 You can have all the items in the Notifications Center sorted by time, or sorted manually in an order you specify, by tapping one of these options.

5 If you choose the manual option in step 4, tap Edit at the top right of the screen to be able to arrange the apps listed on this screen. Set them in the order you want them to appear in Notifications Center.

6 Tap an app to edit its settings.

7 Choosing the None alert style means that neither a banner nor alert will appear.

8 Choosing Banners means that a drop-down banner will appear when the app has a message, and it will go away on its own after a few seconds. These do not interrupt your work when they appear.

9 Choosing Alerts means that a box pops up in the middle of the screen when the app has a message, and you must dismiss it to continue.

10 Turning on Badge App Icon means that the icon will show a number over it when there is a message.

11 Many apps let you set the specific sound used. Tap Alert Sound to specify the sound the app uses.

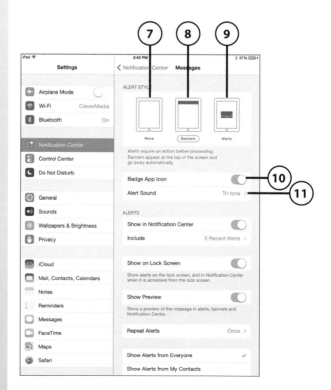

(12) Turn off Show in Notifications Center to exclude these alerts from the Notifications Center screen completely. You will still see the alert when it happens, but it will no longer be in the list when you access Notifications Center.

(13) Tap Include to choose how many alerts appear in the list in Notifications Center.

(14) Show on Lock Screen means that alerts from this app appear, even when the iPad is locked.

(15) Turn off Show Preview so that the small preview of the message does not appear with the alert.

(16) Tap Repeat Alerts to configure whether the alert will repeat after a few minutes, and how many times. It is useful to have an alert repeat in case you missed it the first time.

(17) Tap Show Alerts from My Contacts to remove the blue checkmark beside Show Alerts from Everyone. For the Messages app, this turns off alerts for those not in your contacts list.

Each app has its own set of settings, so take a few minutes to go through them all and see what options are offered. As you add new apps to your iPad, any that use the Notifications Center will be added to this list, so it is a good idea to review your settings occasionally. When a new app wants to send you notifications, it first must ask you for permission. This is where you can go to revoke that permission later on.

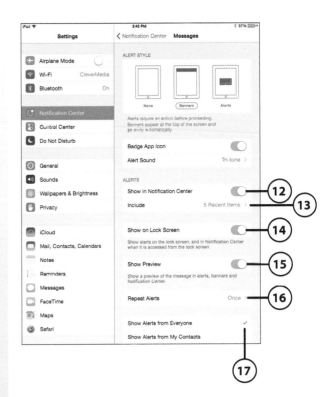

It's Not All Good

Lock It Down

Notifications Center and Control Center put a lot of power on the Lock Screen. You can see a lot of information and control portions of your iPad without ever needing to enter your passcode.

If you prefer to have all of that power hidden behind the passcode, then turn off both options under Access On Lock Screen in the Notifications Center settings. Also turn off Access on Lock Screen in the Control Center settings.

Adding More and More Apps

The Settings app adds new items as you add new apps to your iPad. Some third-party apps do not add a component in the Settings app, so don't be alarmed if you don't see an app you added in the Settings list.

Sync your music and information with your Mac or
PC computer.

Put your favorite
photos on your iPad.

In this chapter, you find out how to connect your iPad to your local Wi-Fi network. You also see how to sync your iPad with your Mac or Windows computer and with Apple's iCloud service.

→ Setting Up Your Wi-Fi Network Connection

→ Setting Up Your 3G/4G Connection

→ Syncing with iCloud

→ Syncing with iTunes

→ Syncing Photos with iTunes

→ Keeping Your iPad Up-To-Date

→ Sharing with AirDrop

Networking and Syncing

Your iPad connects you to the world. You can surf the Web, view all sorts of information, communicate with friends, and share photos. But first, you must connect your iPad to the Internet. You can do that using a Wi-Fi connection. Some iPads also have the capability to connect to a mobile network.

Setting Up Your Wi-Fi Network Connection

One of the first things you need to do with your iPad is to establish an Internet connection.

Chances are that you did this when you started your iPad for the first time. It should have prompted you to choose from a list of nearby Wi-Fi networks. But you need to do this again if you first used your iPad away from home or need to switch to use another Wi-Fi network.

To connect your iPad to a wireless network, follow these steps.

Settings

1. Tap the Settings icon on the Home screen.

2. Choose Wi-Fi from the list of settings on the left.

3. Make sure that Wi-Fi is turned on.

4. Tap the item that represents your network. (If you tap on the blue-circled i button next to each network, you can further customize your network settings.)

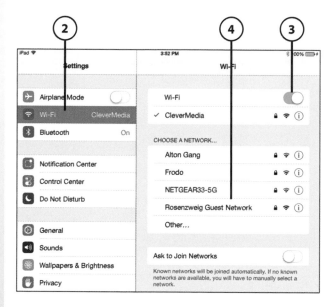

I Don't Have a Wireless Network

If you don't have a Wi-Fi network but do have high-speed Internet through a telephone or cable provider, you have several options. The first is to call your provider and ask for a new network modem that enables wireless connections. Some providers might upgrade your box for free or a small cost.

Another option is to keep your current box and add a wireless base station of your own, such as the Apple Airport Extreme base station.

(5) If the network is protected by a password, you will be asked to enter the password. Once you enter the password, your iPad will remember it. So if you switch between two locations, like work and home, you will be asked to enter the password for each the first time you use that connection. From that point on, your iPad will automatically log on to each connection as you move around.

SECURITY? YES!

>>>Go Further

Your wireless network at home should have security turned on. This means that you should see a padlock next to it in the list of Wi-Fi networks on your iPad. When you select it for the first time, you should be asked to supply a password.

If you don't require a password, seriously consider changing your Wi-Fi network box's settings to add security. The issue isn't simply about requiring a password to use your Internet connection. It is about the fact that a secure network will send encrypted data through the air. Otherwise, anyone can simply "sniff" your wireless connection and see what you are doing online—such as using credit cards and logging on to websites and services. See your network equipment's documentation to set up security.

Setting Up Your 3G/4G Connection

If you have an iPad with 3G/4G capabilities, you can set it up to use AT&T, Verizon, or any other compatible network. You can purchase a monthly data plan or purchase service in shorter increments.

(1) Tap the Settings icon on the Home screen.

(2) Tap Cellular Data on the left.

(3) Turn on Cellular Data. In addition, if you have a 3rd generation iPad, turn on Enable LTE for the faster 4G connection.

(4) Tap View Account.

(5) You have three options to set up an account with AT&T. Other carriers may offer different options. The first one is to set up a completely new account. If you choose this, skip to step 8.

(6) Another option is to add your iPad's data plan as an additional service to your existing AT&T plan. Use this if you are already an AT&T customer. You will be prompted for your mobile phone number, zip code, passcode, and social security number to complete the setup.

(7) This option is for those who already have an iPad data plan but want to transfer it from an old iPad to a new one.

Settings

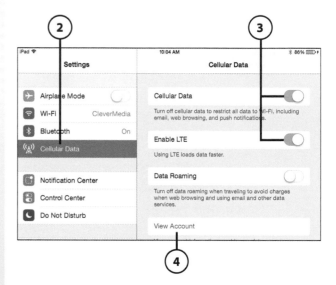

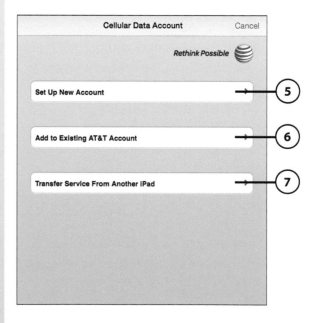

8 To set up a new account, you are prompted for some basic information. You need to enter all your basic information and specify an email address for your account and a password.

9 Choose a data plan that best fits your needs

10 Enter your credit card information. When you are done, you have to approve the service agreement and confirm your purchase. Still, it beats going to the mall and dealing with a salesperson at a mobile phone store, right?

It may take a few more minutes for your 4G service to activate. After establishing 4G service, you can return to this section of the Settings app to view your usage and modify your plan. Then you can see your pay details and status.

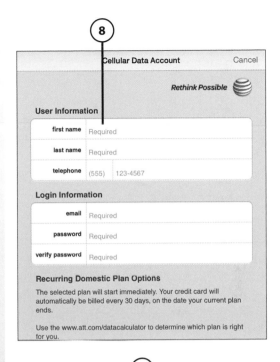

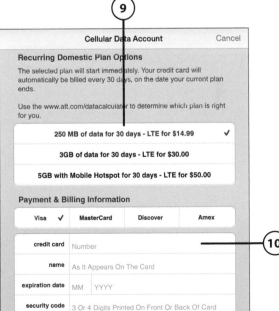

Working with Wi-Fi and 3G/4G

After you establish a 3G/4G plan, your iPad should still connect to your Wi-Fi networks when it is in range and use 3G/4G when it cannot find a Wi-Fi network. You can also return to Settings and turn on or off Cellular Data to specifically prevent your iPad from using the 3G/4G network. This is handy when you are completely out of mobile data range but have local Wi-Fi; for instance, you might be on an airplane flight. Of course, for take-off and landing, you will most likely be asked to use the Airplane Mode available in the Settings as well. That mode comes in handy when you want to quickly take your iPad "off the grid" and have it connected to absolutely nothing.

Looking at the top-left corner of your iPad's screen, you can tell which sort of connection you are currently using. You will see the Wi-Fi symbol, a fan of four curves, when you are connected to Wi-Fi. If you have a 3G/4G plan you will see the name of your network next to it, such as "AT&T," plus a series of bars that show your connection strength. But you are only using that connection if the characters "3G," "4G," or sometimes "LTE" are shown.

It's Not All Good

Watch for Data Roaming

In the Cellular Data settings, you can turn Data Roaming on or off. This is what enables your iPad to connect to wireless data networks that are outside of your data plan, such as networks in other countries. If you leave Data Roaming on and your iPad connects to such a network, you may find a surprise bill in the mail. You can avoid extra charges by leaving Data Roaming off or by purchasing a plan from AT&T for International data roaming.

Syncing with iCloud

When you think of your contacts, calendar events, and email messages, you may be tempted to think of that information as being "on your iPad" or "on your computer." But today this information is usually in both places, and more. This is referred to as "the cloud"—when the actual location of the information isn't important as long as it is where you need it, when you need it.

As an iPad user, you have access to several different cloud services, most notably Apple's system called iCloud. It is a free service that offers email, contacts, calendar, and other types of data stored on Apple's servers and automatically synced to your iPad and the other Apple devices you may own.

Or, you could choose to use other cloud services, such as Gmail or Yahoo!, for mail and calendar events. There's no reason to pick just one—you can use both iCloud and Gmail on your iPad, for instance.

When you use cloud services, you get automatic syncing as long as you have a connection to the Internet. For example, add a contact to your iPad and your iPhone will automatically update to show that new contact. Let's look at how to set up an iCloud account, or link to one you've already created.

(1) Go to the Settings app.

(2) Select iCloud settings.

(3) If you have never set up an
account with Apple before, then
tap Get a Free Apple ID to set
one up. Any account you have
with Apple, such as an iTunes
account, would be an Apple ID,
and you should use that instead
of starting a new account.

(4) If you already have an Apple
ID, even if you have never used
iCloud before, then enter your
ID and password. Apple IDs can
be any email address, not just
an @iCloud.com email address.

(5) Tap Sign In to access your
account. If your account has
only been used for things like
iTunes in the past, then you will
be prompted to set up the new
iCloud part of your account.

(6) If you think you have used
an email address to log on to
iTunes or some other Apple
service before, but you can't
remember the password, then
tap Forgot Apple ID or Password
to reset your password.

Settings

It's Not All Good

Don't Confuse ID with Email

An Apple ID is a unique identifier that allows you to log in to your iCloud account. It can be an Apple email address, like myipadbook@icloud.com, but it can also be a non-Apple email address, like myipadbook@gmail.com. In the former case, the ID is the same as your iCloud email address. But in the latter case, the ID is just an ID. Your email account would be a Gmail account and have nothing to do with your iCloud account.

(7) You can use your iCloud email on your iPad. This would typically be an @icloud.com (or old @me.com or @mac.com) email address. These addresses are part of the free iCloud service. If you happen to be using a non-Apple email address as an Apple ID, note that this setting has nothing to do with that email account.

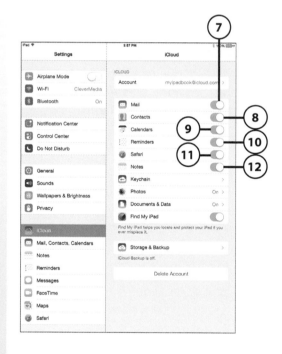

(8) If Contacts is on, iCloud stores all your contacts so they automatically sync with the iCloud servers and then to your other Apple devices.

(9) Likewise, iCloud can store your calendar events when the Calendars switch is on.

(10) Turn on Reminders to have the Reminders app use iCloud to store reminders and automatically sync them with your other devices.

(11) Safari can sync over iCloud as well. Things like your bookmarks, tabs, and reading list would sync across devices when the Safari switch is on.

(12) Turn the Notes switch on so that Notes can also sync over iCloud.

13 iOS 7 allows you to store some passwords while using Safari so you don't need to enter them each time. Syncing these over iCloud means that you can also access these passwords on other Apple devices. Tap Keychain to configure this setting. We'll look at Keychain further in Chapter 7.

14 The Photos option enables you to configure Photo Stream for storage and sharing. We'll look at Photo Stream further in Chapter 9.

15 Some other Apps, like Pages, Numbers, and Keynote, can store documents using iCloud. This way you can access the same document using the same app on your other devices. The files are transferred to iCloud and then to each device without you needing to take any action. Tap Documents & Data to make sure switches for these apps are turned on, if you use them.

16 Find My iPad is an option that lets you locate your iPad on a map using another Apple device or the iCloud.com website. Be aware that if your Location Services are not on, this feature will not work.

17 If you don't have a desktop computer to use to back up your iPad, you can enable iCloud backups by tapping Storage & Backup. Most of your critical information, such as contacts and events, are stored in iCloud anyway if you have them enabled. However, a full backup makes it easier for you to recover from a lost or broken iPad.

It's Not All Good

iCloud.com

In addition to syncing between devices, much of your iCloud information is available if you go to iCloud.com and log in using your Apple ID. You can do this on any computer. So even if you are using your iPad as your only computing device, there still is another way to get to your data should you need it.

Syncing with iTunes

With iOS 7 and iCloud, the iPad can be a truly stand-alone device, no desktop computer needed. If you use a computer, however, you may still want to sync your iPad with it. There are several advantages to doing so:

- Each day you sync your iPad, iTunes stores a backup of its content. You can restore all your data from these backups if you lose your iPad.

- Syncing with a computer is a good way to get a large number of photos from your collection on your iPad.

- Syncing is how you get your music stored in iTunes onto your iPad. If you have a large collection of music, you can opt to copy only a selection of it to your iPad at any one time. You can also do this with iCloud if you use an optional pay service from Apple called iTunes Match.

- It can be easier to arrange your app icons on the Home screen pages using iTunes, rather than doing it on your iPad.

You might get a message on your computer the first time you connect your iPad and open iTunes, asking if it is okay to sync your iPad to this computer. The message won't reappear.

After connecting the first time, iTunes should automatically open when you connect your iPad. While connected, you can always resync to apply changes by clicking the Sync button in iTunes.

You can also check Sync over Wi-Fi connection in your iPad's options in iTunes. This allows you to sync when your iPad isn't connected by the cable. It only needs to be on the same network as your Mac or PC that is running iTunes.

Syncing Options

After your device is in sync, you can change some general options for your iPad from the Summary screen in iTunes. Most of the options are self-explanatory, such as Open iTunes When this iPad Is Connected.

1. Using iTunes 11, look for the devices button at the top right. If you have only the iPad connected, it should show the name of the iPad there, and you can click it and skip step 2. If you have enabled the left sidebar in the View menu of iTunes, then your iPad will appear in that sidebar instead.

2. A list of devices appears. Click on your iPad.

3. You can configure your backups. iCloud backups are convenient for those without regular access to a computer, but it uses Internet bandwidth and can be a problem if you have a slow connection. Backing up to your computer is the best option if you regularly sync to your computer anyway.

4. You can set your iPad to connect via Wi-Fi. From then on, you only need to be on the same network as your computer to sync with iTunes.

5. A handy graph of your iPad's storage is shown.

6. Any changes you make on this screen or any other iTunes sync screen will require that you click Apply to re-sync with the new settings.

One option that dramatically changes how your iPad syncs is Manually Manage Music and Videos, which turns off automatic syncing of music and videos and enables you to simply drag and drop songs and movies from your iTunes library onto the iPad icon on the left. (You might need to scroll down the Summary page to locate this checkbox if your screen size is too small to show the entire page at once.)

As we look at some of the syncing options for the iPad, the Mac version of iTunes is used as an example. The Windows version of iTunes is similar but not exactly the same.

>>>Go Further

BACK IT UP!

Perhaps the most important part of syncing with your computer is backing up your data. Everything you create with apps, every preference you carefully set, and every photo you take could be gone in a second if you drop your iPad or someone swipes it. Even a hardware failure is possible—the iPad isn't perfect.

Choosing This Computer is your best option. This saves all your data on your computer in a backup file. Try to do it once per day. With a good backup you can replace a lost iPad and restore all your data from the backup. It works incredibly well.

You can always plug your iPad into your Mac or PC, launch iTunes, and Control+click (right-click on Windows) your iPad in the left sidebar and select Backup. But it also happens automatically once per day if you set up the sync.

Your other option is iCloud. This will back up your data wirelessly to iCloud. It is your only option if you are not going to sync your iPad with a computer. But it does use up your data storage allotment in your iCloud account, so you may need to upgrade your iCloud account to allow for more data.

Even so, backing up to iCloud is a great alternative, especially if you travel often and use your iPad for critical tasks.

Syncing Music

The easy way to sync music is to select Entire Music Library In iTunes on your computer. If you have more music than can fit on your iPad, though, you must make some choices. Syncing Movies, TV Shows, Podcasts, Tones (ringtones for messaging and FaceTime), iTunes U, and Books all work in a similar way to syncing music, so you can apply what you learn in these steps to those items as well.

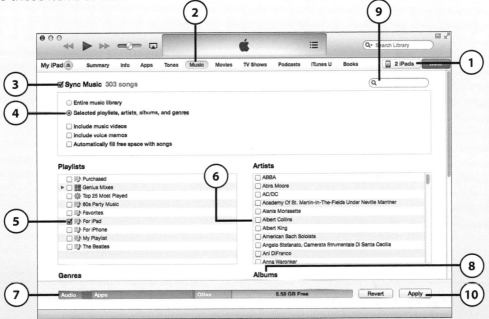

1. Select your iPad at the top of the iTunes window. If you have more than one iOS device, you may have to select your iPad from a short list.

2. Click the Music button of your iPad's settings in iTunes.

3. Select Sync Music, if it isn't already turned on.

4. Click the Selected Playlists, Artists, Albums, and Genres button.

5. Check off any playlists in the Playlists section that you want to include.

6. Check off any artists for which you want to include every song by that artist.

7. Check off any genres to include in their entirety.

8. Check off any albums you want to include.

9. Use the search box to quickly find specific artists.

10. Click the Apply button if you want to apply the changes now.

One Copy Only

Note that songs are never duplicated on your iPad. For instance, if the same song appears in two playlists and is also by an artist that you have selected to sync, the song only has one copy on your iPad. But it appears in both playlists and under that artist, album, and alphabetical list of all songs.

The Kitchen Sync

In addition to Music, you can also sync your Tones, Movies, TV Shows, Podcasts, iTunes U, and Books in a similar way. Each type of media has its own way of syncing, but they are all similar to music. For instance, Tones lets you sync all tones or selected tones, and then you select them individually. There are no playlists for Tones. Movies, TV Shows, and Podcasts can be included in playlists, so syncing options there let you sync by playlist if you like. Explore each page of your syncing settings to see which options you have.

>>>Go Further

MORE WAYS TO SYNC

iTunes Match is a service from Apple. For an annual fee, you can sync your music collection with Apple's servers. Then you can access all your music on your iPad by turning on iTunes Match in the Music settings in the Settings app. When you do this, you no longer need to sync your music. Instead, you see all your music on your iPad, and it will download from Apple's servers when you want to listen to a particular song.

Visit www.apple.com/itunes/itunes-match/ to find out more about Apple's iTunes Match service.

You can also sync your music and videos manually. This sounds like a lot of work, but it can be an easier way to sync your music for many people. If you check off Manually Manage Music and Videos on the iTunes Summary screen for your iPad, you can then drag and drop music from your iTunes music library on to your iPad. It requires a bit of knowledge about how the iTunes interface works, however. You'll need to choose View, Show Sidebar so you can see your iPad in the left sidebar. Then you can look at the Music item listed to see which songs are there. Switch to your iTunes Music library to see what songs you have on your computer and simply drag and drop songs, albums, or artists from the iTunes Music library to your iPad in the left sidebar.

Syncing Photos

The process for syncing photos from your computer to your iPad is very similar to how you move music, videos, and other data to your iPad. So let's use photos as an example. The steps here are very similar if you want to sync something else, like movies, to your iPad. You would just choose the Movies tab in iTunes instead of the Photos tab.

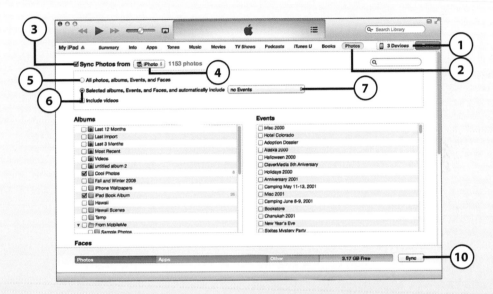

1. Select your iPad.

2. Choose the Photos tab at the top.

3. Click the checkbox to indicate that you want to sync photos.

4. You can choose from any applications that are compatible with iTunes and store photos. For instance, on Mac you can choose iPhoto and also Aperture if you use it. You can also simply select a folder to use as the location for your photos. The rest of the steps here assume you are using iPhoto.

5. Click All photos, albums, Events, and Faces to sync all your photos. Only do this if you have a fairly small collection.

6. Choose Selected albums, Events, and Faces, and automatically include button to select which albums and events to sync.

7. You can also have a number of recent events, or photos taken over a recent period of time, automatically sync. For instance, you can have it sync all events from the past 6 months.

(8) Choose which albums you want to sync. Albums are collections of photos, like music playlists, that allow you to compile your favorite or related photos into a group.

(9) You can also select individual iPhoto events.

(10) When you are satisfied with your selections, click Sync to begin the transfer.

No Duplicates

Like with music, you get only one copy of each photo, no matter how many times the photo appears in albums, events, and faces. The photos appear in all the right places but take up only one spot in memory on your iPad.

It's Not All Good

One Way Only

As with the iPhone and iPod touch, syncing photos works only one way. For the photos you sync from your computer to your iPad, you cannot pull photos from your iPad back to your computer. The original is on your computer, and there is merely a copy on your iPad. So, it is important that you maintain your real photo library on your computer and remember to back it up.

Syncing music, movies, and other items works basically the same way. For instance, with music you can choose albums, artists, playlists or simply your entire music collection. With movies you can choose individual videos or everything.

Syncing Apps

iTunes keeps your apps on your computer and your iPad in sync and helps you organize them.

Note that you cannot run apps on your computer, just store them. You can store all of the apps you have downloaded and purchased on your computer and only have a subset of those set to sync on to your iPad.

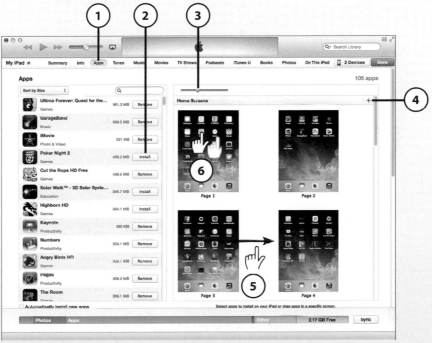

(1) Click the Apps button of your iPad's settings in iTunes.

(2) Use the Remove or Install buttons next to each app to remove or install the app, depending on its current state and what you want to do. Install appears next to apps that are currently not on the iPad, and you can click it to install it the next time you sync.

(3) Use this slider to adjust the size of the screens so you can see more screens at a time, or make them larger to see the icons more clearly.

(4) Click here to add a new screen.

(5) You can swap entire pages by dragging them around in this area.

(6) Double-click a screen to enlarge it.

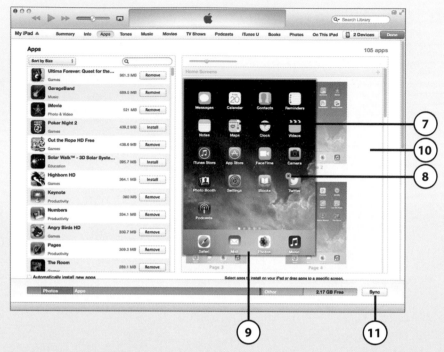

(7) Now you can grab icons on this screen and move them around to change their positions. You can also drag them out of this screen. Then the screen will shrink back and allow you to move the icon onto another screen.

(8) Move the cursor over an app and an X appears. You can use this to remove the app from your iPad.

(9) You can also drag apps in and out of the iPad's dock area at the bottom.

(10) To shrink a screen back to normal size, click an area outside of the screens.

(11) Click the Sync button if you want to apply the changes now.

Syncing Documents

Apps sometimes have documents. For example, Pages is a word processor, so it would naturally have word-processing documents. Documents are stored on your iPad, but you might want to access them on your Mac or PC as well.

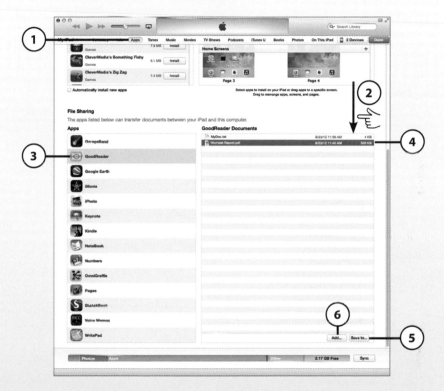

1. Click the Apps button of your iPad's settings in iTunes.

2. Scroll down to the bottom of the Apps page.

3. In the File Sharing section, choose an app.

4. Select a document from the right.

5. Click the Save To button to save the document as a file on your computer.

6. Click the Add button to import a file from your computer to your iPad. Each app has its own document space on your iPad. So if you have two PDF readers, and you want the PDF document available to both, you need to add it to each app's documents.

Keeping Your iPad Up-to-Date

Apple periodically comes out with updates to iOS. And Apple and other developers come out with updates to apps all the time. Usually all these updates are free and contain useful and important new features. So, there is no reason not to keep your iPad up-to-date. In fact, updates sometimes include important security patches, so you should pay careful attention when an update is available.

To check for iOS and software updates, follow these steps:

(1) Tap the Settings icon on the Home screen and then tap General.

(2) Tap Software Update.

(3) If you have the latest version of iOS, you will see a message like this one. Otherwise, follow the instructions provided to update your iPad.

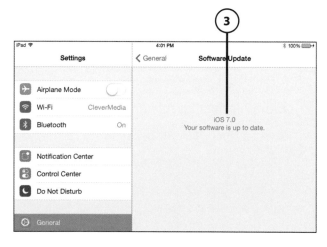

(4) Updating your apps is also important. iOS 7 can do this for you automatically. Make sure you have automatic updates enabled by going to the Settings app and choosing iTunes & App Stores on the left.

(5) Under Automatic Downloads, you should have Updates turned on. This means iOS 7 will download app updates in the background. It will actually attempt to do this at times when you are not using your iPad and have a Wi-Fi connection.

(6) On the Home screen, find and tap the App Store app. You may also notice a number in a red circle attached to the icon. This tells you how many apps you have that have updates available.

(7) Tap the Updates button. This takes you to a screen with a list of all recent app updates.

(8) Here you can see a list of all apps that have been updated recently. It also shows a list of changes to these apps.

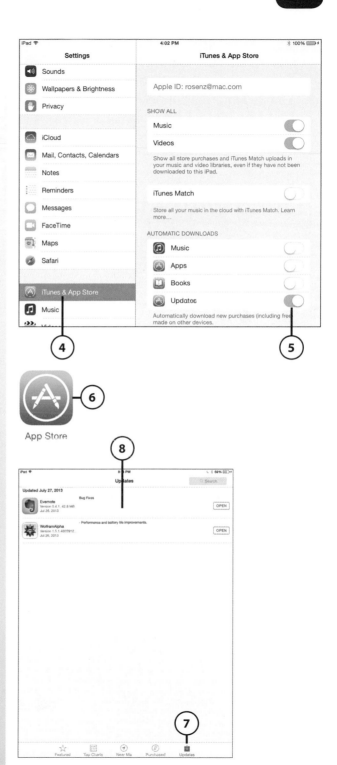

Bandwidth Concerns?

If you often find yourself in a situation where you are worried about Wi-Fi bandwidth, you may want to turn off automatic updates. For instance, if you pay for a limited Internet connection at home, but have a fast, unlimited connection at work, you can turn off automatic updates and use the Updates section of the App Store app to manually update your apps only while at work.

Sharing with AirDrop

A new way to get files from your iPad to another iOS device is using AirDrop. This technique uses Wi-Fi, but instead of going through a Wi-Fi network, it goes directly from iOS device to iOS device. So the devices don't need to be on the same network—they don't need to be on any Wi-Fi network at all.

AirDrop requires the latest Wi-Fi hardware in your iPad, so it only works with the 4th generation iPad or newer, or an iPad mini. Using AirDrop is pretty simple.

To use AirDrop, follow these steps:

1. To use AirDrop, make sure you have turned it on. Do this by accessing Control Center. See "Using Control Center" in Chapter 1. Make sure that it is set to "Everyone."

2 Let's use the Notes app as an example. You can use any app that can share items, such as the Photos app, Contacts app, and so on. While editing a note, tap the Share button.

3 In addition to sharing options such as Message and Mail, you'll see a list of other AirDrop-compatible devices that are within range. You will see whatever image the user has chosen as a user icon, plus their name. If you do not see your other device, it could be asleep, or have AirDrop disabled, or possibly is not a model that has AirDrop available.

4 After you tap the icon, you see a "Waiting" message below it. In the meantime, the recipient will get an alert asking them to accept the transfer.

For You, Friend

The real power of AirDrop is sending between friends. For instance, if you are standing with your iPad next to a friend with an iPhone 5, you can send her a picture without both of you needing to share a common Wi-Fi network or exchanging email addresses. You just Share, select her for the AirDrop, and she accepts.

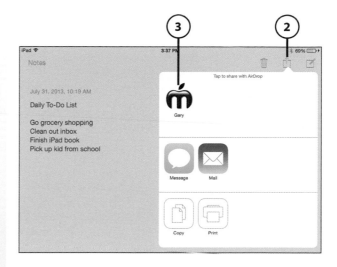

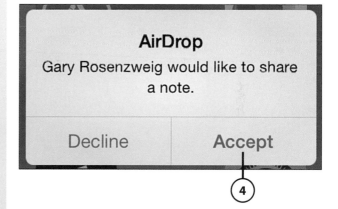

Purchase music and
buy or rent videos.

Play your
music.

Listen to Podcasts.

In this chapter, you learn how to use the Music and Video apps to play music and watch video. You also learn how to use iTunes Radio.

→ Playing a Song
→ Building a Playlist
→ Making iTunes Purchases
→ Downloading Podcasts
→ Playing Video
→ Using AirPlay to Play Music and Video on Other Devices
→ Home Sharing
→ Listening to iTunes Radio

Playing Music and Video

The iPad handles playing music as well as any iPod or iPhone ever has, plus it has a big screen for you to use to browse your collection. In Chapter 3, you learned how to sync music to your iPad from your computer. That's one way to get music onto your iPad. You can also use the iTunes app to purchase music, or the iTunes Match service to sync all your music from iCloud.

No matter how you put music on your iPad, you play your music using the Music app.

Playing a Song

So let's start by simply selecting and playing a song with the Music app.

(1) Tap the Music icon, which is most likely along the bottom of your Home screen.

(2) Tap Songs on the bottom, if it isn't already selected.

(3) Tap the name of a song to start it. You can also tap and drag up and down on the screen to scroll through the list, or use the letters on the right to jump to a position in the list.

Music

Playing iTunes Match Music

If you are using iTunes Match, you will see all your music in the list, even songs not currently on your iPad. You can still tap the name of a song to start it. The song will download and play, assuming you are connected to the Internet. You can also tap the iTunes Match (cloud) icon for each song to simply download each song so it is ready to listen to later, even if you are not connected. You would want to do this for some songs if you are going to be away from your Internet connection and plan to listen to music.

Visit www.apple.com/itunes/ itunes-match/ to find out more about Apple's iTunes Match service.

4 At the top of the screen, the Play button changes to a Pause button. The red time progress bar to the right begins to move.

5 Use the volume slider at the top to adjust the volume, or use the physical volume controls on the side of your iPad.

6 Tap the Now Playing button at the top to view album artwork for the current song.

7 Tap the repeat button to choose whether to repeat this song over and over again, or repeat the playlist or album you are currently listening to.

8 Tap the Shuffle button to make your iPad play the songs in the album or playlist in a random order.

9 Tap the list button to view the album that contains the song you are currently listening to.

10 Tap the left-facing arrow button at the top left to return to the main Music app interface.

How Else Can I Listen to Music?

You can also listen to music using third-party apps. Some apps access your music collection on your iPad, but the most interesting ones play streaming music from over the Internet. We look at apps, such as Pandora, in Chapter 13. You can also use iTunes Radio to listen to streaming music. We look at that later in this chapter.

(11) Tap any of the buttons at the bottom of the screen—Playlists, Songs, Artists, and Albums to sort the list of songs.

(12) A list of album artwork is shown. Tap on any album to view the album and the songs in it. Tap a song name to play it.

(13) Tap in the Search field at the top of the list to search your songs.

Siri: Playing Music

You can use Siri to play music. Here are some examples:

"Play The Beatles"
"Play Georgia On My Mind"
"Play some blues"
"Play my driving music" (plays the playlist named "driving music")
"Shuffle all songs"
"Skip"
"Pause"

>>>Go Further

CONTROLLING MUSIC PLAYBACK

To control music playback

- Tap and move the red line in the progress bar to move around inside a song.

- Use the Back and Forward buttons that appear on either side of the play/pause button to move from song to song in the list of currently selected songs.

- Press the Pause button at any time to pause the music. Use the same button, which has become a Play button, to restart the music. Many headphones, including the Earpods that Apple sells, have a pause button on the cable that allows you to pause and resume playback and control the volume.

Building a Playlist

Playlists are a way to take the songs you have on your iPad and arrange them in ordered groups. For instance, you can create one to listen to while working, while working out, while trying to go to sleep, or make a party mix for your next get-together.

You can create playlists on your Mac or PC in iTunes, but you can also build actual playlists on your iPad.

(1) Tap the Playlists button at the bottom of the main Music app screen.

(2) A list of current playlists appears. Tap the New Playlist button.

(3) Give the new playlist a name and tap Save.

Genius Playlists

If you turn on the Genius feature in your Mac or PC copy of iTunes, you can use the Genius playlist feature to create playlists. After you click the Atom icon, select a song to use as the start of the Genius playlist. iTunes selects other songs from your collection that are similar and creates a playlist using the name of that song.

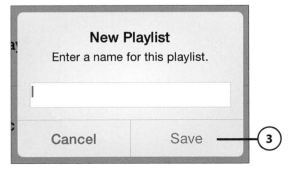

4 In the expanded list of your music, tap the + buttons next to each song you want to add to the playlist.

5 Tap the Sort buttons at the bottom of the screen to sort through your music.

6 Use the Search field at the top to find songs faster.

7 Tap the Done button when you have selected all the songs you want to add to the playlist.

8 The playlist will remain on the screen. You can also return to it any time by tapping on the Playlists button at the bottom of the screen and selecting this playlist. If you want to edit the playlist, tap Edit.

9 On the playlist edit screen, remove songs from the playlist by tapping on the red buttons.

10 Tap and drag on the three-line buttons to rearrange the songs.

11 Tap the + button to add more songs to the playlist.

12 Tap Done to exit editing the playlist.

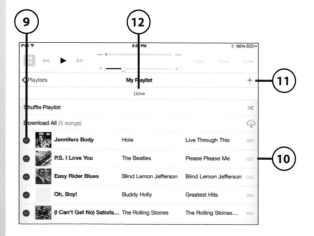

Making iTunes Purchases

You have lots of options when it comes to adding more music to your iPad. You can simply add more music to your iTunes collection on your computer and then sync those songs to your iPad. In that case, you can buy them from iTunes, from another online source, or import them from music CDs.

How Else Can I Get Music?

You can purchase music on your iPad only through the iTunes app. But you can sync music from your computer that you get from any source that doesn't use special copy protection, like CDs you import into iTunes. You can buy online from places such as Amazon.com, eMusic.com, cdbaby.com, or even directly from the websites of some artists.

In addition to syncing music to your iPad from your computer, you can purchase music, movies, TV shows, and audio books directly on your iPad using the iTunes app and using the same account that you use in iTunes on your computer.

(1) Tap the iTunes app icon on your Home screen to go to the iTunes store.

iTunes Store

(2) Use the buttons at the top of the screen to choose which genre of music to view.

(3) Swipe left and right to browse more featured albums.

(4) Drag the screen up to reveal more lists, such as top albums, top songs, and music videos.

(5) Use the Search field at the top to search for an artist, album, or song by name.

(6) Select a suggestion from the list, or tap the Search button on the keyboard to complete the search.

Syncing Devices

After you make an iTunes purchase, the music, TV show, or movie you downloaded should transfer to your computer the next time you sync your iPad. From your computer, you can sync your new purchase to any other device you use that uses your iTunes account.

You can also set iTunes on your computer and your other devices to automatically download new purchases. So when you buy on your iPad, you'll get the new music everywhere. On your iPad, that setting is found in Settings, iTunes & App Stores, Automatic Downloads. In iTunes on your computer, it is found in the menu iTunes, Preferences, Store, Automatic Downloads.

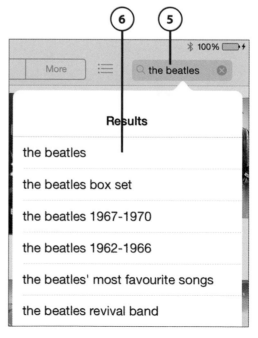

7. Find a song or album you want to buy, and tap its artwork to view more information.

8. If you move down the page by swiping upward, you'll also find ringtones, music videos, movies, and even books that match your search.

9. Tap a song name to listen to a sample of the song.

10. Tap outside of the album window to close it and return to the previous view.

11. To buy a song, album, or any item in the iTunes music store, tap the price of that item and then tap again on the Buy button.

How About My Home Videos?

If you shoot a home video with a video camera, or iPod touch or iPhone, you can bring that into iTunes on your Mac or PC and sync it to your iPad. They appear as Home Movies in the menu along the top of the Videos app.

What About My DVDs?

If you can import CD music content into iTunes, you'd think you'd be able to import video content from your DVDs. Well, technically it is possible (although not necessarily legal) by using programs like Handbrake (http://handbrake.fr/) for your Mac or PC to import DVD content and then drag the resulting file into iTunes. Then you can sync it with your iPad. These may also show up as Home Movies, since your iPad doesn't recognize them as official movie content.

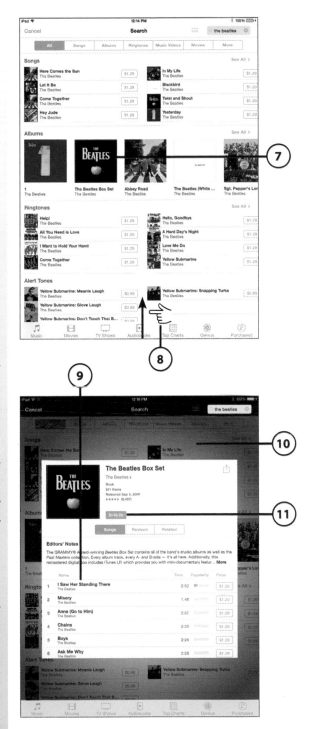

BUYING AND RENTING VIDEO

Although buying video is similar to buying music, some significant details are different and worth taking a look at.

Copy Protection   Although music in the iTunes store recently became copy-protection free, videos are a different story altogether. Purchased videos can be played back only on the Apple devices you own that use your iTunes account. You can't burn videos to a DVD, for instance, or watch them on a TV unless it is hooked up to an Apple device. Rentals are even more strict because you can watch them only on the device you rent them on.

Collecting Movies   Thinking of starting a collection of videos by purchasing them from Apple? These videos take up a lot of space on your hard drive. An iPad, even a 128GB version, quickly fills up if you start adding dozens of movies.

Time-Delayed Rentals   Rentals have some strict playback restrictions. After you download a rental, you have 30 days to watch it. After you start watching it, you have only 24 hours to finish it. This means you can load up your iPad in advance with a few movies to watch on an airplane flight or while on vacation.

TV Show Season Passes   You can purchase seasons of TV shows that aren't complete yet. When you do this, you are basically pre-ordering each episode. You get the existing episodes immediately but have to wait for the future episodes. They usually appear the next day after airing on network television.

Multi-Pass   In addition to season passes, you can also get a Multi-Pass, which is for TV shows that broadcast daily. When you purchase a Multi-Pass, you get the most recent episode plus the next 15 episodes when they become available.

HD Versus SD   You can purchase or rent most movies and TV shows in either HD (high definition) or SD (standard definition). Look for the HD/SD button to the right of the buy buttons on movie purchase pages. The difference is the quality of the image, which affects the file size, of course. If you have a slow connection or limited bandwidth, you might want to stick to SD versions of the shows.

iCloud Movies   If you use iCloud, some movies that you purchase (not rent) will appear in your Videos app as well, even if they are not actually on your iPad. You will see a little iCloud icon appear next to them. You can tap that icon to start downloading that movie to your iPad from Apple's servers. This allows you to purchase movies from Apple and not have to worry about where to store them. Simply download them from Apple any time you want to watch. But this only works if the movie studio has given Apple the rights to store and distribute the movie in this manner.

Downloading Podcasts

Podcasts are episodic shows, either audio or video, produced by major networks, small companies, and individuals. You'll find news, information, tutorials, music, comedy, drama, talk shows, and more. There is something covering almost any topic you can think of.

To subscribe to and listen to or watch podcasts, you need to get the Podcasts app from Apple. You can find it in the App Store and add it to your iPad for free. See "Finding and Listening to Podcasts" in Chapter 13 for a step-by-step on how to get a new app.

(**1**) Tap the Podcasts app icon on your Home screen.

(**2**) Tap the Podcasts button to look at the podcasts you've already downloaded. If you start off by looking at your library, you'll see an equivalent button labeled Store at the bottom left that takes you back to this screen.

(**3**) Use the Search field to search for a podcast by name or key-word.

(**4**) Tap a podcast to get more information about it. You can also swipe right to left to view more in the list.

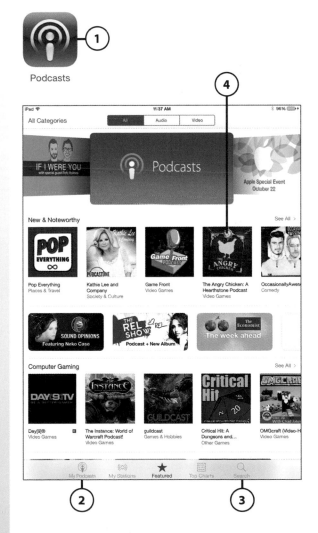

5 Tap Reviews to see what others have to say.

6 Tap the Download button next to a single episode to download just that episode.

7 Tap Subscribe to subscribe to the podcast. This will download the latest episode and also automatically get new episodes as they become available.

8 Using the Library button from step 2, you can go to the list of podcasts and view them by icon or in a list. Tap the list button to see them as a list with each episode shown on the right.

9 Tap the episode to watch or listen to it.

10 Tap the info button to get more details about an episode and to mark it as played without listening. Swipe left to right across an episode to delete it.

11 Tap the settings button to set the sort order and auto-download preferences for the podcast. You would want a current events podcast to put the newest at the top, while a podcast that tells a story or is a learning series would be better suited for oldest on top.

12 Tap Edit to be able to delete podcast episodes from your library.

13 Tap the Edit button at the top left and then use the red buttons next to the podcast names to remove a podcast subscription.

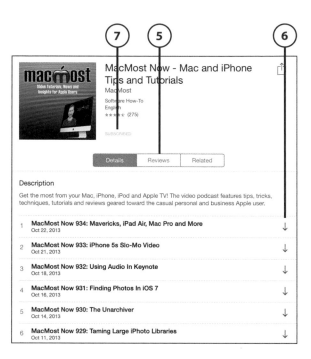

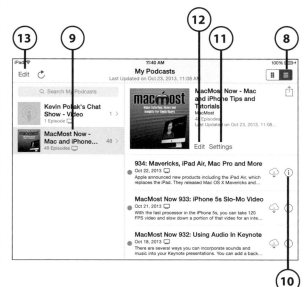

Playing Video

After you have movies, TV shows, and Home videos on your iPad, you need to play them using the Videos app.

(1) Tap the Videos app icon on your Home screen.

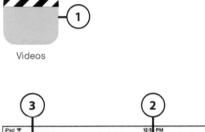

Videos

(2) The Movies you have on your iPad display by default. Tap TV Shows, Music Videos, or Home Videos to switch lists. If you don't have videos in one or more of these categories, then that button may not appear at all.

(3) Tap a movie to view more information about it.

Any Video Alternatives to Apple?

You bet. There is a Netflix app for the iPad that Netflix subscribers can use to stream movies. Amazon also has an Amazon Instant Video app for subscribers to their service. Some companies, such as ABC, have also provided their own apps for viewing their shows on the iPad. You can also view video from any site that has video in standard MP4 formats. The site www.archive.org/details/movies has public domain movies and videos, often in MP4 format. The popular video site http://blip.tv also works well with the iPad.

(4) Tap the Play button to start the movie.

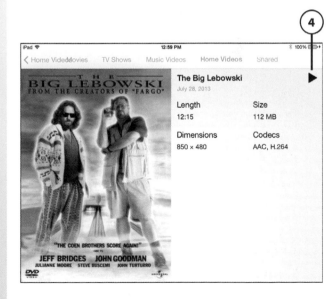

(5) After a movie is playing, tap in the middle of the screen to bring up the controls at the top and bottom of the screen.

(6) Tap the Done button to exit the movie and return to the movie information screen.

(7) Tap the Pause button to pause the movie and then again to resume.

(8) Adjust the volume with the volume control.

(9) Drag the dot along the line to move to a different section of the movie.

(10) Use the Back and Forward buttons to jump between chapters.

(11) Use the AirPlay button to send the video stream to another device, such as an Apple TV. See "Using AirPlay to Play Music and Video on Other Devices" later in this chapter.

Changing the Orientation

For most video content, you can rotate your iPad to view in a horizontal orientation and use the Zoom button at the upper right to crop the left and right sides of the video so that it fits vertically on the screen. This is similar to watching a movie on a standard TV.

What Happened to the YouTube App?

In iOS 5 and previous versions of iOS, there was a special YouTube app that enabled you to view YouTube videos. As of iOS 6 this was removed. But a new and improved app has since been released—it just doesn't come preloaded on your iPad. So you can head over to the App Store, search for YouTube, and download the app. See Chapter 12 for more information about the YouTube app.

Using AirPlay to Play Music and Video on Other Devices

In iTunes, with the Video app and many other apps that play music or video, you have the option to send the audio or video stream from your iPad to another device that is connected to the same Wi-Fi network, such as an Apple TV.

You need to enable AirPlay on those devices first. For instance, using the Apple TV (2nd generation models or newer), you need to go into settings on the device and turn on AirPlay. You also need to make sure that the device is using the same Wi-Fi network as your iPad.

1 Look for the AirPlay button in the app you are using. Tap it to bring up a list of available devices.

2 Your iPad will show as the first device. Use this to switch back to playing the media on your iPad if you have switched to something else.

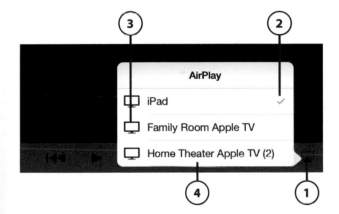

3 Next to each device, you will see either a screen icon or a speaker icon. This tells you whether you can stream video or just audio using that device.

4 Tap on another device, and the music or video currently playing will start to play over that device.

AirPlay Everything

You can also use AirPlay to mirror your iPad's screen with an up-to-date Apple TV 2. In Control Center (see "Using Control Center" in Chapter 1), there is an AirPlay button. Use that to turn on mirroring and send your screen to the Apple TV. Some apps, however, specifically block this. If you simply want to play video from the Videos app or another app that shows video, use the app's AirPlay button, not the Control Center one.

Home Sharing

If you are using iTunes on your Mac or PC, you can play this iTunes content on your iPad if it is on the same local network.

(1) In iTunes on your Mac or PC, choose Turn On Home Sharing from the File menu. You are prompted to enter your Apple account ID and password.

(2) In the Settings App, tap Music.

(3) Enter the same Apple account ID and password used in step 1.

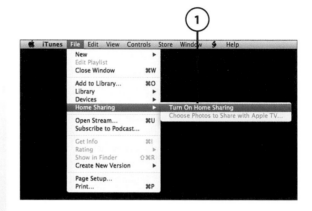

4 In the Music app, tap the More button at the bottom of the screen.

5 Tap Shared, and then choose the name of the library you want to access. The content in your Music app changes to reflect the content in the iTunes library on your Mac or PC. You can now play songs from your computer without having to transfer them to your iPad first.

What if My Library Doesn't Appear?

Home Sharing is tricky. It requires that you use the same iTunes account IDs on both your iPad and on your Mac or PC. It also requires that you have the iPad on the same local network as your Mac or PC. In addition, network firewalls and other software may get in the way. It usually works effortlessly, but some users have reported trouble getting Home Sharing to work at all with their particular home network setup.

Listening to iTunes Radio

New in iOS 7 is iTunes Radio. It is very similar to existing services like Pandora and Last.fm. You choose a music genre, artist, or song, and then you hear a continuous stream of songs based on that starting point. That stream is saved as a "station," and you can return to it at any time. Meanwhile, you can create other stations with other starting points and switch between them. The music comes from Apple's servers and includes music you already own, as well as music you don't.

Using iTunes Radio is very easy. You can choose from some sample stations or create your own.

(1) Tap the Radio icon at the bottom of the Music app.

(2) If this is your first time using iTunes Radio, tap the Start Listening button. Note that you must be signed in to your iCloud account to use iTunes Radio. You can sign in using the Settings app in the iTunes & App Stores section.

(3) You can start listening to music right away by tapping one of the Featured Stations at the top.

(4) Tap the New Station box to create a station of your own.

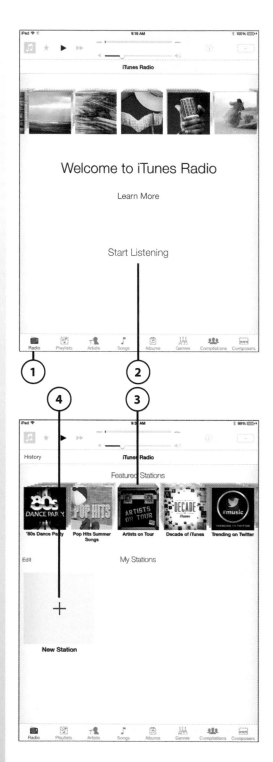

5 Type the name of an artist, genre, or song to search for iTunes content.

6 If you search for an artist, you usually get a "& more" station suggestion at the top. Select that to create a station based on that artist.

7 A song from that artist, or possibly from another artist that is similar, will start playing.

8 You'll now see your station in the My Stations list. You can create more stations and then switch between them by tapping on the icons in this list.

9 Tap the information button for the song that is currently playing.

10 You can purchase the current song from iTunes.

11 You can create a new station from the current artist. You can also do this using the Create button at the top of the Music app while listening to a song you own. So while listening to your favorite playlist, you can tap the Create button and then tap New Station from Song to create an iTunes Radio station and jump to it.

12 You can share your station via text message, email, or other methods. This basically sends information to your friends that lets them create the same iTunes Radio station on their iOS device, or in iTunes on their computer.

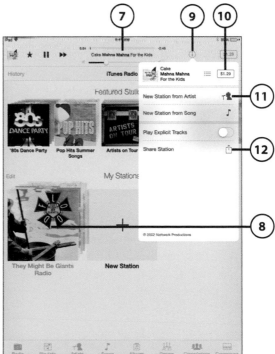

13 Tap the Star button at the top.

14 You can tap Play More Like This to fine-tune your station. This song will be added to the information used to pick which song to play next.

15 Alternatively, you can tap Never Play This Song to stop the song and tell the app to avoid songs like that in the future. By using the Play More Like This and Never Play This Song buttons, you can highly customize your station.

16 Tap the skip button to skip the current song without adding it to the Never Play This Song list for the station.

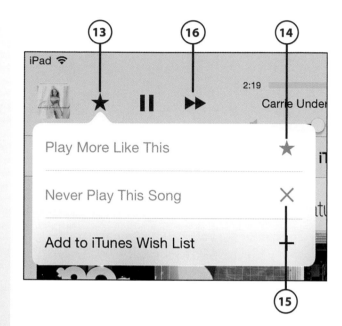

What About Bandwidth?

iTunes Radio streams music from the Internet. This means it uses bandwidth. If you are using your iPad with a mobile network or have limited bandwidth at home, that is something to be aware of. However, audio streams do not use as much as video streams, so you may be surprised at how little bandwidth an hour or so of music uses compared to watching a few YouTube videos.

And Now a Message from Our Sponsor

iTunes Radio is free, but it also includes commercials. Every so often you'll hear a sponsored message between songs. But if you have an iTunes Match account and are signed into it, as a bonus you get iTunes Radio commercial-free!

Purchase and read books with the
iPad's ebook reader.

Find out how to purchase books from the iBooks store and how to read them on your iPad.

→ Buying a Book from Apple
→ Reading a Book
→ Using Reading Aids
→ Adding Notes and Highlights
→ Adding Bookmarks
→ Organizing Your Books
→ Using iBooks Alternatives

5

Reading Books

We finally have a better way to enjoy books. As an ebook reader, your iPad can give you access to novels and textbooks alike, storing hundreds inside and allowing you to purchase more right from the device.

A single app, the iBooks app, allows you to both read and purchase new books. You can also download and add books from other sources.

Buying a Book from Apple

The first thing to do with the iBooks app is to get some books! You can buy books using the store in the app. You can also find some free books there.

1. Tap the iBooks app icon to launch iBooks.

2. Tap the Store button to switch to the iBooks store.

iBooks

Don't Want to Purchase from Apple?

You don't necessarily need to buy books from Apple. You can buy from any seller that sends you an ePub or PDF formatted file with no copy protection. After you have the file, just drag and drop it into iTunes. It will add it to your books collection there, ready to be synced to your iPad.

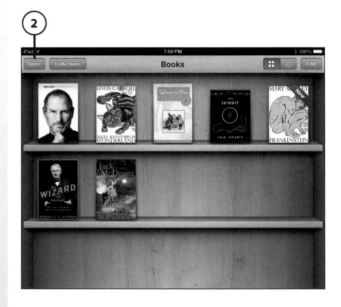

3 Swipe left and right to browse more featured books.

4 Tap the Move button to go to a list of book categories.

5 Tap Top Charts button to see a list of bestsellers.

6 Swipe up to see more featured categories.

7 Use the search field to search for book titles and authors.

8 Tap any book cover to view more information about the book.

9 Tap the price next to a book to purchase it. The price button changes to Buy Book. Tap it again to continue with the purchase.

10 Tap the Get Sample button to download a sample of the book.

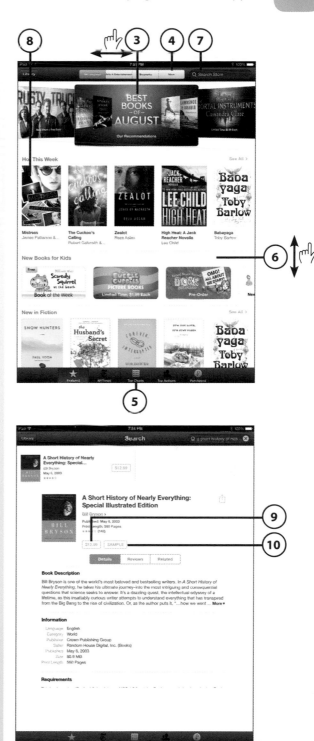

Reading a Book

Reading books is a simple process. Following are the basics of reading your downloaded books.

(1) Tap the iBooks app icon to launch iBooks.

iBooks

(2) If you are still in the store section of the app, tap Library at the top left to go to your iBooks library. Then, tap a book to open it.

Can't Find Your Book?

Did you download a book only to discover that you can't see it in your Library? Try tapping the Collections button at the top of the screen and switching to a different collection. For instance, by default, PDF documents are put in the PDF collection, not in the Books collection.

(3) To turn a page, tap and hold anywhere along the right side of the page, and drag to the left. A virtual page turns.

(4) Tap and drag from the left to the right or simply tap the left side of the page to turn the page back.

(5) To move quickly through pages, tap and drag the small marker at the bottom of the page along the dotted line. Release to jump to a page.

(6) Tap the Table of Contents button at the top to view a table of contents.

(7) Tap anywhere in the table of contents to jump to that part of the book.

(8) Tap the Resume button to return to the page you were previously viewing.

(9) Tap the Library button to return to your books. If you return to the book later, you return to the last page you viewed.

Tired of the Special Effects?

If you tire of the page-turning special effect, a quick tap on the right or left side of the screen also turns pages. The effect still shows, but it's quick.

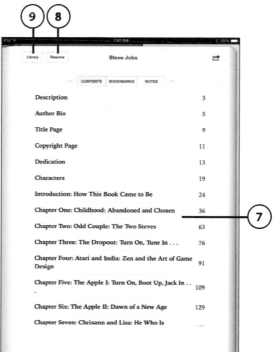

Using Reading Aids

iBooks has a variety of ways you can customize your reading experience. You can change the font size, the font itself, and even turn your iPad on its side to see two pages at one time.

(**1**) While viewing a page in iBooks, tap the display adjustment controls at the top of the screen.

(**2**) Drag the brightness control left or right. Dragging to the left makes the screen dim, which you might use if you're reading in a dark room. Dragging to the right makes it bright, which could make reading easier while outdoors.

(**3**) Tap the smaller "A" button to reduce the size of the text.

(**4**) Tap the larger "A" button to increase the size of the text.

(**5**) Tap the Fonts button to choose from a few font options.

(**6**) Tap the Themes button to select one of three color themes (White, Sepia, or Night). You can also choose to switch to Full Screen to get rid of the book-like border, or switch from flipping pages to vertical scrolling.

(**7**) Turn your iPad on its side to change to a two-page view. (Make sure your orientation lock is not on.)

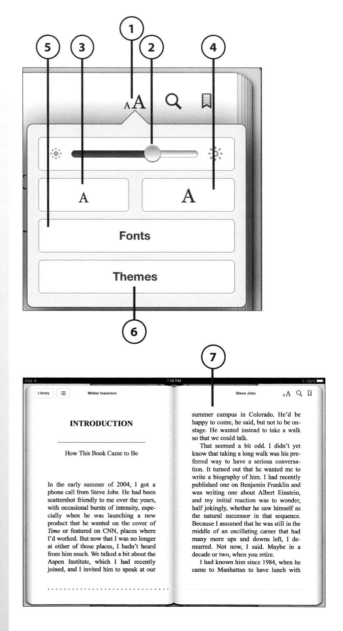

Where Did the Buttons Go?

If you tap in the middle of the screen, the buttons at the top and the dotted line at the bottom disappear. You can still turn the pages; you just don't have access to these buttons. To see the buttons again, tap in the middle of the screen.

Adding Notes and Highlights

Each time you launch iBooks, your iPad returns you to the page you were last reading. However, you might want to mark a favorite passage or a bit of key information.

(**1**) Go to a page in a book in iBooks.

(**2**) Tap a word and hold your finger there for about a second.

(**3**) Release your finger and you see six choices: Copy, Define, Highlight, Note, Search, and Share.

Define and Search

Tapping Define brings up a definition of the word. Tapping Search brings up a list of the locations of the word throughout the text.

Sharing from iBooks

When you choose Share, you can send the excerpt you have selected to someone else using email, a text message, Twitter, or Facebook.

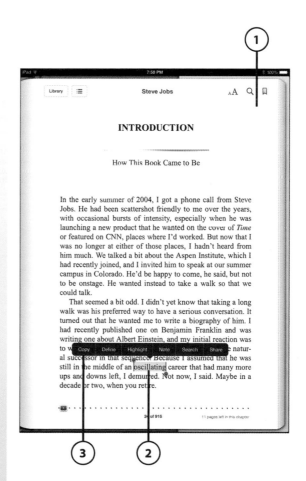

(4) Drag the blue dots to enlarge the section of text highlighted.

(5) Tap Highlight. Alternatively, you can tap a word and hold for a second and then immediately start dragging to highlight text.

(6) The text is now highlighted.

(7) Tap the first button to change the type of highlighting. You can choose from various colors or a simple red underline.

(8) Tap the second button to remove the highlight completely.

(9) Tap Note instead of Highlight to bring up a yellow pad of paper and add a note.

(10) Tap in the note to bring up the keyboard and start typing.

(11) Tap outside the yellow paper to finish the note. It will then appear as a small yellow sticky note to the right side of the page. Tap it any time you want to view or edit the note. You can delete a note by removing all text in the note.

walk was his preferred way to have a serious conversation. It turned out that he wanted me to write a biography of him. I had recently published one on Benjamin Franklin and was writing [Copy] [Define] [Highlight] [Note] [Search] [Share] n was to wonder, half jokingly, whether he saw himself as the natural successor in that sequence. Because I assumed that he was still in the middle of an oscillating career that had many more ups and downs left, I demurred. Not now, I said. Maybe in a decade or two, when you retire.

That seemed a bit odd. I didn't yet know that taking a long walk was his preferred way to have a serious conversation. It turned out that he wanted me to write a biography of him. I had recently published one on Benjamin Franklin and was writing one abo al reaction was to wonder, half jokingly, whether he saw himself as the natural successor in that sequence. Because I assumed that he was still in the middle of an oscillating career that had many more ups and downs left, I demurred. Not now, I said. Maybe in a decade or two, when you retire.

iPad 7:59 PM 100%

[Library] [≡]   Steve Jobs   AA Q 🔖

INTRODUCTION

How This Book Came to Be

In the early summer of 2004, I got a phone call from Steve Jobs. He had been scattershot friendly to me over the years, with occasional bursts of intensity, especially when he was launching a new product that he wanted on the cover of *Time* or featured on CNN, places where I'd worked. But now that I was no longer at either of those places, I hadn't heard from him much. We talked a bit about the Aspen Institute, which I had recently j   t our summer campus in Co   said, but not to be onstage   lk so that we could talk.

That seem   taking a long walk was his   nversation. It turned out th   phy of him. I had recently   klin and was writing one about Albert Einstein, and my initial reaction was

Adding Bookmarks

You can also bookmark a page to easily find it later.

1 Tap the bookmark button at the top of a page to bookmark the page. You can bookmark as many pages as you want in a book.

2 Tap it again to remove the bookmark from the page.

3 Tap the Table of Contents button to go to the table of contents.

4 Tap the Bookmarks button at the top of the table of contents to see a list of all the bookmarks, highlights, and notes you have added to the book.

5 Tap any bookmark, note, or highlight to jump to it.

Organizing Your Books

Like to read a lot? You aren't alone. I'm sure many people gather massive collections of ebooks on their iPads. Fortunately, iBooks includes a few great ways to organize your ebooks.

(**1**) Go to your iBooks main page— your Library.

(**2**) Tap the Collections button.

(**3**) Tap a Collection name to jump to that collection. You can think of collections as different book-cases filled with books.

(**4**) Tap New to create a new collec-tion.

(**5**) Tap Edit to delete or re-order collections in the list.

(**6**) Tap the Edit button to enter edit mode.

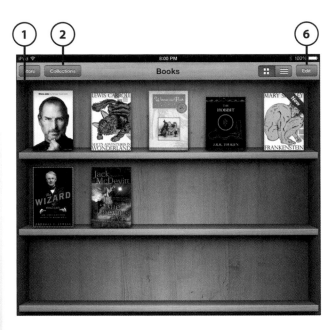

Books in the Cloud

When you view your Purchased Books collection, you will see all the books you have bought in the past, even if that book is no longer on your iPad because you removed it. These books will have a little iCloud icon in the upper-right corner; when you select one, it will download.

(7) Tap one or more books to select them.

(8) Tap the Move button to move those books to another collection.

(9) Tap the Delete button to delete those books.

(10) Tap and hold your finger over a book to drag it to a new position in the library. You can also do this in normal mode or in edit mode.

(11) Tap Done to exit edit mode.

12 Tap the List View button.

13 Now you can see a vertical list of your books. Scroll up and down by dragging and flicking.

14 Tap the Titles, Authors, and Categories buttons at the bottom of the screen to change the order of the list.

15 Use the search field to search your library. If you don't see a search field, tap and drag down on the whole list to reveal it. You can also drag down the screen to reveal the search box in the normal icon view of books and type in a search keyword there.

Another Way to Delete
You can also delete books in list view by swiping from left to right across the title of a book. A Delete button appears to the right. Tap it to delete the book.

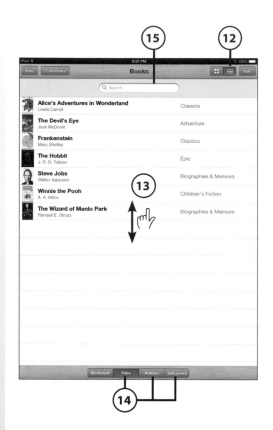

Using iBooks Alternatives

Copy protection prevents you from taking your ebooks from one platform to the other. Thankfully there are Kindle and Nook apps for the iPad, so you can read the books you purchase from those stores.

1 When you launch the Kindle app, you see a screen that displays your library. Tap a book to open it.

2 Tap the middle of the page to bring up controls at the top and bottom.

3 Tap the Font button to change the font size, brightness, and background.

4 Tap the right side to flip to the next page.

5 Use the slider at the bottom to quickly move to other pages in the book.

6 The "Go to" button allows you to jump to chapters or specific pages.

7 You can add your own bookmarks just like in iBooks.

8 Tap the Search button to search text in the book.

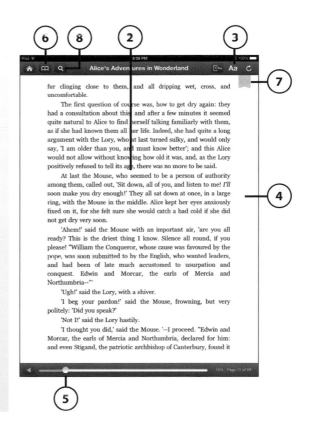

Cloud Versus Device

The new Kindle app has a Cloud/Device control at the bottom of the screen. Selecting Cloud shows you all the books you have purchased. Selecting Device shows you which books are on your iPad and ready to read. You can tap on a book on the Cloud screen to download it to your device. You can tap on it again after it has been downloaded to read it.

More eBook Alternatives

If you like to buy your books from Barnes & Noble, you can also get the Nook app. This lets you read books that can be purchased in the Nook store. If you own a Nook and have already bought books, you can access those books and load them onto your iPad.

Another App you can get is the Google Play Books app. This works with books purchased in the Google Play store, which is similar to the Amazon Kindle store or the iBookstore. You can choose whether you want to buy from Apple, Amazon, Barnes & Noble, or Google.

Track your
appointments
and events.

Set reminders.

Store and
search
all your
contacts.

Take notes
and create
lists.

In this chapter, we learn how to add and look up contacts and calendar events. We also look at the Notes app.

6

Organizing Your Life

Whether you are a well-connected businessperson or just someone who has lots of friends, you can use the iPad to organize your life with the default Contacts, Calendar, Reminders, and Clock apps. Let's take a close look at some of the things you can do with these apps.

Adding a Contact

If you use Contacts on your Mac or a contact management application on Windows, all your contacts can transfer to your iPad the first time you sync. If you have been using iCloud on your Mac or another iOS device, then your contacts will automatically appear on your iPad when you sign in to iCloud. You can also add new contacts directly on your iPad.

(1) Tap the Contacts app icon to launch the app.

(2) Press the + button near the top of the screen. A New Contact form and keyboard appear.

(3) Type the first name of the contact. No need to use Shift to capitalize the name because that happens automatically.

(4) Tap the return key on the keyboard to advance to the next field and type the last name for the contact.

(5) To add more information, like a phone number, tap the green + button next to the field name.

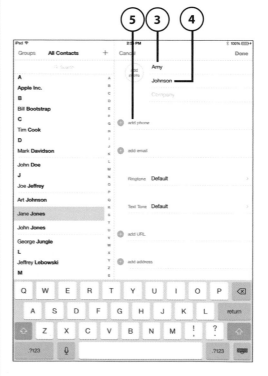

6 Type the phone number.

7 If you ever want to remove some information from the contact, you can use the red – buttons.

8 You can add more than one phone number per contact. Some contacts may have many: home, work, mobile, and so on.

9 Tap Add Photo to add a photo from one of your photo albums.

Don't Worry About Formatting
You don't need to type phone numbers with parentheses or dashes. Your iPad formats the number for you.

10 You can add one or more email addresses to the contact as well. These will be used in your Mail app when you compose a new message. You will only need to type the person's name, or choose them from a list, instead of typing their email address.

11 You can add one or more physical addresses for the contact.

12 You can select a specific ringtone for the contact that is used when they call you via FaceTime. You can also set a specific Text tone.

13 You can swipe up to see more fields. You can even add custom fields and notes to a contact.

14 Tap the Done button to complete the new contact.

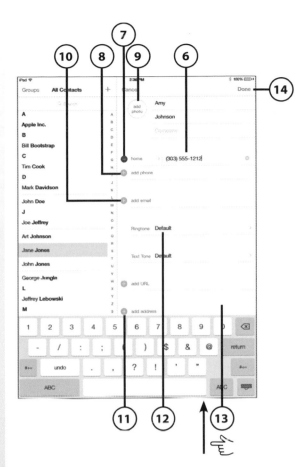

Contacts Sync

Contacts that you add to your iPad sync back to your iCloud account right away, as long as you have a connection. They will then also sync right away to your other iCloud-enabled devices. If you are not using iCloud, they will sync to your computer the next time you connect and sync using iTunes.

Siri: Call Me Ray

You can set a nickname field in a contact. When you do this, and the contact happens to be yours, Siri will call you by that name. You can always tell Siri: "Call me *name*" and it will change your nickname field even if you are not in the Contacts app at the moment.

You can also set relationships in your contacts by saying things like "Debby is my wife."

Searching for a Contact

If you didn't have a lot of friends before, I'm sure you gained quite a few since you got a new iPad. So how do you search though all those contacts to find the one you want?

(1) Tap the Contacts app icon to launch the app.

Contacts

2 Tap in the Search field. A keyboard appears at the bottom of the screen.

Other Ways to Find Contacts

You can also drag (or flick to move quickly) through the contact list to find a name. In addition, the list of letters on the left side of the Contacts app enables you to jump right to that letter in your contacts list.

Siri: Show Me

You can also use Siri to find a contact. Try these phrases:

"Show me John Smith."
"Show me my contact."
"Show me my wife."

3 Start typing the name of the person you are looking for. As soon as you start typing, the app starts making a list of contacts that contain the letters you've typed.

4 Keep typing until you narrow down the list of names and spot the one you are looking for.

5 Tap the name to bring up the contact.

6 Tap the Cancel button to dismiss the search.

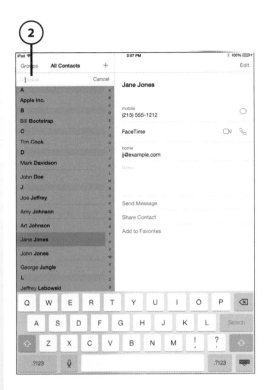

Working with Contacts

After you have contacts in your iPad, you can do a few things from a contact in the Contacts app.

(1) Tap and hold the name to copy it to the clipboard buffer.

(2) Tap and hold the phone number to copy it to the clipboard buffer.

(3) Tap the message button to send a text message to the user using that phone number. This uses Apple's iMessage system, so it will only work for other Apple users, not those who use mobile carrier's SMS systems.

(4) Tap the FaceTime button to start a video chat with the user, providing they are also on an iOS device (or a Mac) and have set up FaceTime. You can start a FaceTime video call, or tap the phone-like button for an audio-only call.

(5) Tap the email address to start composing a new email in the Mail app.

(6) Tap to the right of Notes to add more information without entering Edit mode.

(7) Tap Share Contact to send the contact information via a text message, email, or using AirDrop.

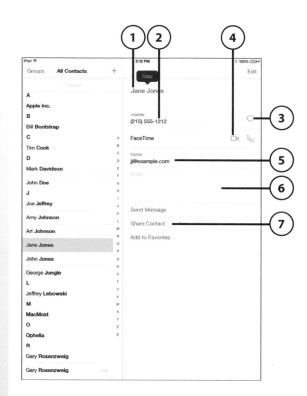

8 Tap Add to Favorites to add this contact to your Favorites group for easier access.

9 Tap Edit to enter Edit mode, which gives you the same basic functionality as entering a new contact.

Creating a Calendar Event

Now that you have people in your Contacts app, you need to schedule some things to do with them. Let's look at the Calendar app.

1 Tap the Calendar app icon on the Home screen.

(2) Tap the + button at the upper right.

(3) Enter a title for the event.

(4) Enter a Location for the event, or skip this field.

(5) Tap the Starts field to bring up a control for setting the starting time.

(6) Tap the Ends field to bring up a control for setting the ending time for the event.

(7) If the event covers the entire day, or a series of days, then slide the All-day switch on. The Starts and Ends fields will now be dates only, and won't include a specific time.

(8) Tap Repeat to set an event to repeat every day, week, 2 weeks, month, or year.

(9) Tap Invitees to send an email invitation to another person for this event, if your calendar system allows this. If you and the other person are both using iCloud, they will get a notification of the event and have the option to accept or decline. If they accept, the event will be added to their calendar. You will then be able to look at your event's invitation list in this same location and see if they have accepted or declined.

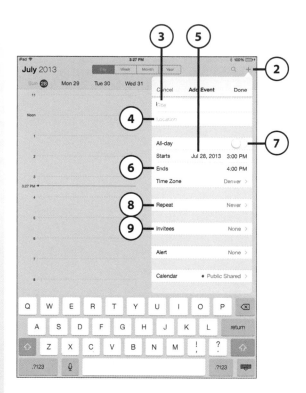

10 Tap Alert to set the time for a notification alert to appear. This can be at the time of the event, or before the event, such as 5 minutes, 15 minutes, or even as much as a week before.

11 Tap Done to complete the event.

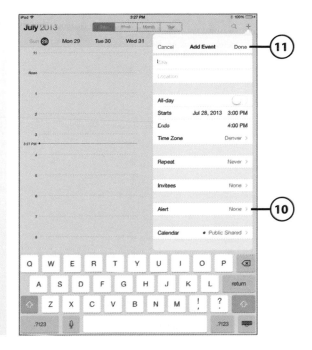

Siri: Creating Events

You can use Siri to create new events even when the Calendar app is not on your screen.

"Schedule a doctor appointment for 3 PM next Wednesday."
"Set up a meeting with John tomorrow at noon."
"Cancel my dentist appointment."

Using Calendar Views

There are three main ways to view your calendar: Day, Week, and Month. Let's take a look at each.

Exploring Day View

The Day view is broken into two halves: the left side shows a timeline from morning until evening. Events are shown as blocks of color in this vertical timeline. The right side shows information for the event selected, if any.

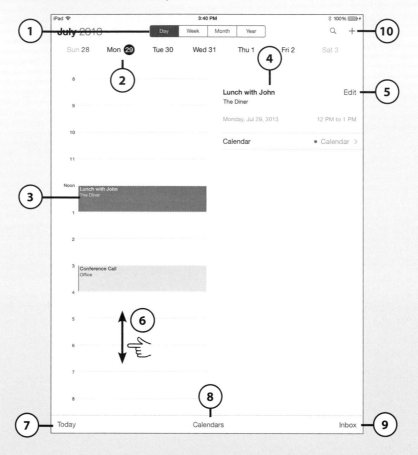

(1) Tap Day to enter Day view mode.

(2) You can tap any day shown at the top to jump to the list of events for that day. You can also drag left and right here to see previous days and upcoming ones.

(3) Tap any event shown to view information about that event.

(4) The information appears on the right.

(5) You can tap Edit to edit that event and change any aspect of it, or delete it.

(6) You can drag up and down to view the entire day.

(7) Tap Today to jump to the current day, in case you have moved to another day and want to return quickly.

(8) Tap Calendars to select which calendars are shown. This is useful if you have set up multiple calendars in iCloud, or have subscribed to public calendars.

(9) Tap Inbox to view any invitations you may have received via email or messages. You can accept or reject them. Accepted invitations will be added to your calendar.

(10) Tap + to add a new event.

Exploring Week View

To get a view of all the events for the week, switch to Week view. This gives you seven days across, but less space to preview each event. You can still select and edit events.

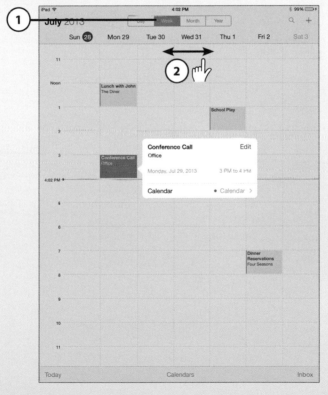

(1) Tap Week to go to the Week view.

(2) You can move to the previous week or the next by tapping and dragging in any blank part of the calendar. You can also drag vertically to see earlier in the morning or late in the evening.

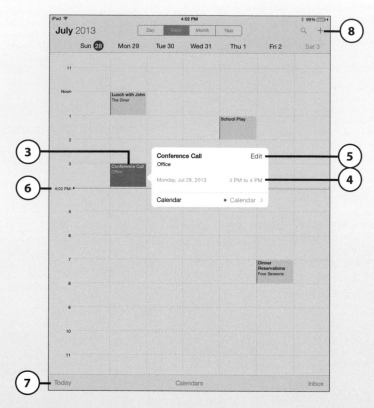

(3) Tap an event to view more information about it.

(4) The information appears in a box to the left or right of the event.

(5) You can tap Edit to edit the event right here. The familiar editing interface will appear in an expanded box while you remain in the Week view.

(6) You can see the current time represented by a red line.

(7) Tap Today if you have navigated away from the current week and want to get back.

(8) Tap + to add a new event while remaining in Week view.

Exploring Month View

To see the "big picture," you may want to use Month view. This gives you a grid of seven days across and six or more weeks vertically. While this view is similar to a monthly calendar, it doesn't necessarily have to show a single month. It can be used to show any group of six consecutive weeks.

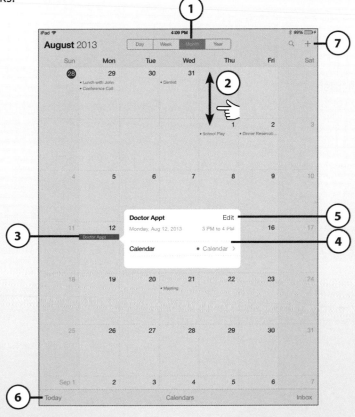

(**1**) Tap Month to enter Month view.

(**2**) While in Month view, you can tap and drag in blank areas to scroll up and down.

(**3**) Tap an event to view more information.

(**4**) The information appears in a box, like in Week view.

(**5**) Tap Edit to edit the information right here in Month view. The editing interface will appear inside an enlarged box.

(**6**) Tap Today to return to the current day if you have scrolled away from it.

(**7**) Tap + to add a new event right here in Month view.

Siri: Checking Your Schedule

You can use Siri to see what events you have coming up.

"What do I have going on tomorrow?"
"What is on my calendar for this week?"
"When is my dentist appointment?"

Year View

There is also a Year view, as you may have already noticed since there is a Year button at the top of the screen. This shows you 12 very small monthly calendars, with colored-in spaces on days where you have events. You can use this view to quickly navigate to an event in a different week or month. Or, you can use it to see when the days fall in the week.

Creating Calendars

You may have noticed in the previous tasks that you can select a calendar when you create an event. You can create multiple calendars to organize your events. For instance, you may want to have one for work and one for home.

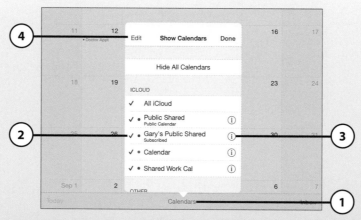

1. From any calendar view, tap the Calendars button at the bottom center.

2. You can scroll up and down this list and disable or enable calendars by tapping on the checkmarks. A calendar without a checkmark is hidden and won't appear in your views.

3. You can also view and change information about a calendar, such as changing the color used as a background for events. You can also share calendars with other iCloud users.

4. Tap Edit to go into editing mode.

(5) In Editing mode, you can also select calendars to change their color and who they are shared with.

(6) Tap Add Calendar to create a new calendar.

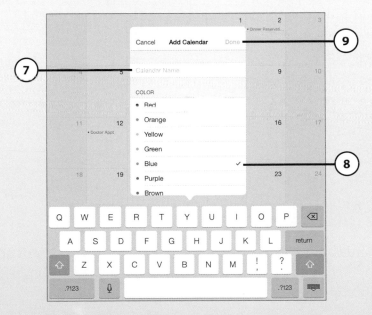

(7) Give the new Calendar a name.

(8) Set the color for the calendar.

(9) Tap Done.

Deleting a Calendar

You can delete a calendar by following the previous steps 1–4 and then selecting a calendar to edit. Scroll to the bottom below the list of colors and choose Delete Calendar.

Default Calendar

Which calendar will be used when you create a new event? The default calendar is a setting you can find in the Settings app, under Mail, Contacts, Calendars, way near the bottom of the list of preferences on the right.

>>>Go Further

SHARING CALENDARS

When you edit a calendar's information, you can also use the Add Person button that appears above the list of colors to share a calendar with a specific iCloud user. Below the colors list you can choose to set the calendar to "public" and then share an Internet link that others can use to subscribe. For instance, you can create a schedule for your softball team and make it public, and then put a link to the calendar on the team's website. Anyone can subscribe to this calendar, but only to view it. By default, others can edit it, but you can turn off Allow Editing by tapping the i button for the calendar, and then View & Edit next to the person's name with whom you are sharing it.

Creating Notes

Another organization app that comes with your iPad is the Notes app. Although this one is much more free-form than a Contacts or Calendar app, it can be useful for keeping quick notes or to-do lists.

(1) Tap the Notes icon on your Home screen.

(2) Notes opens up the note you were previously working on. To type, tap on the screen where you want the insertion point, and a keyboard appears.

What's in a Name

The filename for a note is just the first line of the note, so get in the habit of putting the title of a note as the first line of text to make finding the note easier.

(3) To start a new note, tap the Compose button at the upper right.

(4) To view a list of all your notes, and to jump to another note, tap the Notes button.

(5) Tap the name of the note you want to switch to.

(6) Tap and type in the Search field to find text inside of notes.

(7) Turn your iPad to horizontal orientation, and you'll have a permanent list of notes on the left, you don't need to tap Notes as you did in step 4 to see the list.

(8) Tap the Trash button at the top-right of the screen to delete notes.

(9) Tap the Share button at the top-right of the screen to share the note in a number of ways. For instance, you can start a new email message in the Mail app using the contents of the note, or print the note using AirPrint.

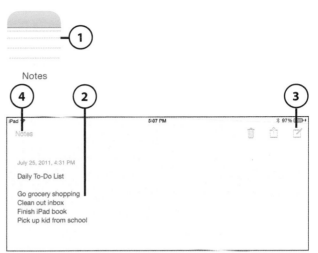

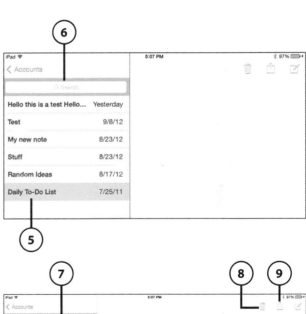

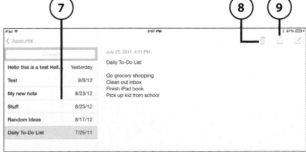

Notes Isn't a Word Processor

You can't actually use Notes for any serious writing. There aren't any styles or formatting choices. You can't even change the display font to make it larger. If you need to use your iPad for writing, consider Pages or a third-party word processing app.

Notes in the Cloud

What happens to notes after you create them can be confusing. Notes usually are attached to cloud services accounts like iCloud in the same way email messages are. If you are using the same cloud account on your Mac, for instance, you should see the notes appear almost instantly on your Mac, synced through iCloud. They will also appear on your other iOS devices.

Setting Reminders

Reminders is a to-do list application available on iPad, iPod touch, iPhone, and Macs running OS X 10.8 Mountain Lion or newer. This app is for creating an ongoing list of tasks you need to accomplish or things you need to remember. These reminders can be similar to calendar events with times and alarms. Or, they can be simple items in a list with no time attached to them.

(1) Tap the Reminders icon on your Home screen.

Reminders

2 Select the list you want to add a new Reminder to.

3 Tap in a new line to create a new reminder.

4 Type the reminder and close the keyboard when done.

5 Tap the i button next to the reminder to bring up the Details dialog. If you don't see an i button, then tap any reminder item first.

6 Tap here to edit the reminder.

7 Slide the Remind me on a day switch to on to set a reminder alert.

8 Set a time for the alert to occur.

9 Add a note to the reminder if you want to include more details.

10 Tap outside of the Details box when you are finished editing the reminder.

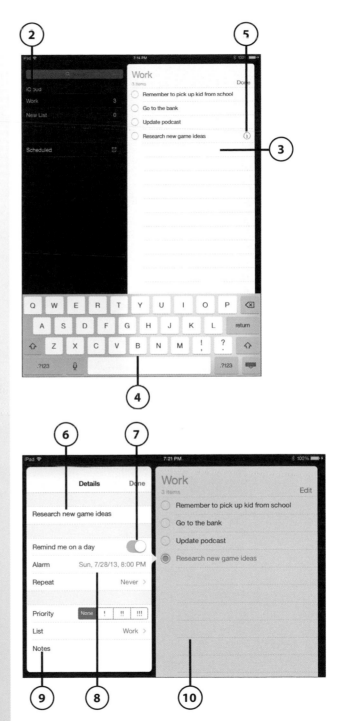

11 Tap the button next to the reminder when you have completed the task. It will remain in the list temporarily.

12 Tap Add List to add a new reminders list.

13 Tap Show Completed to see completed reminders.

14 You can also search for reminders by typing the title or something from the content.

15 Tap Edit to remove reminders.

16 Tap the red button next to a reminder to delete it.

17 Tap and drag the right side of the reminders to re-order them.

18 Tap Done when you are finished deleting and re-ordering the reminders.

19 You can also delete the entire list.

Reminders sync by using the iCloud service from Apple. So, they are automatically backed up and should also appear on your Mac in the Reminders app, if you have OS X 10.8 Mountain Lion or newer. And if you use an iPhone, they should appear there as well.

Siri: Remind Me

You can create new reminders using Siri like this:

"Remind me to watch Doctor Who tonight at 8 PM."
"Remind me to pick up milk when I leave work."
"Remind me to check my stocks every day at 9 AM."

Setting Clock Alarms

The advantage of using an alarm rather than a reminder is that an often-recurring alarm, like your morning wake-up call, or a reminder on when to pick up your child at school, won't clutter up your Reminders list or calendar.

(1) Tap the Clock app.

(2) The main screen shows up to six clocks in any time zone you want. Tap a clock to have it fill the screen.

(3) Tap an empty clock to add a new city.

(4) Tap Edit to remove or rearrange the clocks.

(5) Tap Alarm to view and edit alarms.

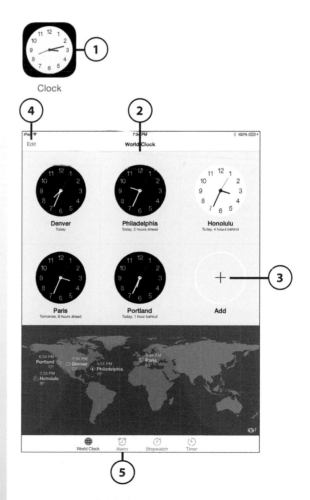

Clock

6 To add a new alarm, tap the + button.

7 Select a time for the alarm.

8 Select the days of the week for the alarm. Leaving it set to Never means you just want the alarm to be used once, as you might do if setting an alarm to wake you up early so you can catch a plane the next day. Otherwise, you can select from seven days of the week. So, you can set an alarm for Monday through Friday and leave out the weekend.

9 Tap Label to give the alarm a custom name.

10 Select a sound for the alarm. You can choose from preset sounds or your ringtone collection.

11 Leave the Snooze switch on if you want the ability to use snooze when the alarm goes off.

12 Tap Save to save all your settings and add the alarm.

13 The alarm now appears in the special Clock calendar.

14 You can switch off the alarm, while leaving it in the calendar for future use.

15 Tap Edit on an alarm to edit or delete it.

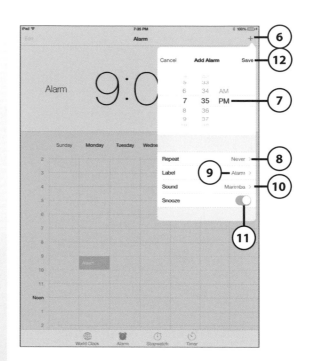

16. The alarm will sound and a message will appear when it is time. Even if your iPad is sleeping, it will wake up.

17. If you've enabled snooze, tapping here will silence the alarm and try again in 9 minutes.

18. To silence the alarm normally, assuming it has sounded while the iPad is asleep and locked, you need to swipe the lock switch. If the iPad was awake when the alarm went off, you simply get a button to tap.

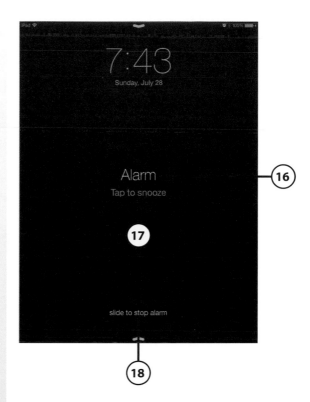

Wake Up!

When you set an alarm, it will sound even if you lower your volume to nothing, mute the sound with the side switch or Control Center, and switch into Do Not Disturb mode. This way, you can't accidentally turn off an alarm just because you wanted to avoid other distractions.

Siri: Create Alarms

You can use Siri to create and delete alarms. Try these phrases:

"Set an alarm for weekdays at 9 AM."
"Create an alarm for tomorrow at 10 AM."
"Cancel my 9 AM alarm."
"Turn on my 9 AM alarm."
"Turn off my 9 AM alarm."

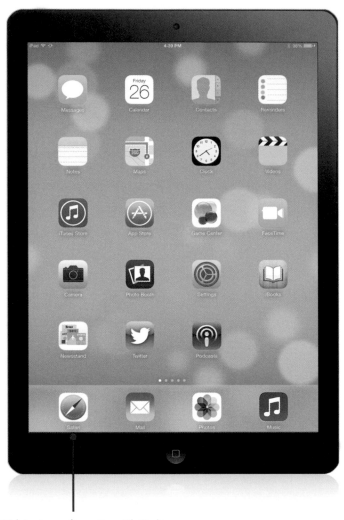

The Web is at your fingertips with iPad's
Safari web browser.

In this chapter, you learn about Safari, the browser built-in to the iPad. You can use it to browse the Web, bookmark web pages, fill in forms, and search the Internet.

→ Browsing to a URL and Searching
→ Viewing Web Pages
→ Bookmarks, History, and Reading List
→ Deleting Your Bookmarks
→ Creating Home Screen Bookmarks
→ Filling in Web Forms
→ Opening Multiple Web Pages with Tabs
→ Copying Text from a Web Page
→ Copying Images from Web Pages
→ Viewing Articles with Safari Reader
→ Saving Time with AutoFill

Surfing the Web

The iPad is a beautiful web surfing device. Its size is perfect for web pages, and your ability to touch the screen lets you interact with content in a way that even a computer typically cannot.

Browsing to a URL and Searching

Undoubtedly, you know how to get to web pages on a computer using a web browser. You use Safari on your iPad in the same way, but the interface is a little different.

At the top of the Safari browser is a toolbar with just a few buttons. In the middle, the largest interface element is the address field. This is where you can type the address of any web page on the Internet, or enter a search query.

1 Touch the Safari icon on your iPad to launch the browser. It might be located at the bottom of the screen, along with your other most commonly used applications.

Safari

2 Tap in the field at the top of the screen. This opens up the keyboard at the bottom of the screen. If you were already viewing a web page, the address of that page remains in the address field. Otherwise, it will be blank.

Clear the Slate

To clear the field at any time, tap the X button located inside the field all the way to the right.

3 Start typing a search term or a URL such as apple.com or macmost.com.

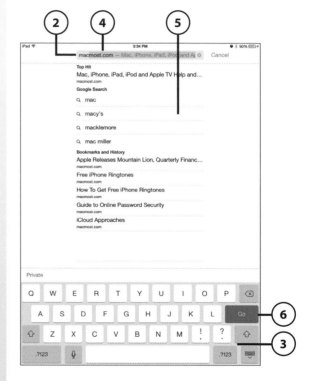

4 The area to the right of where you are typing will fill with a complete address and description, trying to predict the URL you want. You can ignore this and keep typing until you have completed the URL. You can then skip to step 6.

5 As you type, suggestions based on previous pages you have visited and past web searches from other users appear. To go directly to one of these pages, tap the page in the list.

6 Tap the Go button on the keyboard when you finish typing. If you typed or selected a URL, you will be taken to that web page.

(7) Notice that the address field at the top of the screen shows you the domain name for the website you are visiting, but doesn't display the complete URL of the specific page of that site you are on.

If you typed a search term, or selected a search from the list, the term will remain at the top and you will get a page of search results.

(8) Tap on any result to jump to that page.

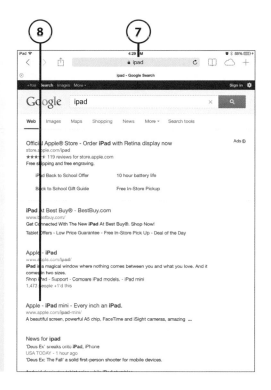

TIPS FOR TYPING A URL

- A URL is a Universal Resource Locator. It can be a website name or a specific page in a website.

- For most websites, you don't need to type the "www." at the beginning. For instance, you can type **www.apple.com** or **apple.com** and both take you to Apple's home page. You never need to type "http://" either, though occasionally you need to type "https://" to specify that you want to go to a secure web page.

- Instead of typing ".com." you can tap and hold the period button on the iPad keyboard. You can select .com, .edu, .org, .us, or .net.

Nothing Special, Please

Some websites present you with a special iPad version of the site. This is not as common as the special iPhone or iPod touch versions that many sites offer. If a website does not look the same on your iPad as it does on your computer, you might want to check to see if a switch is on the web page provided by the site to view the standard web version, instead of a special iPad version. This is especially useful if a site has lumped the iPad together with the iPhone and provided a needlessly simplified version.

Search This Page

Below Google Suggestions in the search suggestions drop-down menu is a list of recent searches and the occurrences of the phrase on the web page you are viewing. Use the latter to find the phrase on the page.

>>>Go Further

TIPS FOR SEARCHING THE WEB

- You can go deeper than just typing some words. For instance, you can put a + in front of a word to require it and a – in front to avoid that word in the results.

- You can use special search terms to look for things such as movie times, weather, flight tracking, and more. See http://www.google.com/landing/searchtips/ for all sorts of things you can do with a Google search.

- Using iPad's Settings app, you can choose the search engine that Safari uses as its default. Tap the Settings icon and choose Safari on the left, and then look for the Search Engine setting. You can choose Bing or Yahoo! instead of Google, for instance.

- Using Google, you can search for much more than text on web pages. Look at the top of the search results, and you see links such as Images, Videos, Maps, News, and Shopping. Tap "more" and you can also search for things such as Blogs and Books.

- To explore the search results without moving away from the page listing the results, tap and hold over a link to see a button that enables you to open a link in a new tab, leaving the results open in the current tab.

- You can use many search settings with Google. These are not specific to the iPad but work on your computer as well when performing searches. Tap Google's settings button (looks like a small gear) and then the Search Settings link in the upper-right corner of the search results page to choose a language, filters, and other settings. Set up a Google account (same as a Gmail account) and log in to save these search preferences and use them between different devices.

Siri: Search the Web

You can use Siri to search the web, even if you are not currently looking at the Safari screen. Sometimes Siri will also answer general questions by suggesting a web search:

"Search the web for iPad tutorials."
"Search for local plumbers."
"Search for MacMost.com."
"Search Wikipedia for Paris."
"Show me some websites about geology."
"Google Denver news."
"Search for iPad tutorials on MacMost.com."

Viewing Web Pages

Whether you typed in a URL or searched for a web page, after you have one open on your iPad screen, you can control what you view in several ways. You need to know these techniques to view the complete contents of a web page and navigate among web pages.

1 Navigate to any web page using either of the two techniques in the previous step-by-step instructions. When you arrive at the page, only the domain name shows at the top.

2 When you are viewing a page, you can touch and drag the page up and down with your finger. As you do so, notice the bar on the right side that gives you an indication of how much of the complete web page you are viewing at one time.

Flick It

If you release your finger from the iPad screen to stop scrolling while dragging, the screen will continue to scroll with a decelerating affect and then come to a stop quickly.

3 To zoom in on an area in the page, touch the screen with two fingers and move your fingers apart. This is called an unpinch. You can also move them closer together (pinch) to zoom back out. A double-tap restores the page to normal scaling. This works well on websites made for desktop computers, but mobile sites usually are set to already fit the screen at optimal resolution.

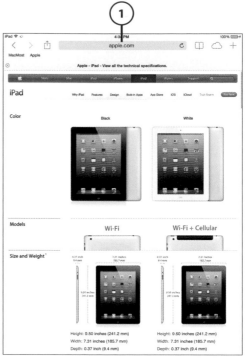

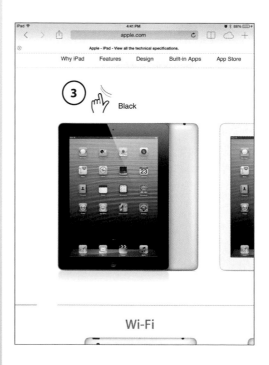

4 You can also double-tap images and paragraphs of text to zoom in to those elements in the web page. A second double-tap zooms back out.

5 While zoomed in, you can also touch and drag left and right to view different parts of the web page. You see a bar at the bottom of the screen when you do this, just like the bar on the right side in step 2.

6 To move to another web page from a link in the current web page, just tap the link. Links are usually an underlined or colored piece of text; however, they can also be pictures or button-like images.

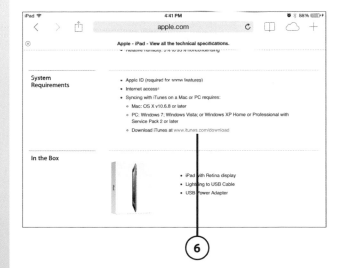

It's Not All Good

Where's the Link?

Unfortunately, it isn't always easy to figure out which words on a page are links. Years ago, these were all blue and underlined. But today, links can be any color and may not be underlined.

On the iPad, it is even more difficult to figure out which words are links. This is because many web pages highlight links when the cursor moves over the word. But with the touch interface of the iPad, there is no cursor.

Bookmarks, History, and Reading List

You can always visit a web page by typing its address in the field at the top of Safari. But the app also has a way for you to get to your most frequently visited sites easily, find a page you recently visited, or save a page to read later.

Using Bookmarks and Favorites

Bookmarks allow you to save the web pages you visit most often and then access them with just a few taps. Favorites are bookmarks that appear at the top of the Safari browser for easier access.

1. Use Safari to navigate to any web page.

2. Tap the Share button at the top of the screen.

3. Tap Bookmark.

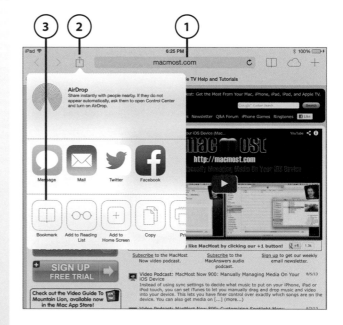

(4) Edit the title of the bookmark. The official title of the web page is prefilled, but you can use the keyboard to change it. You can tap the X to clear the text and start fresh.

(5) Tap Location to place the book-mark in a bookmarks folder.

(6) You can choose to place the bookmark in Favorites, so it will appear at the top of the Safari window where you can easily find it.

(7) Or you can put it in Bookmarks, where you can select it from the Bookmarks menu.

(8) Tap Save to finish creating the bookmark.

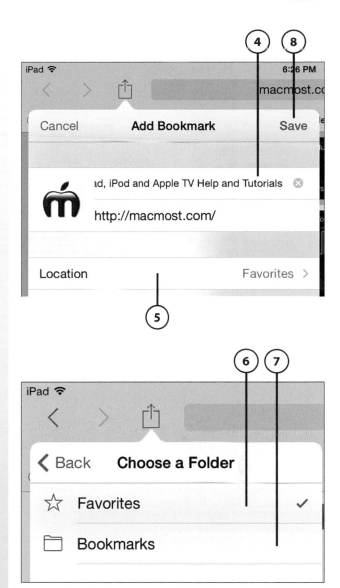

9 To use a bookmark, first tap the Bookmarks button.

10 Find the bookmark in the list and tap it to go to that web page.

11 If you put the bookmark in Favorites, or another folder, you have to tap that folder name first to dig down to find the bookmark.

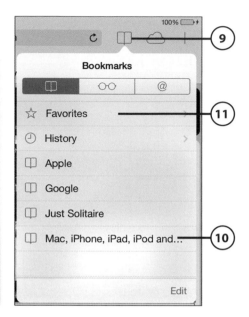

TIPS FOR BOOKMARKING WEBSITES

- The titles of web pages are often long and descriptive. It is a good idea to shorten the title to something you can easily recognize, especially if it is a web page that you plan to visit often.

- Only save the most important bookmarks to the Favorites folder. These always show up at the top of your Safari screen unless you have disabled Favorites in the Settings app under Safari. If use shorter names for these bookmarks, you can fit more onto the Favorites bar.

- To create folders inside the Bookmarks folder, tap the Bookmarks button at the top of the Safari screen. Then choose the Bookmarks button at the top. At the bottom of that menu, tap Edit and then tap New Folder.

- You can create folders of bookmarks under Favorites. These appear as their own pop-up menu when you tap them, giving you direct access to a subset of your bookmarks.

- Favorites also appear when you close all tabs in Safari, or start a new tab by tapping the + button. Instead of a blank page, you get a screen full of icons, one for each Favorite you have added. This makes these "blank" web pages a good launch point for Web surfing.

>>>Go Further

Using History

Safari keeps track of which web pages you have visited. You can use this history to find a page you went to earlier today, yesterday, or even several days back.

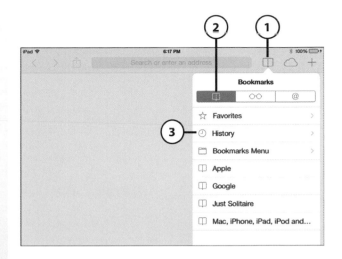

(1) After using Safari to view several pages, tap the Bookmarks button at the top of the screen.

(2) Tap the first tab at the top of this menu to view your bookmarks and history folders.

(3) You may already be viewing your history at this point. If the top of this menu reads History instead of Bookmarks, then you are. Otherwise, tap the History item to go into your history.

(4) Tap any item in the list to jump to that web page.

(5) Previous pages you have visited are broken into groups by date.

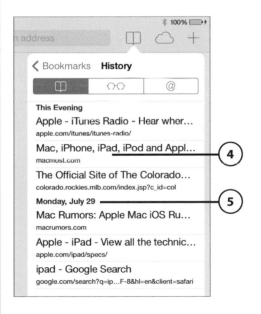

History/Bookmarks

Safari treats both history and bookmarks the same. They are both just lists of web pages. Think of your history as a bookmark list of every site you have visited recently.

Deleting Your Bookmarks

Adding and using bookmarks is just the start. You eventually need to delete ones you don't use. Some might link to missing or obsolete pages, or some you simply no longer use. There are two ways to delete a bookmark. The results of the two methods are the same; however, you might find the second method gives you a little more control.

Delete a Single Bookmark

The first method uses the Bookmarks list to locate and delete a single bookmark.

1. Tap the Bookmarks button at the top of the Safari screen.

2. Navigate to the Bookmarks section of that menu.

3. Tap Edit.

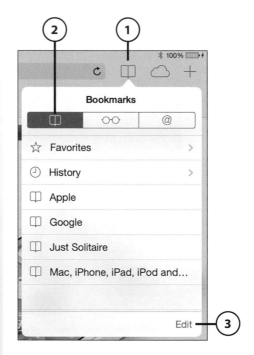

(4) Tap the red button next to a bookmark.

(5) Tap the Delete button to remove the bookmark. The bookmark is instantly deleted.

(6) Tap Done when you finish deleting bookmarks.

Sync Your Bookmarks

If you are using iCloud, your bookmarks should sync between all your iOS and Mac devices. Safari on your computer gives you greater control over moving and deleting bookmarks. So just do your wholesale editing on your computer and those changes should be reflected in your iPad's bookmarks as well.

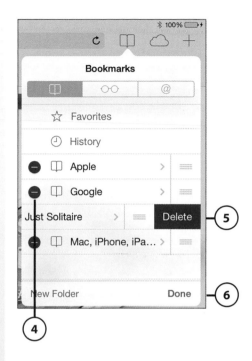

Creating Home Screen Bookmarks

If a web page is somewhat important, you might want to create a bookmark for it. If it is extremely important and you need to go to it often, you might want to make sure that bookmark is saved to your Bookmarks Bar so that it is easily accessible.

However, if a web page is even more important to you than that, you can save it as an icon on your iPad's Home screen.

(1) Use Safari to navigate to any web page.

(2) Tap the Share button at the top of the screen.

(3) Tap Add to Home Screen. Note that the icon shown here will change to use the icon for that website or to a small screen capture of the site.

Managing Home Screen Bookmarks

You can arrange and delete Home screen bookmarks just like icons that represent apps.

(4) You can now edit the name of the page. Most web page titles are too long to display under an icon on the Home screen of the iPad, so edit the name down to as short a title as possible.

(5) You can tap Cancel to leave this interface without sending the bookmark to the Home screen.

(6) Tap Add to complete adding the icon to the Home screen.

(7) Press the Home button to return to your Home screen.

(8) Look for the new icon on your Home screen that represents this bookmark. You may need to swipe through the pages of your Home screens to find it. Then, you can move it to any page or into a folder. The icon acts just like the app icons on your Home screen.

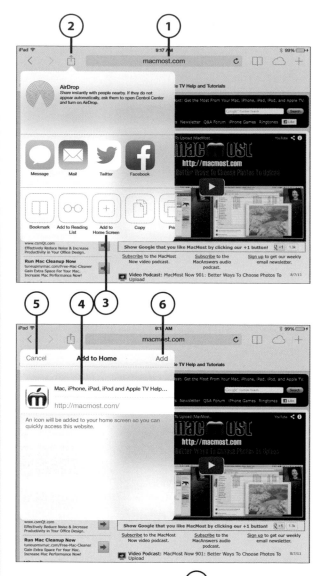

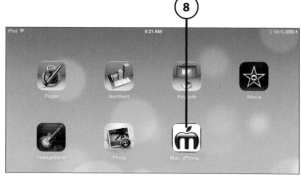

Website Icons

The icon for this type of bookmark can come from one of two sources. Web page owners can provide a special iPhone/iPad icon that would be used whenever someone tries to bookmark her page.

However, if no such icon has been provided, your iPad will take a screen shot of the web page and shrink it down to make an icon.

Building a Reading List

Your reading list is similar to bookmarks. You can add a page to your reading list to remember to return to that page later. When you do, it will be removed from the Unread section of your reading list, but still appear in the All section.

In addition, pages you add to your reading list are downloaded to your iPad so that you can read them later while not connected to the Internet.

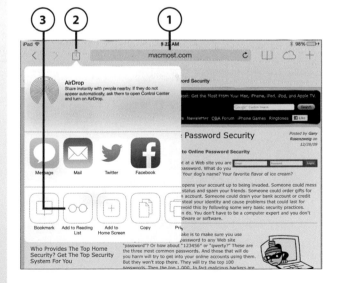

1. Find an article you want to read later.

2. Tap the Share button.

3. Tap Add to Reading List.

(4) To see your reading list, tap the Bookmarks button.

(5) Tap the Reading List button.

(6) Tap any item to view the page. Even if you are not connected to the Internet, the page will show because Safari stored the content when you added the page to the Reading List.

(7) At the bottom you see either Show All or Show Unread. This lets you switch between the two lists. Show All shows everything in your Reading List. Show Unread does not show items you have already opened from the Reading List.

Reading List Syncing

The Reading List also syncs across your iOS devices and Macs using iCloud. So you can add it on your Mac and then see it appear in your Reading List on your iPad.

Shared Links

In addition to Bookmarks and Reading List, there is a third button that looks like an @ symbol that appears only if you are signed into social media networks like Twitter or Facebook in the Settings app. Here you find shared links. Recently shared links from those networks appear in this list.

Filling in Web Forms

The Web isn't a one-way street. Often you need to interact with web pages, filling in forms or text fields. Doing this on the iPad is similar to doing it on a computer, but with a few key differences.

The keyboard shares screen space with the web page, so when you tap on a field, you bring up the keyboard at the bottom of the screen.

Also pull-down menus behave differently. On the iPad, you get a special menu showing you all the options.

(1) Use Safari to navigate to a web page with a form. For demonstration purposes, try one of the pages at http://apple.com/feedback/.

(2) To type in a text field, tap that field.

(3) The keyboard appears at the bottom of the screen. Use it to type text into the field.

(4) Tap the Go button when you finish filling in all the required fields.

(5) To select a check box or radio button, tap it just as you would click on it on your computer using the mouse.

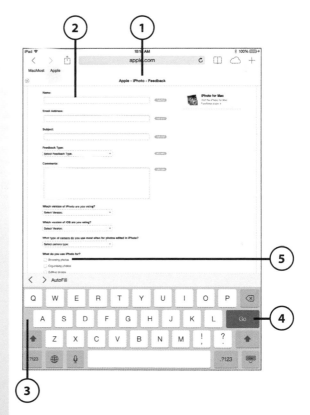

6 To select an item in a pull-down menu, tap the menu.

7 The special iPad pull-down menu reacts like any other iPad interface. You can tap an item to select it. You can touch and drag up and down to view more selections if the list is long.

8 A check mark appears next to the currently selected item. Tap that item or any other one to select it and dismiss the menu.

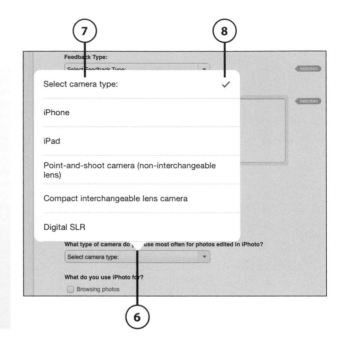

Special Menus

Some websites may use special menus that they build from scratch, rather than these default HTML menus. When this is the case, you get a menu that looks exactly like the one you get when viewing the web page on a computer. If the web page is well coded, it should work fine on the iPad, though it might be slightly more difficult to make a selection.

>>>Go Further

TIPS FOR FILLING IN FORMS

- You can use the AutoFill button just above the keyboard to fill in your name, address, and other contact info instead of typing on the keyboard. To enable AutoFill, go into your iPad Settings and look for the Passwords & AutoFill preferences under Safari. Also make sure your own information is correct and complete in your card in the Contacts application.

- To move between fields in a form, use the flat left and right arrow buttons just above the keyboard that move to the Previous or Next field. You can quickly fill in an entire form this way without having to tap on the web page to select the next item.

Opening Multiple Web Pages with Tabs

Safari on the iPad enables you to open multiple web pages at the same time. You can view only one at a time, but you can hold your place on a page while you look at something on another page.

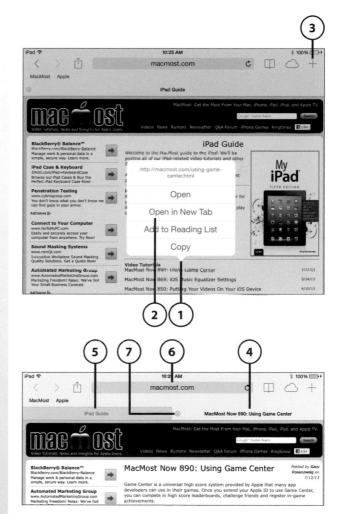

1 Instead of tapping on a link, tap down and hold your finger there until a contextual menu pops up above your finger.

2 Tap Open in New Tab.

3 Alternatively, you can tap the + button at the top of the screen to open a new tab that shows icons linking to the websites you have put in your Favorites.

4 You see two tabs at the top of the screen now. The one on the right is in front of the one on the left and represents the page you are looking at below.

5 You can switch tabs by tapping on the other tab; that tab now appears front of the one on the right, and the screen area below shows that page.

6 When you enter a new web address, search, or use a bookmark, it changes the page of the current tab, but doesn't affect the other tab.

7 You can close the current tab by tapping the X button to the left of the tab's name.

iCloud Tabs

If you have iCloud set up on multiple iOS devices and/or Macs running Mountain Lion, you may see a cloud icon in the Safari toolbar next to the Bookmarks button. Tap that and you will see tabs that are currently open on those other devices. You can select one item to open that page. This means you can surf on your Mac for a while, and then switch to the iPad and easily find the pages you were just looking at on your Mac.

Copying Text from a Web Page

You can select text from web pages to copy and paste into your own documents or email messages.

1. Use Safari to navigate to a web page.

2. Tap and hold over a piece of text. You don't need to be exact because you can adjust the selection later. The word Copy appears above the selected area that is highlighted in light blue.

3. You can tap and drag one of the four blue dots to change the selection area. When your selection gets small enough, it changes to only two blue dots indicating the first and last character of the selection.

4. Tap outside the selection at any time to cancel the selection.

5. Tap the Copy button over the selection to copy the text.

6. You can now go to another application such as Mail or Pages and tap in a text area to choose Paste and paste the text into the area. You can also do this in a form on a page in Safari, such as a web-based email form.

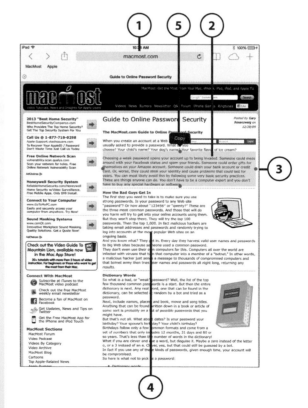

What Does That Mean?

If you select only a single word in Safari, or just tap and hold any word in the text of a web page, you get the menu with Copy as an option as well as a second option: Define. Use this to get a quick definition of a word in a little window that overlays the web page.

Copying Images from Web Pages

Along with copying and pasting text from Safari, you can copy images and save them to your photo collection.

(1) Use Safari to navigate to a web page that has an image you want to save.

(2) Tap and hold your finger on that image until the contextual menu appears.

(3) The menu shows you the title of the image and some options. If the image is also a link to another web page, you might see options to Open that page here as well.

(4) Select Copy to copy the image to the Clipboard. You can then go to a program such as Mail or Pages and paste that image into the document you are composing.

(5) Alternatively, you can tap Save Image and put a copy of the image in your Camera Roll. This may be a good option because many apps use the Camera Roll to allow you to import, edit, share, and do other things to images.

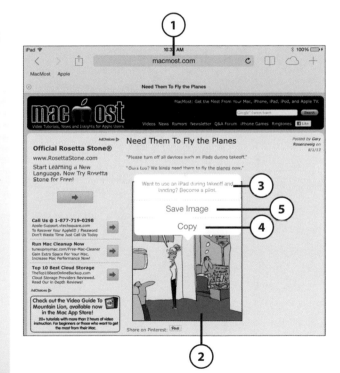

Viewing Articles with Safari Reader

Web pages on the iPad can be vibrant and pretty. But sometimes the website tries to cram so much text and other junk onto a page that it can be painful to read. You can clear away all the clutter to reveal the text of a news article or blog post using the Reader feature.

(1) Look for the Reader button in the address field. It will only appear on some news articles and blog posts. Tap it to enter the Reader mode.

(2) In Reader mode, only the text and inline images of the article appear.

(3) Tap Reader again to return to the regular view of the page.

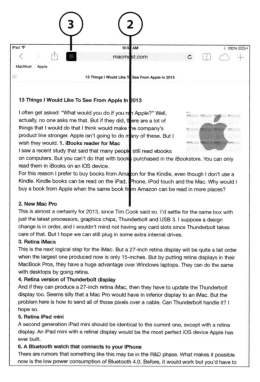

Reader Font Size

Previous versions of Reader have allowed you to change the font size at the top of the page. You can still change the font size, but not as easily, and not just for Reader. In the Settings app, go to General, TextSize. You can drag a slider there to increase the font size used by Safari's Reader feature. This will affect other apps as well, such as Mail and Notes.

Saving Time with AutoFill

When you go to websites and fill out forms, it can be annoying to type out basic information like your name and address, or your user ID and password. Furthermore, if you have to type your password every time you visit a site, or even on a daily or weekly basis, this encourages you to use simple, easy-to-guess passwords so you don't have to type long complex strings of characters.

The Keychain function built into Safari allows you to automatically fill in forms and login prompts. After you enter your information the first time, you never have to do it again for that website.

Setting Up AutoFill

To set up AutoFill in Safari, start by going to the Settings app.

① Tap Safari in the Settings app.

② Tap Passwords & AutoFill.

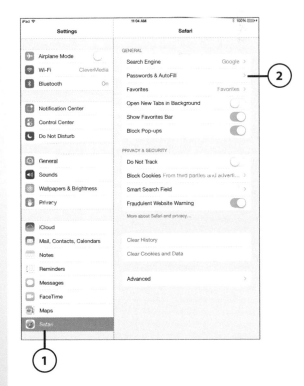

3 Slide the Use Contact Info switch on, if it's not. Now any time you go to a web page with a form that asks for basics like name, address, or telephone number, AutoFill uses your contact information in the Contacts app to fill those fields automatically.

4 Tap My Info to tell Safari which contact in the Contacts app is you.

5 Slide the Names and Passwords switch on to have Safari remember user IDs and passwords when you log on to websites. As you will see in the next section, Safari prompts you each time you enter a new User ID and Password so you can decide the passwords that are saved.

6 After you have visited some sites and saved some passwords, you can access the list of saved passwords by tapping Saved Passwords.

7 Tap on any entry to view the ID, password, and the website it belongs to.

8 You can enter Edit mode to delete entries.

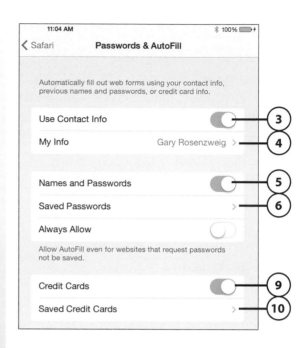

(9) Safari can also remember credit card information. Slide the Credit Cards switch to on for this information to be saved.

(10) Tap Saved Credit Cards to see a list of your saved credit cards and to add new ones. When you add a credit card, include your name, the card number, the expiration date, and a short description. However, the security code for the card is not saved. Most websites will ask you for this even after Safari has autofilled in the information it has saved.

>>>Go Further

SAFETY AND SECURITY

If you add your passwords and credit card information for Safari to automatically fill in, isn't that incredibly insecure? Well, it is if you have not set a passcode for your iPad. The Settings app recommends this when you turn these options on.

You should set a passcode under Settings, General, Passcode Lock. Then, you should set the Require Passcode option to Immediately so as soon as you lock your iPad by closing the Smart Cover or pressing the sleep button, the passcode is required to use it.

Even with the security enabled, using a simple passcode like 1234 or letting it sit around unlocked still presents a problem. You don't need to use AutoFill on every website. You could use it for unimportant sites like games and forums, and avoid using it for bank accounts and social media sites.

The advantage to using AutoFill for passwords is that you can use a long, random password for an account rather than a short, memorable one. It is more likely that your account will be broken into remotely when you use a short, common password than someone stealing your iPad and using it to gain access to that website. And even if they do, you can simply change your important passwords if your iPad is stolen.

Using AutoFill

After you have AutoFill set up, using it is relatively simple. You can use it with a form that asks for basic contact information, or for a login form. The process is the same. Let's look at using it with a simple login form.

(1) Enter an ID or password at a website.

(2) If AutoFill is enabled, you may be prompted by Safari to save the password.

(3) Tap Save Password to save the user ID and password.

(4) Alternatively, you can tell Safari that you don't want to save the password for this site, and not to ask again.

(5) You can also skip this for now. This is useful if you have multiple logons for a site and don't want to save the one you are using at this moment.

(6) Log out and then return to the same website.

(7) You'll notice that the ID and password are already filled in. The fields turn yellow to show that AutoFill has been used to fill them in.

(8) Tap the button used by the site to complete the login.

(9) On some websites, the information might not fill in automatically. You can try tapping the AutoFill Password button to force it.

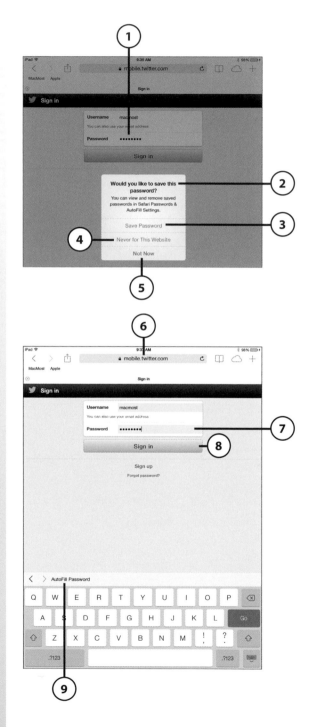

Changing Passwords

So what happens if you change passwords for a site? Simply use the keyboard to erase and retype the password when logging into that site the next time. AutoFill will prompt you, asking if you want to save the new password, replacing the old one in its database.

It's Not All Good

AutoFill Not Working?

AutoFill works because forms use typical names for fields: id, password, name, firstname, last-name, zip, and so on. If a website wants to get creative, or intentionally block AutoFill functions of browsers, then the site may obfuscate the names of fields to make it impossible for AutoFill to tell which field is which.

Therefore, some websites might not work with AutoFill, while others do. This may be intentional, depending on the sites you visit.

Send and receive
messages from other iOS
and Mac users.

Keep up with
your friends on
Twitter.

Send and receive email from your ISP or a
variety of popular email services.

Next, we look at how to configure and use the Mail program on your iPad to correspond using email and how to use the Messaging and Twitter apps to send and receive messages.

8

Communicating with Email, Messaging, and Twitter

Now that you have an iPad with a battery that seems to last forever, you have no excuse for not replying to emails. You need to be comfortable using the built-in Mail app that enables you to connect with your home or work email using standard protocols such as POP and IMAP. You can even connect with more proprietary systems such as AOL, Exchange, and Yahoo! You can also send messages to your friends using Apple's iMessage system or Twitter.

Configuring Your iPad for Email

It's easy to set up your email if you use one of the popular email services like iCloud, Gmail, Yahoo, AOL, or Microsoft. But if you use another kind of service, such as the email given to you by your local ISP, you need to collect some information to set things up. Here is a list of information you need to set up your iPad for a basic email account

- Email Address
- Account Type (POP or IMAP)
- Incoming Mail Server Address
- Incoming Mail User ID
- Incoming Mail Password
- Outgoing Mail Server Address
- Outgoing Mail User ID
- Outgoing Mail Password

>>>Go Further

IMAP VERSUS POP

POP (Post Office Protocol) fetches and removes email from a server. The server acts as a temporary holding place for email. It is difficult to use POP if you receive email using both your iPad and a computer. You need to either deal with some email going to one device and some to another, or set up one device to not remove email from the server so that the other device can also retrieve it.

IMAP (Internet Message Access Protocol) makes the server the place where all messages are stored, and your iPad and computer simply display what is on the server. It is more ideal in situations where you have multiple devices getting email from the same account.

Popular email services like iCloud and Gmail use an IMAP-like system so you can easily manage your email from both your iPad and your desktop computer—and even your phone.

If you wonder why you shouldn't skip all the setup and just use webmail on your iPad, it's because you can't use emailing features in other apps—such as emailing web page links or emailing photos—if you don't configure the email settings.

If you are using iCloud, Gmail, or any of the other services listed on the Add Account screen, all you need to do is enter your email address and password. Your iPad will set up the account from those two pieces of information. But if you are using another type of email account, you need to enter several details about your account.

Settings

1. Tap the Settings icon on your Home screen.

2. Tap Mail, Contacts, Calendars.

3. Tap Add Account.

4. If you have an iCloud, Microsoft Exchange, Gmail, Yahoo! Mail, AOL, or Hotmail account, tap the corresponding button. From there, simply enter your user ID and password information, and your iPad figures out the rest. You can skip the rest of the steps!

5. Tap Other if you have a traditional POP or IMAP account from work, your Internet providers, or a traditional hosting company.

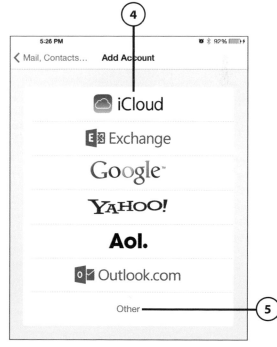

(6) Tap Add Mail Account.

(7) Tap in the Name field and enter your name.

(8) Tap in the Address field and enter your email address.

(9) Tap in the Password field and enter your password.

(10) The Description field should automatically fill with a copy of your email address. Keep it or use another description for the account.

(11) Tap Next.

(12) Tap IMAP or POP as the email account type.

(13) Tap in the Incoming Mail Server, Host Name field and enter your email host's address.

(14) Tap in the Incoming Mail Server, User Name field and enter your user name.

(15) Tap in the Incoming Mail Server, Password field and enter your password.

(16) Repeat the previous three steps for Outgoing Mail Server.

(17) Tap Next, and the verification process, which can take up to a minute, begins.

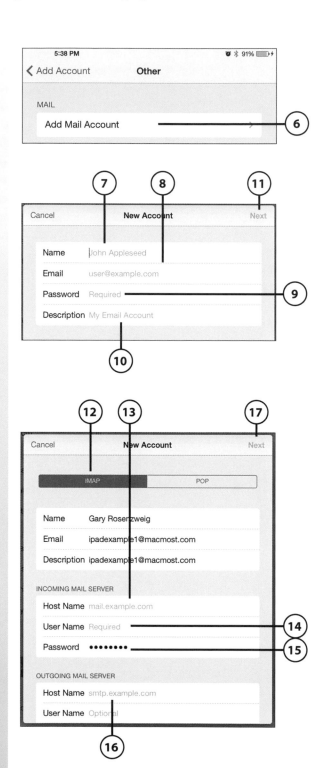

What if the Settings Won't Verify?

If your settings fail to verify, you need to double-check all the information you entered. When something is wrong, it often comes down to a single character being mistyped in one of these fields. For instance, some email systems expect yourname+example.com as the user ID if your email address is yourname@example.com. Be careful you don't miss little things like that.

Reading Your Email

You use the Mail app to read your email, which is much easier to navigate and type with your iPad turned horizontally. Let's start by reading some email.

Mail

(1) Tap the Mail app icon on the Home screen.

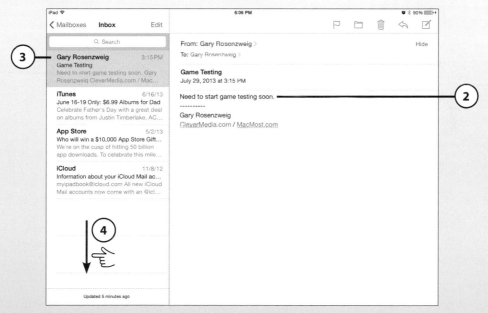

(2) On the left, you see a list of incoming mail. On the right, you see the selected message.

(3) Tap a message in the list to view it.

(4) If you want to check for new mail, drag the list of messages down and release. It will spring back up and ask the server to see if there are new messages.

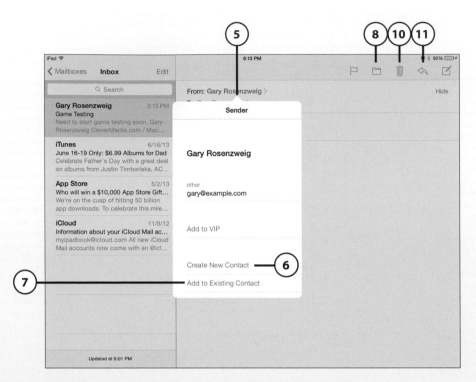

5. Tap the name or email address of the sender.

6. Tap Create New Contact to add the sender to your contacts.

7. Tap Add to Existing Contact to add the email address to a contact you already have in your Contacts app.

8. Tap the Folder button at the top of the message.

9. Tap a folder to move the current message to that folder.

10. Tap the Trash button at the top of the message to send the message directly to the Trash folder.

11. Tap the arrow button at the top of the message to reply or forward the message.

Multiple Inboxes

If you have more than one email account, you can choose to look at each inbox individually or a single unified inbox that includes messages from all accounts. Just tap the Mailboxes button at the upper-left corner of the screen and choose All Inboxes. You can also choose to look at the inbox of a single account, or dig down into any folder of an account.

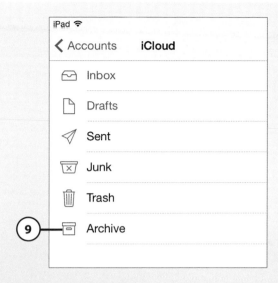

How Do You Create Folders?

For most email accounts—particularly IMAP, Gmail, and iCloud accounts—you can create folders using the Mail app. Use the back arrow at the upper-left corner of Mail and back out to the list of inboxes and accounts. Choose an account. Then tap the Edit button, and you'll see a New Mailbox button at the bottom of the screen.

VIPs

You can make a contact a VIP when you select the sender's name in an incoming email. Then, their messages will continue to appear in your inbox as normal, but they will also appear in the VIP inbox. So if you get a lot of email and want to occasionally focus only on a few very important people instead of everyone, choose your VIP inbox rather than your inbox.

If you are using VIPs with your iCloud email accounts, you'll see the same VIPs for your Mac and other iOS devices using that iCloud account.

Composing a New Message

Whether you compose a new message or reply to one you received, the process is similar. Let's take a look at composing one from scratch.

(1) In the Mail app, tap the Compose button.

(2) Enter a To: address.

(3) Alternatively, tap the + button to bring up a list of contacts, and choose from there.

(4) Tap in the Subject field and type a subject for the email.

Siri: Sending Email

You can use Siri to send email by asking it to "send an email to" and the name of the recipient. It will ask you for a subject and a body to the message, and then display it. You can choose to send it or cancel.

---

(5) Tap below the subject field in the body of the email, and type your message.

(6) Tap the Send button.

Including Images

You can copy and paste inside a Mail message just like you can inside of any text entry area on your iPad. But you can also paste in images! Just copy an image from any source—Photos app, Safari, and so on. Then tap in the message body and select Paste. You can paste in more than one image as well.

Creating a Signature

You can create a signature that appears below your messages automatically. You do this in the Settings app.

1. In the Settings app, choose Mail, Contacts, Calendars.

2. Tap Signature, which is way down in the list on the right.

(3) If you have more than one email account set up, you can choose to have one signature for all accounts or a different signature for each account.

(4) Type a signature in one of the signature text fields. You don't need to do anything to save the signature. You can tap the Home button on your iPad to exit Settings if you like.

Case-By-Case Signatures

You can have only one signature, even if you have multiple email accounts on your iPad. But the signature is placed in the editable area of the message composition field, so you can edit it like the rest of your message.

Deleting and Moving Messages

While viewing a message, you can simply tap the Trash Can icon and move it to the trash. You can also move a group of messages to a folder or the trash.

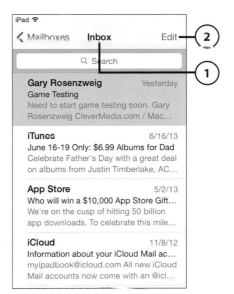

1. In the Mail app, go to any mail-box and any subfolder, such as your Inbox.

2. Tap the Edit button.

3. Tap the circles next to each message to select them.

4. They will be added to the middle of the screen in a neat stack.

5. Tap the Trash button to delete the selected messages.

6. Tap the Move button, and the left side of the screen changes to a list of folders. You can select one to move all the messages to that folder.

7. Tap the Cancel button to exit without deleting or moving any messages.

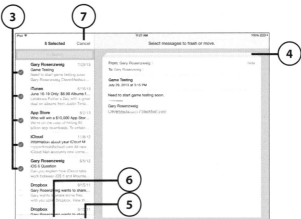

Where's the Trash?

If you are just deleting the single message that you happen to be viewing, you can tap the trashcan icon at the top. But sometimes that icon isn't there. Instead, you may see an icon that looks like a file box. This is an Archive button. Some email services, like Gmail, insist that you archive your email instead of deleting it. To facilitate this, they provide a nearly infinite amount of storage space, so you might as well use that Archive button.

What About Spam?

Your iPad has no built-in spam filter. Fortunately, most email servers filter out spam at the server level. Using a raw POP or IMAP account from an ISP might mean you don't have any server-side spam filtering, unfortunately. But using an account at a service such as Gmail means that you get spam filtering on the server and junk mail automatically goes to the Junk folder, not your Inbox.

Searching Email

You can also search your messages using the Mail app.

(1) In the Mail app, from a mailbox view, tap in the Search field.

(2) Type a search term.

(3) Select a message to view from the search results.

(4) Tap the keyboard hide key at the bottom right to hide the keyboard.

(5) Tap Cancel to exit the search and return to the mailbox you were previously viewing.

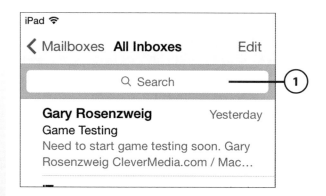

Search What?

Searches work on From, To, Subject fields and the body of the message. However, this only works on messages stored on your iPad. If you are using a server-based email solution, such as IMAP, iCloud, Gmail, and so on, you may not get all the results you expect.

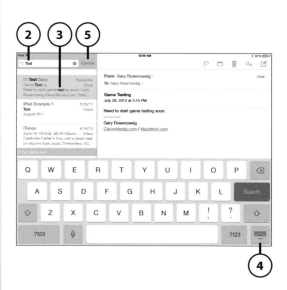

Configuring How Email Is Received

You have more settings for email beyond the basic account setup. You can decide how you want to receive email, using either push delivery (iCloud, IMAP, and Microsoft Exchange) or fetch delivery (all other email accounts).

(1) Go to the Settings app and tap on Mail, Contacts, Calendars.

(2) Tap Fetch New Data.

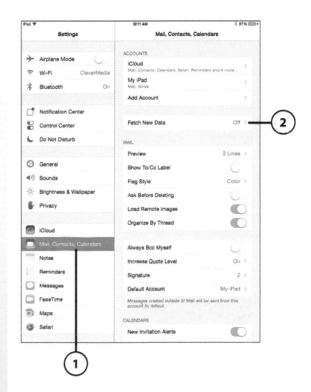

3 Turn on Push to use push email reception, if you use email accounts that can send email via push. Push means that the email servers alert your iPad when new mail arrives, instead of waiting for your iPad to check for new mail every so often.

4 Otherwise, select how often you want your iPad to go out to the server and fetch email.

5 Tap one of your email accounts to customize the settings for that particular account.

6 For each account you can set your preferences to Fetch, Manual, or Push if available for that email account.

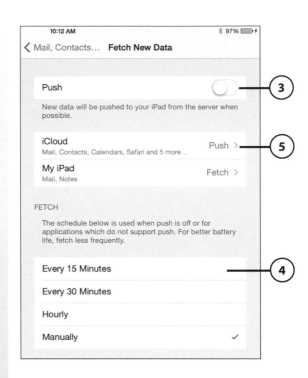

Push Settings

The two choices for most email accounts are Fetch and Manual. If you have a push account, such as iCloud, you have three choices: Push, Fetch, and Manual. You can switch a Push account to Fetch or Manual if you prefer. You might want to use Manual if you are concerned about bandwidth, like when traveling internationally and only want to check email when using Wi-Fi.

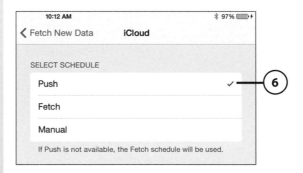

Siri: Checking Email

You can ask Siri for a quick list of new email messages by saying "check my email." You'll get a list from within the Siri interface, and you can tap on a message to read it in the Mail app.

More Email Settings

You can change even more email settings in the Settings app. Let's take a look at some of them.

(1) Tap Preview to choose how many lines of message preview to show when stacking messages up in the list view.

(2) Turn Show To/Cc Label on to view "To" or "Cc" in each email listed so that you know if you were the primary recipient or someone who was just copied on an email to someone else.

(3) Turn Ask Before Deleting on to require a confirmation when you tap the trash can button in Mail.

(4) Turn Load Remote Images off so that images referenced in an mail, but stored on a remote server, are not shown in the message body.

(5) To group replies to a message under the original message, select Organize By Thread. This is handy when you subscribe to email discussion lists.

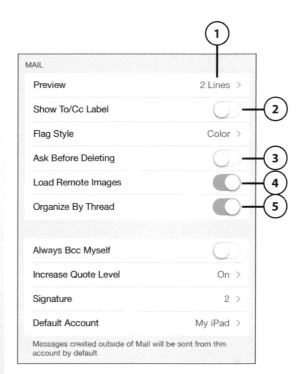

6 Turn Always Bcc Myself on if you want to get a copy of every email you send so that later you can move your copies of emails to your Sent folder on your computer. This might be a good idea if you are using an older email system. Modern email systems like iCloud and Gmail should save your sent messages to the server just like other messages.

7 Choose whether to indent the quoted text from the original email when replying to a message.

8 Tap Default Account to determine which account is used to send email by default if you have more than one account set up on your iPad.

9 In most apps from which you send emails, you can type a message and also change the account you use to send the email. To do this, tap on the email address shown next to From: and you get a list of all your accounts, including alternate email addresses for each account.

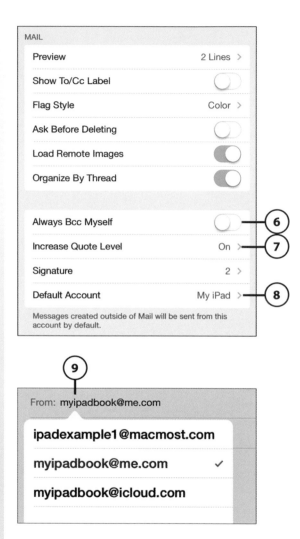

Why Not Show Remote Images?

The main reason to not show remote images is bandwidth. If you get an email that has 15 images referenced in it, you need to download a lot of data, and it takes a while for that email to show up completely. However, remote images are often used as ways to indicate whether you have opened and looked at messages. So, turning this off might break some statistics and receipt functionality expected from the sender.

Siri: Sending Email

You can use Siri to send email through a series of responses. First, activate Siri and say something like "Send an email to John." You are asked for the subject of the message. After dictating that, you are asked for the message text. Then, you are shown the message to review it. You are then asked "Ready to send it?" If you respond "yes," Siri sends the email. Otherwise, respond "no" to cancel.

Setting Up Messaging

Even though your iPad isn't a phone, you can send text messages. The catch is that you can only message others who are also using Apple's iMessage system. This would include anyone using iOS 5 or newer with an iPad, iPhone, or iPod touch, as long as they have signed up for the free service. Mac users can also send messages with the iMessage system.

(1) Launch the Messages app.

(2) If this is your first time, you need to enter your Apple ID and password. Otherwise, you can go to step 3.

(3) Tap Sign In.

Messages

4 You can further customize how you send and receive messages in the Settings app. Go to the Settings app and choose Messages.

5 If you turn this option on, when someone sends you a message they will also get an indication when you have viewed the message. This can save you from having to send simple "OK" messages in response.

6 You can use any valid email address that you own for Messages, even if it is not the same as your Apple ID email address. You can control which email addresses can be used to find you, adding more and removing others.

7 Apple's iMessage system can include a subject line along with the message, though most people don't use this.

8 Tap Blocked to add email addresses to block so individuals cannot send you messages.

Conversing with Messages

After you have set up an account with Messages, you can quickly and easily send messages to others. The next time you launch Messages, you will be taken directly to the main screen.

1 Tap the New Message button at the top of the screen.

2 In a new message, tap in the To field and enter the email address of the recipient. Note that they should already be signed up for iMessage or you will not be able to send them anything. Some iPhone users may use their phone number as their iMessage ID instead of, or in addition to, their email address. As long as the phone number is tied to an iMessage account, you can still converse with them using Messages on your iPad.

3 Tap the text field above the keyboard to type your message.

4 If you want to include a picture with your message, tap the camera button. This allows you to choose a picture from your photo library, or take a new one with your iPad's camera.

5 Tap Send to send your message.

6 You will see the conversation as a series of talk bubbles. Yours will appear on the right.

7 When your friend responds, you will see their talk bubbles as well.

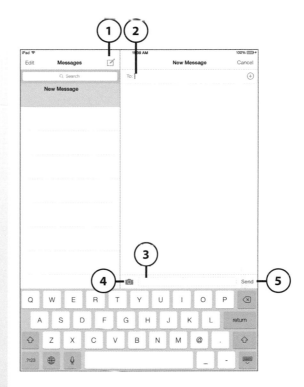

8 A list of conversations appears on the left. You can have many going on at the same time, or use this list to look at old conversations.

9 Tap the Compose button to start a new conversation.

10 Tap Edit to access buttons to delete old conversations.

11 Tap on the Contact button to do various tasks such as adding them to your contacts, or starting a FaceTime video chat.

12 Tap and hold on any message to bring up more options.

13 Use the More button to bring up options like selecting and deleting individual messages in the conversation.

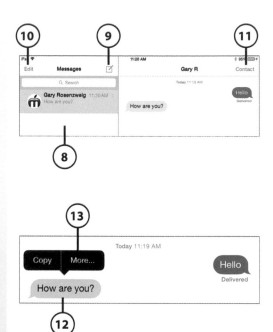

Siri: Sending Messages

You can use Siri to send messages. Simply tell Siri something like "Send a text message to Gary" and Siri will respond by asking you what you want to say in your message. You can review the message before it is sent for a truly hands-free operation. When you get a message, you can also ask Siri to "Read me that message" and you can listen to the message without ever glancing at your iPad's screen.

Setting Up Twitter

Another way to message is to use the popular service Twitter. But instead of a private conversation, Twitter is all about telling the world what you are up to. If you already have a Twitter account, you can use the official Twitter app that comes with your iPad. Otherwise, you can set up a new account.

1. If you don't already have it, install the Twitter app by going to Settings and tapping Twitter on the left side. Launch the Twitter app from the Home screen.

Twitter

2. If you already have an account, tap Sign In.

3. If you need to create a Twitter account, you can do so here by tapping Sign Up. Then enter the required information for a new account.

4. Enter your Twitter Username and Password.

5. Tap Sign In.

Following People on Twitter

Even if you don't tweet much yourself, you can have fun with Twitter by following others. You can even learn things and stay informed. The key is to figure out who you want to follow and then add them.

1. With the Twitter app open, tap the Search button.

2. Type in the name or Twitter handle of the person you want to follow. You can also use terms that describe them, like which website or company they are associated with.

3. Tap the profile that matches your search, and then use the picture to help identify the right person.

4. Tap the Follow button to add them to the list of people you follow.

Who to Follow?

This depends on what you want from Twitter. If you just want to know what your friends are up to, then only follow your friends. If you want to hear what celebrities have to say, then search for some of your favorites. You can also search for professional and industry experts to learn more and stay informed. And don't limit your search to people. Local and worldwide news publications and organizations also have Twitter feeds.

How to Tweet

Thinking about adding your voice to the conversation? You can send a tweet easily with the Twitter app.

(1) With the Twitter app open, tap the Compose button.

(2) Enter the text of your tweet. It must be 140 characters or less.

(3) You can add a photo or video to your tweet. This will upload the image to the service you have selected in your Twitter account and put a link to the file in the tweet.

(4) You can add your GPS location to the tweet.

(5) Tap Tweet.

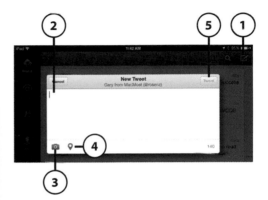

Siri: Tweeting

You can send a tweet with Siri simply by asking it to "send a tweet." You will then be prompted to speak the message. Like with sending email, you can review and confirm the message before it is sent.

Take pictures with the
iPad's cameras.

Edit your photos using
iPhoto.

Browse your photos on the iPad's
brilliant screen.

In this chapter, we use the Camera app to take photos, the Photos app to view your pictures and create slideshows, and the iPhoto app to edit photos and create journals.

Taking and Editing Photos

In addition to replacing books, the iPad replaces photo albums. You can literally carry thousands of photos with you on your iPad. Plus, your iPad's screen is a beautiful way to display these photos.

To access photos on your iPad, you first must sync them from your computer. Then you can use the Photos app to browse and view your photos.

With the iPad's cameras, you can also take photos with your iPad. You can view those in the Photos app as well.

Taking and Editing Photos

All iPads after the 1st generation include two cameras that you can use to take photos. The primary app for doing this is the Camera app.

Camera

(1) Tap the Camera app icon on the home screen. This brings up the Camera app, and you should immediately see the image from the camera.

(2) The camera app has three modes: Video, Photo, and Square. The first one is for movie filming mode, and the others take rectangular and square photographs. To switch between modes, tap and drag up and down where you see Video, Photo, and Square. The three words will move vertically while the yellow dot remains in the same place. The option with the yellow dot is the mode you are currently using.

3 Tap the button at the top right switch between front and rear cameras.

4 Tap anywhere on the image to specify that you want to use that portion of the image to determine the exposure for the photo.

5 After you have tapped on the image, and if you are using the rear-facing camera, you can zoom in. To do that, use your fingers to pinch apart. After you do so, you will see a zoom slider at the bottom of the screen. Drag it to the right to increase the zoom.

6 Tap the HDR button to turn on High Dynamic Range Imaging.

High Dynamic What?

High Dynamic Range Imaging is a process where multiple pictures are taken in quick succession, each using a different exposure. Then the multiple images are combined. For instance, if you are taking a picture of a person with a bright sky behind them, one picture will do better with the person, and the other with the sky. Combining the multiple images gives you a picture that shows them both better than a single shot would.

When you use HDR, be sure to hold your iPad steady so each shot captures the same image. They will be taken a fraction of a second apart. So, HDR does not work well with moving objects or a moving camera.

7 Tap the large camera button at the right side of the screen to take the picture.

8 Tap the button at the lower right to go to the Camera Roll and see the pictures you have taken.

(9) If you don't see buttons at the top and bottom of the photo, tap the middle of the image from the Camera Roll to bring up controls on the top and bottom of the screen.

(10) Use the thumbnails at the bottom to flip through images you have taken that are in your Camera Roll. Or just swipe left and right through the thumbnails to flip through your photos.

(11) Tap Camera Roll to exit viewing this one image and jump to an icon view of all of your Camera Roll photos.

(12) Tap Done to exit this screen and return to take more pictures.

(13) Tap the Trash icon to delete the photo.

(14) Tap the Share icon to send the photo to someone else via message, email, AirDrop and a variety of other methods depending on which apps you have installed. This is also where you can copy the image so you can paste it into an email or another app.

(15) Tap Edit to adjust the photo.

(16) Tap Rotate to rotate the image 90 degrees counterclockwise.

(17) Tap Enhance to have the app examine the brightness and contrast in the photo and try to bring out the best image.

(18) Tap Filters to access a choice of several filters to apply to the photo, such as Mono, Noir, Fade, Chrome, Transfer, and Instant.

(19) Tap Red-Eye, and then tap red eyes in the photo and they are automatically corrected.

(20) Tap Crop to crop the image and get rid of unwanted things at the edges or to focus on a specific object in the photo.

(21) You can tap Revert to Original at any time to throw away all the edits you might have made with the options in steps 16 to 20. You can try different adjustments without permanently committing to them. You can also tap Undo to throw away only the very last adjustment you made.

(22) You can also tap the Cancel button to throw away changes and return to the previous screen.

(23) If you want to make the changes stay with the photo, you can tap the Save button.

IT'S HIP TO BE SQUARE

The square format of the Camera app comes from a trend to post square images online. Social media icons are square, and square images often look better in online posts. The popularity of the Instagram photo sharing service is another reason we see a lot of square photos.

Square format works great for things like faces or objects where landscape or portrait photos have wasted space on the sides or top and bottom. Photographers can debate the merits of both formats. Some think that landscape photos look good when the subject is off to one side and the background is at the center of the image, whereas square photos look good when the subject is right at the center.

Using Photo Booth

In addition to the basic picture-taking functionality of the Camera app, you can also use the included Photo Booth app to take more creative shots using one of eight special filters.

(1) Launch the Photo Booth app.

Photo Booth

(2) You'll start by seeing all the filters you can choose from. Tap one of the filters to select it.

(3) Now you'll see just that one filter. In addition, you have some buttons. Tap on the button at the bottom right to switch between the front and rear cameras.

(4) Tap the button at the bottom left to return to the 9-filter preview.

(5) Tap the camera button at the bottom to take a picture.

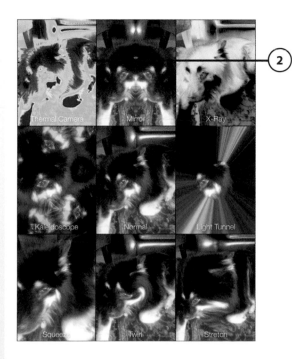

6 Some filters also allow you to tap the live video image to adjust the filter. For instance, the Light Tunnel filter enables you to set the position of the center of the tunnel.

7 All you do with Photo Booth is take photos. Then they are sent right to your Camera Roll. See the next section to learn how to browse your photos in the Camera Roll.

A Kind of Flash
When you take a picture with the camera on the front of the iPad, you get a kind of flash effect from the screen. It simply turns all white for a second. This helps in low light situations.

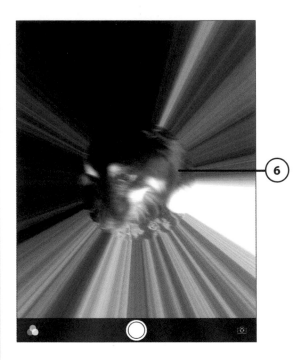

6

Browsing Your Photos

After you have synced to your Mac or PC, you should have some photos on your iPad, provided you have set some to sync in either iPhoto or iTunes. Then you can browse them with the Photos app.

Photos

(**1**) Tap on the Photos app icon to launch it.

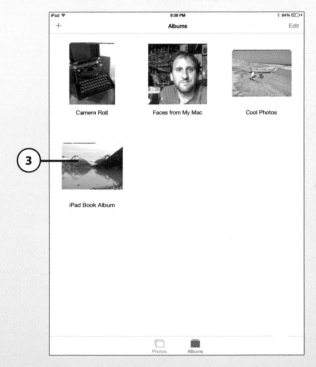

(**2**) Tap to view your photos by photo collections or albums. For this example, we'll use albums. These are both just different ways of sorting the photos on your iPad.

(**3**) Tap an album to view the photos in it.

4 Tap a photo to view it. For most photos, you might want to rotate the iPad to its horizontal orientation for wide-screen viewing.

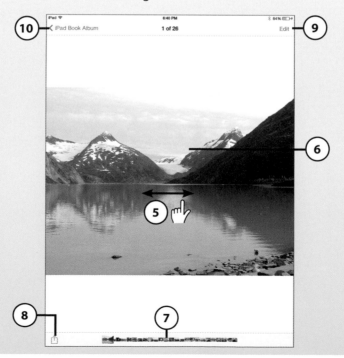

(5) To move to the next or previous photo, drag left or right.

(6) To bring up controls at the top and bottom of a photo, if they are not already present, tap in the center of the screen.

(7) You can tap and run your finger over the small thumbnails at the bottom of the screen to move through that album's photos.

(8) Tap the Share button to copy the photo, or send it to a friend or another app.

(9) Tap Edit to adjust the photo, the same way you did in the task "Taking and Editing Photos" earlier in this chapter, steps 16 to 23.

(10) Tap the name of the album at the top of the screen to return to the list of photos.

ZOOM AND ROTATE

>>> Go Further

Here are a few tips on how to navigate your photos as you view them:

- Pinch or unpinch with two fingers to zoom out and in.

- Double-tap a photo to zoom back out to normal size.

- While a photo is at normal size, double tap to zoom it to make it fit on the screen with the edges cropped.

- If you pinch in far enough, the picture closes, and you return to the browsing mode.

Sharing Photos

There are many ways you can share photos from the Photos app.

(1) While viewing a single image in the Photos app, or in the Camera app right after taking a new photo, tap the Share button in the lower-left corner.

(2) The image is selected, but you can also select other images in the album by swiping to the left and right and tapping the checkmark circle at the bottom of each image. This way you can share a set of photos instead of just one.

(3) If any other iOS devices using AirDrop are nearby, you will see them in this area and can tap their icon to send the photo via AirDrop.

(4) Tap the Message button to send a text message that includes the selected image(s) using iMessage to another person. See "Setting Up Messaging" in Chapter 8.

(5) Tap Mail to send the current photo in an email message.

(6) After you tap Mail, a message composition screen appears and starts a new message. The photo is attached to the message.

It's Not the Original Image

If you sync a photo from your computer to your iPad, and then email it to people, they actually receive a reduced image, not the original. iPad albums contain reduced images to save space. If you want to send the original, email it from your computer.

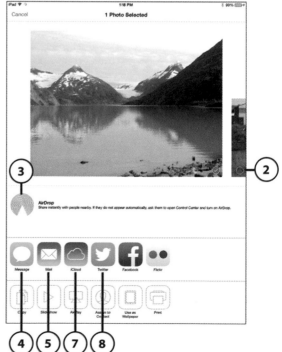

7 If you are using iCloud's Photo Stream feature, you can send the photo to Photo Stream— even if it is not a photo you have taken with the iPad's camera, such as a photo taken with your iPhone. We'll look at using Photo Stream in the next section.

8 You can also send (tweet) the photo using your Twitter account. Tap the Twitter button and a small Twitter composition dialog appears, which allows you to add a message to go along with the photo.

9 Likewise, tap the Facebook button to post the photo, along with a message, to your Facebook wall.

10 If you use Flickr, tap the Flickr button to post the image to your Flickr account. Go to the Flickr section of the Settings app to configure your Flickr account first.

11 Tap Copy to copy the photo to your clipboard. Putting the photo on the clipboard enables you to paste it into documents or email messages in other apps.

12 Tap Slideshow to start a slideshow with the selected pictures. It can display on the iPad's screen, or you can select to view it on an AirPlay device like an Apple TV on the same network.

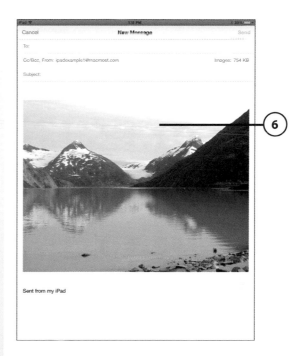

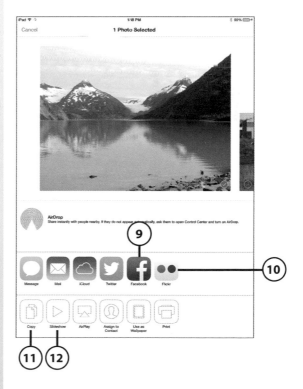

13 You can also show a single photo on a TV using an Apple TV. This only appears if you are using AirPlay on your network.

14 Tap Assign to Contact to display a list of all your contacts so that you can add the photo to the contact's thumbnail image.

15 Tap Use as Wallpaper to assign the image to either the Lock Screen background or the Home Screen background, or both.

16 Tap Print to send the photo to your networked printer.

You can share your photos in many ways, and it is likely that more will be added in the future. What you can use depends on what you have set up on your iPad. For instance, if you have Messaging and Twitter set up, you can use the Message and Tweet buttons to share using those services.

Using Photo Stream

Photo Stream is a feature of iCloud that can do two things: First, it can automatically upload new photos you take on your iPad to iCloud. Then these photos will sync to your other iOS devices and your Mac using iPhoto. This can essentially replace syncing your iPad to your computer to transfer your photos.

A second feature of Photo Stream is the ability to create online photo galleries that your friends and family can view. This also happens wirelessly using iCloud.

Setting Up Photo Stream

To use these Photo Stream features, you first need to enable Photo Stream in the Settings app.

1. In the Settings app, first go to the iCloud settings and make sure you are signed in to your iCloud account. See "Syncing with iCloud" in Chapter 3.

2. Once again in the Settings app, tap Photos & Camera.

3. Turn on My Photo Stream, which automatically saves the photos you take to iCloud.

4. Turn on Photo Sharing, which enables you to create online photo galleries.

After you have Photo Stream enabled, each photo you take with your iPad will be placed in an album titled for the current month. These albums will also appear, with their photos, on your other iOS devices and in iPhoto on a Mac, if you have one. Of course, your iPad must be connected to the Internet for this to happen.

Photo Stream in iPhoto

If you are a Mac user, you can set up Photo Stream in iPhoto on your Mac as well. Go to iPhoto, Preferences, Photo Stream and turn it on. Turn on My Photo Stream and Automatic Import. You will see Photo Stream show up in the left sidebar. When you take a picture on your iPad, it will upload to Photo Stream as long as you have an Internet connection. Then it will appear in the Photo Stream section of iPhoto on your Mac a minute later.

Sharing Photos with Photo Stream

After you have turned on Photo Sharing in Settings, you can create shared streams that others can view in a web browser.

(**1**) In the Photos app, tap Shared at the bottom.

(**2**) Tap New Shared Stream.

(**3**) Enter a name for the stream and tap Next.

(**4**) Enter contact names or email addresses of people who will be able to see the photo stream. You will be able to modify this later to add more. Tap Create when you are done.

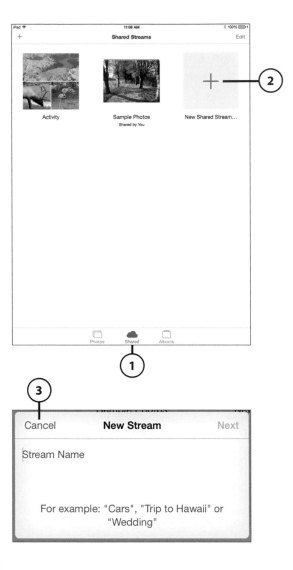

5 You now see your list of shared photo streams again. Tap the new one to enter it.

6 There are no photos here yet, so tap the + button to add one.

7 Select photos you want to add.

8 Tap Done.

9 Enter a message to accompany the posting of these new photos. The message will become the description for the photos when viewed.

10 Tap Post.

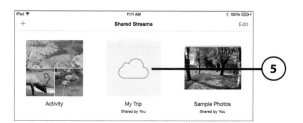

11 You are returned to the stream and can see the photos have been added.

12 Tap People for more shared photo stream settings.

13 You can always remove people from the shared list by tapping the name and then choosing Remove Subscriber from the options presented.

14 You can invite new people.

15 If Subscribers Can Post is turned on, the people on your list can upload photos from their iOS devices and iPhoto to this stream.

16 You can also enable Public Website to make the whole photo stream public. You will get a public URL that you can share with people or post to your blog or social media networks. Anyone can view the photos using that link.

17 Shared photo streams allow likes and comments to photos. Leave Notifications on if you want to get a notification on your iPad when someone interacts with your stream.

18 Delete Photo Stream is the option that enables you to delete the entire stream. This is handy if your photo stream was only meant to be a temporary way for family and friends to see what was going on during a trip or event.

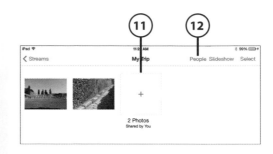

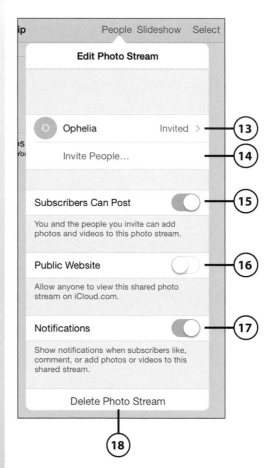

Photo Stream, Interrupted

So what happens when you take a new picture but Photo Stream can't connect to the Internet at that moment? Or, you choose to share a photo and there is no connection?

Like a typical cloud service, you can perform all the steps, and your iPad will simply complete the upload next time it has a connection.

Viewing Photo Collections

When you use the Photos app, you can view your photos in several ways. One way if by collections. Collections are groups created by the Photos app from the information stored in your photos, such as time and location of the photo. You don't create collections; you just leave that up to iOS. In the next section, we look at viewing based on albums, which are groups you define.

(1) The top level of the collections hierarchy is Years. Go to the Photos app and tap Photos at the bottom. If you do not see Years as the title at the top, use the button at the top left to move up the hierarchy to Years.

(2) Your photos are then divided up into years. Every year that has enough photos will show, and years that have only a few photos will be grouped with other years. For instance, you may see 2008-2010 as a group.

(3) Each year shows a list of locations. Tap this list, not the photo thumbnails, to jump to the map view.

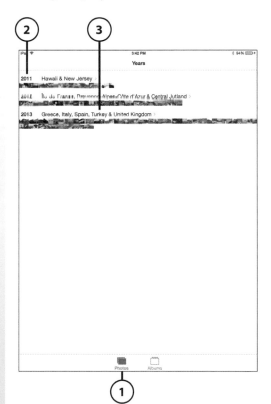

(4) A map appears with groups of photos over various locations. If you only use a camera that does not have GPS capability, then you may not see any. The scale of the map will change depending on where your photos for that year were located. Tap Years to return to the previous screen without working with the map.

(5) Tap a collection of photos over a location to go to that set of phot

(6) Now you are viewing the photos in that collection. You can tap the year button at the top to jump back up to the map.

(7) Tap Slideshow to start an automatic slideshow with all the photos.

(8) Tap Select to be able to select multiple photos from this collection for sharing.

(9) Tap a photo to view it full screen.

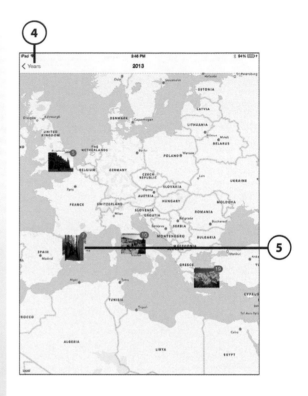

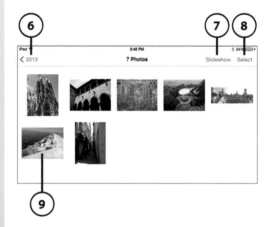

10 When viewing photos, you may want to turn your iPad to horizontal orientation—most pictures are wider than they are taller.

11 Use the thumbnails at the bottom to select another photo from the collection, or simply swipe left or right from the center of the screen to move between photos.

12 Tap Edit to edit the photo from here. See the task "Taking and Editing Photos" earlier in this chapter, steps 15 to 23.

13 You can share the photo, using the same controls from the "Sharing Photos" task earlier in this chapter.

14 To return to the collection, tap the button at the top left. Tap in that area twice more to return all the way back to the list of photos by Years that we started with in step 1.

15 On the Years screen, tap and hold over any tiny thumbnail to see a larger version of it appear above your finger. Then you can move your finger around the screen to view larger versions of other thumbnails.

16 Tapping any thumbnail, as opposed to tapping the list of place names, takes you to a different screen.

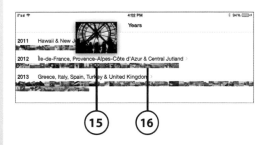

(17) This screen shows collections of photos in smaller selections of time, called "Moments." Tap any thumbnail to jump into a collection.

(18) You can tap any photo to view it full screen, just like in step 9.

(19) You can drag up and down to look at other Moments. You can also do this on the Collections screen.

(20) If you want to quickly share the entire set of photos that comprise one Moment, tap the Share button.

(21) You can return to the previous screen by tapping Collections in the upper left corner.

Collections Are Not for Organizing

When given a collection, such as a collection of photos, our instinct is to organize it. That's what albums are for. Collections can be frustrating for some, as you do not have many options to organize the photos. They are simply grouped based on the data in the photos, which was added when the photo was taken.

If the time or location of a photo is wrong, there is no way to change it in the Photos app. There are some third-party apps in the app store that can do this, and you can also do this in iPhoto on your Mac.

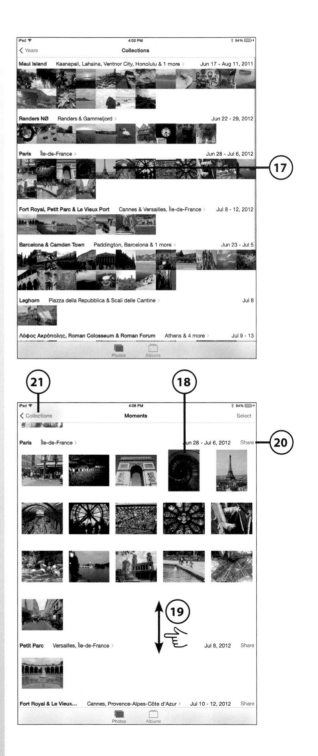

Viewing Albums

Using the Photos button at the bottom of the Photos app is a great way to find the photos you want to view. But, if you would rather organize your photos yourself, you can do so by creating albums.

Albums can be made in iPhoto or Aperture on your Mac, Photoshop Albums or Photoshop Elements on Windows, or by using file system folders on Mac and windows. When you sync to your iPad, you'll see these albums using the steps that follow.

(**1**) In the Photos app, tap the Albums button.

(**2**) Tap on an album to expand it to see all the photos.

(**3**) Tap any photo to view it.

(**4**) Tap the album name to return from viewing the photo, and then tap the Albums button on the next screen to return to the list of albums.

Getting Back to the Album

After you finish digging down into an album, you can go back to the list of albums by tapping the Albums button, or a similarly named button, at the top left. But you can also pinch in all photos to group them in the middle of the screen and then release to move back to the albums list.

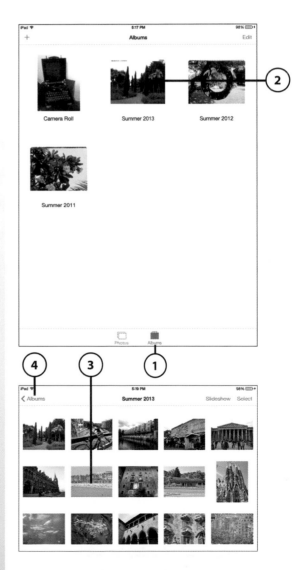

Faces Too

iPhoto and Aperture on the Mac have the ability to find faces in your photos. If you use this feature and you sync your photos to your iPad, you will also have an option to view groups of photos that correspond to those faces. You can even select faces to sync to your iPad in iTunes on your Mac.

Creating Albums

Syncing with iTunes isn't the only way to organize your photos into albums. You can create new albums right on your iPad. The process involves naming a new album and then selecting the photos to appear in the album.

1 In the Photos app, tap Albums at the bottom to view your albums.

2 Tap the + button to create a new album.

3 Enter a name for the album.

4 Tap Save.

5 Now you can start adding some photos to this empty album. You will see all your photos appear in the Moments view, just as they did in step 17 of the task "Viewing Photo Collections," earlier in this chapter.

6 Tap and drag vertically to flip through your photos to locate the ones you want to include in this new album.

7 If you prefer Albums view, you can tap Albums to switch to that view.

8 You can also tap Collections to move up to Collections view.

9 Tap a single photo to add it to the album. Tap again to undo the selection.

10 You can also select an entire collection.

11 When you have added all the photos you want to the album, tap Done. You can always add more by viewing that album, tapping the Select button at the top, and then tapping the Add button at the top.

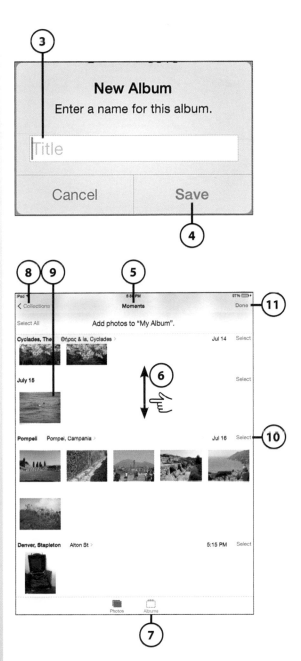

Creating a Slideshow

Another way to look at your photos is as a slideshow with music and transitions. You can quickly and easily create a slideshow with any group of photos in the Photos app that shows a Slideshow button at the top—for example, an album synced to, or that you created on, your iPad.

(1) In the Photos app, tap Albums.

(2) Tap an album to select it.

(3) Tap the Slideshow button at the top of the album.

(4) Tap Transition to select a transition that you want to appear between images. There are several to choose from.

(5) Slide the Play Music button on or off. If you toggle it on, you will be able to select a song from your iTunes collection.

(6) Tap Start Slideshow.

Stopping a Slideshow

Tap on the screen anywhere to stop a slideshow.

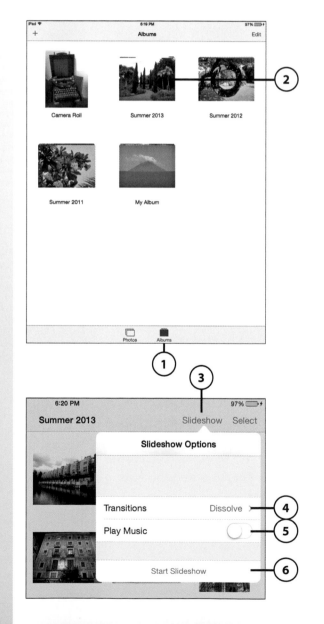

Capturing the Screen

You can capture the entire iPad screen and send it to your Photos app. This feature is useful if you want to save what you see to an image for later.

(1) Make sure the screen shows what you want to capture. Try the Home screen, as an example.

(2) Press and hold the Wake/Sleep button and Home button at the same time. The screen flashes and you hear a camera shutter sound, unless you have the volume turned down.

(3) Go to the Photos app.

(4) Tap on the Camera Roll album. The last image in this album should be your new screen capture. Tap it to open it.

(5) Tap the last image in your Camera Roll, which should be the screenshot you just took.

(6) The example is a vertical capture of the Home screen, so it might be confusing to look at. Turn your iPad horizontally.

(7) Tap the Share icon to email the photo or copy it to use in another application. Or you can leave the photo in your Camera Roll album for future use.

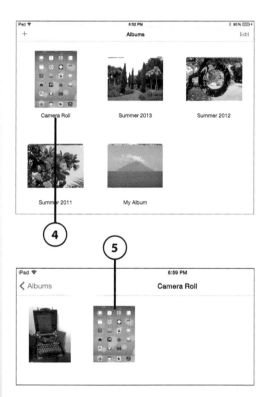

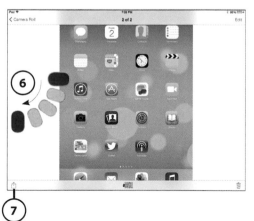

Deleting Photos

You can only delete photos from the Camera Roll album (sometimes referred to as the "Saved Photos" album) and your Photo Stream.

1. In the Photos app, tap Albums.
2. Tap on Camera Roll.
3. Tap a photo to view it.

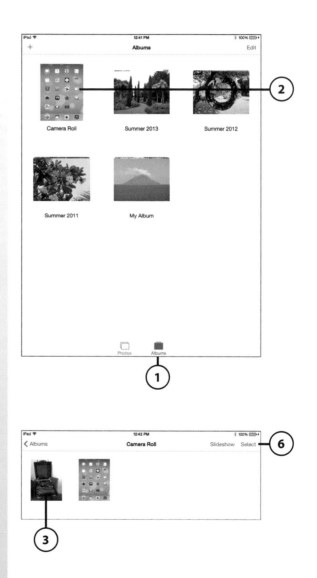

4 Tap the Trash Can button.

5 Tap Delete Photo.

6 Alternatively, you can go back to step 3 and then tap the Select button.

7 Tap multiple photos to select them.

8 Tap the trashcan button, and then tap the Delete Selected Photos button that appears.

So How Can I Delete Other Photos?

The Camera Roll album is special; it contains photos created on your iPad. The rest of the albums are just copies of photos synced from your computer. You can't delete them from your iPad any more than you can delete music synced to your iPad.

To delete these photos, go back to iPhoto on your computer, and remove them from any albums that you have set to sync to your iPad. Also, go into iTunes on your computer, and make sure the photo syncing options there—such as to sync Last 12 Months—won't copy that photo.

If you think of your photos like you think of your music, understanding which photos are synced and why makes more sense.

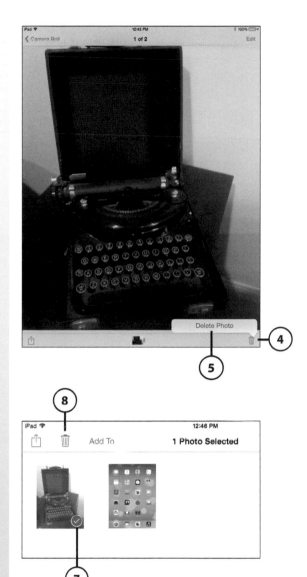

Adjusting Photos in iPhoto

Although the Photos app gives you the ability to make basic adjustments to your pictures, the iPhoto app goes much further. iPhoto does not come preloaded with the iOS—you need to add it from the App Store. Then, you can use the iPhoto app to apply a variety of filters, adjustments, and special effects to your photos.

(1) After you download iPhoto, tap its icon to run it.

(2) First, you need to select a photo to edit. Tap Albums to view your photos grouped into the same albums as in the Photos app.

(3) You can view the photos you have taken with your iPad's camera in the Camera Roll. You can also see photos you have created in other apps here.

(4) If you have already edited a photo, you will see the Edited album. This contains all altered photos. You can go here to continue to work on them.

(5) Tap Photos to see one long list of all the photos on your iPad.

(6) Tap an album to dig into that album's photos.

iPhoto

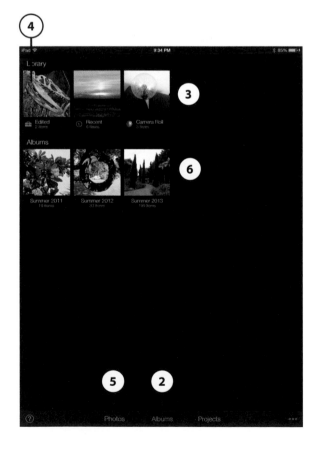

(7) You will see one of the photos from the album in the center of the screen. This is the photo you are currently editing.

(8) Tap the Thumbnail Grid button to see the rest of the photos in the album at the bottom so that you can switch between them.

(9) Tap any photo to switch to it. Alternatively, you can swipe left or right to move between photos.

(10) Tap the Help button to bring up labels for all of buttons and controls in iPhoto.

(11) Try the Auto-enhance button if you want to let your iPad figure out how to adjust the brightness, contrast, and other alterations that should improve the look of the picture.

(12) Tap the Exposure button to reveal the brightness and contrast controls.

(13) Drag the brightness control left or right to adjust the general brightness of the photo.

(14) Drag the contrast controls left or right to adjust the contrast.

(15) Drag the shadows control to adjust the exposure for the dark areas of the photo.

(16) Drag the highlights control to adjust the exposure for the light areas of the photo.

(17) Tap the Color adjustments button.

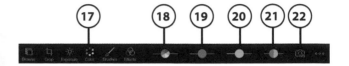

(18) Drag the Saturation control left and right to saturate or desaturate the image. The first enhances the color in your photo, and the second removes color, bringing it closer to black and white.

(19) Adjust the blue tones in the picture.

(20) Adjust the green tones in the picture.

(21) Adjust the skin tones in the picture.

(22) Tap to bring up manual controls for white balance and to adjust the image for specific lighting conditions. These include sun, cloudy, flash, shade, incandescent, fluorescent, or underwater.

Cropping, Straightening, and Rotating

In addition to color effects and adjustments, you can also crop and rotate your pictures. The Crop & Straighten button is at the bottom-left corner and enables you to trim the edges down and straighten the image. To rotate an image 90 degrees, tap the Browse icon at the bottom-left. Using two finger, tap and spin the image in the direction you want it to rotate.

Using Brushed Effects on Photos in iPhoto

There are also adjustments that you can make on parts of a photo rather than the entire image.

1. Tap the Brushes button.

2. Select a brush to use.

3. Use your finger to manually brush the area you want the effect applied to. For instance, you can desaturate everything in this photo except the flower.

4. Tap the undo button to revert to how the image was before you tried the brush. Using the undo button, you can try a variety of brushes and other effects knowing that you can undo the change easily.

5. Tap the Show Original button if you want to quickly compare your changes to the original photo without undoing the changes.

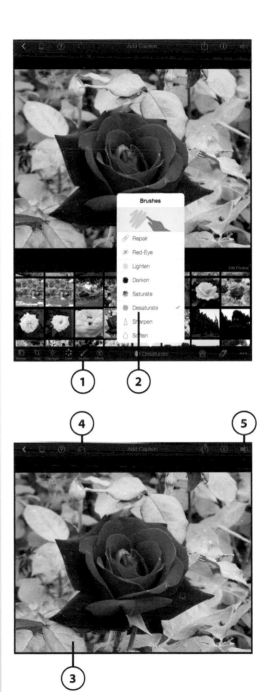

Applying Special Effects to Photos in iPhoto

You can also apply a variety of filters to your entire photo.

(1) Tap the Effects button.

(2) Select one of the effects sets.

(3) All of the effects in the category you chose appear at the bottom of the screen.Tap one and try it with the current image.

(4) Use undo to revert back to the original image before trying another one.

(5) Tap the Show All Effects button to choose from a different category of effects.

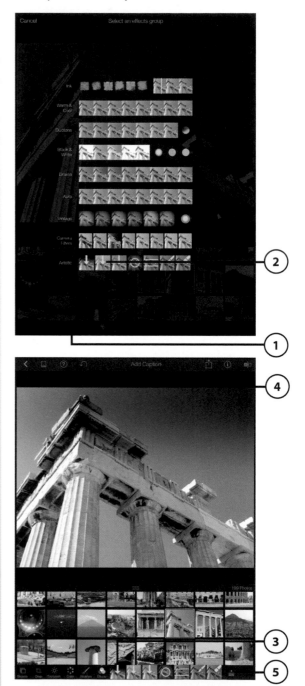

Ordering Prints with iPhoto

If you want printed copies of some of your photos, you can order some from right within iPhoto on your iPad. You pay for the service with your iTunes account, just like buying music or apps.

(**1**) While viewing photos in an album, tap the Share button.

(**2**) Tap Order Prints.

(**3**) If you had previously selected several photos, you can simply use the Selected button to jump to step 7. If the album you are viewing is 100 photos or less, you can tap the All button to order copies of every photo in the album.

(**4**) To select photos to order at this stage, simply tap Choose Photos.

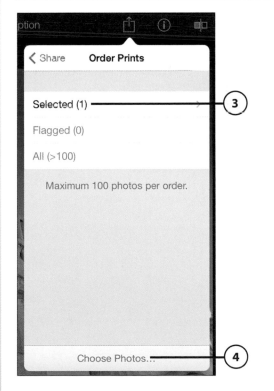

(5) Tap on photos to select them. You see a checkmark on each photo you select.

(6) Tap Next.

(7) Choose a photo sizing option. Each sizing option has further options to choose from.

(8) Review your photos and then tap the price to order them. You will be prompted for an address and then you will finish on a final confirmation screen before the order is complete.

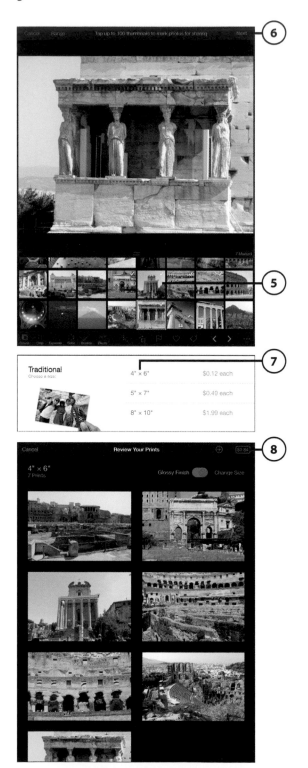

Making Photo Books with iPhoto

An alternative to individual prints is to create a book with your photos. If your plan is to put the photos into an album anyway, this saves you the time and gives you some interesting and creative options.

(1) While viewing photos in an album, tap the Share button.

(2) Tap Photo Book.

(3) You can select photos just as you did in the previous task. Or, just tap All to use all the photos in the album.

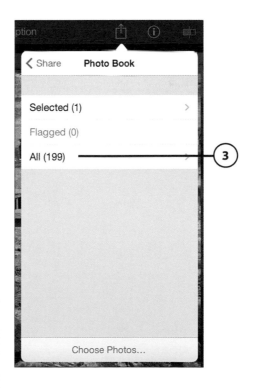

(4) Tap in the name field to type a name for your book and choose a size.

(5) Select a basic book theme.

(6) Tap Create Photo Book.

(7) iPhoto automatically creates and populates a book with your selected photos. When it is done, tap Show to view the book.

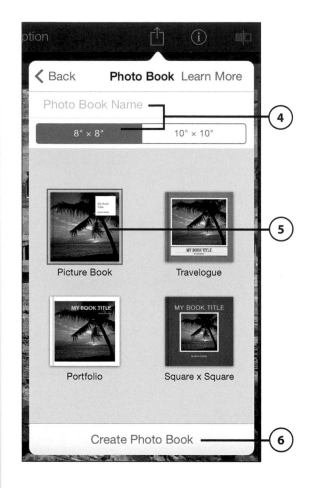

8 You can scroll through the pages of the book, or double-tap a page to view it closer.

9 Tap any photo for options to edit it, replace it, or remove it.

10 You can also drag a photo from the unused photos list at the bottom and replace any photo on the pages. You can also drag a photo to another photo on the pages to swap them.

11 Tap the Page button at the top.

12 You can now change the layout style of the left or right page.

13 You can also change the background pattern.

14 If you like, you can insert a new page or spread of two pages.

15 Tap the back button to view the whole book again.

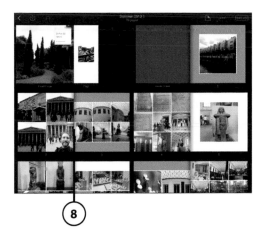

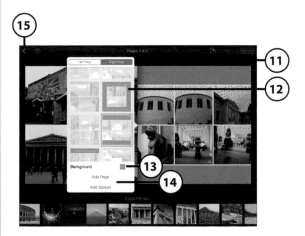

(16) Tap the options button to review the book's options and make changes.

(17) The price of the book will vary depending on the number of pages you have. Tap the price to begin the process of ordering the book, just like ordering prints from the previous task.

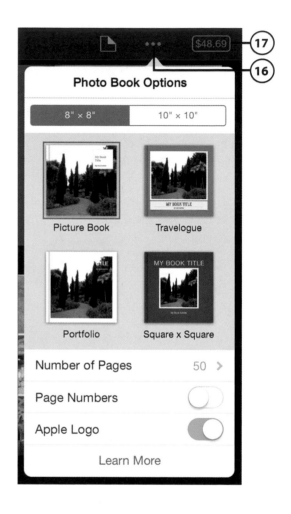

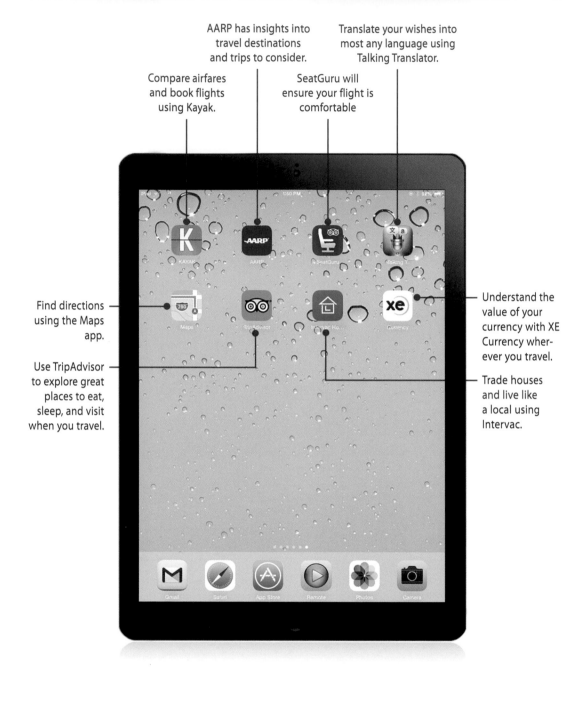

Compare airfares and book flights using Kayak.

AARP has insights into travel destinations and trips to consider.

SeatGuru will ensure your flight is comfortable

Translate your wishes into most any language using Talking Translator.

Find directions using the Maps app.

Use TripAdvisor to explore great places to eat, sleep, and visit when you travel.

Understand the value of your currency with XE Currency wherever you travel.

Trade houses and live like a local using Intervac.

In this chapter, you learn to take advantage of some of the best iPad apps for planning and managing your travel needs.

- → Use Kayak to create and manage your next trip.
- → Find interesting locations to visit using the AARP app.
- → Use SeatGuru to make your in flight time as comfortable as possible.
- → Let Talking Translator help you communicate while traveling abroad.
- → Find your way using the Maps app.
- → Take advantage of other's travel experiences using TripAdvisor.
- → Travel the world living like a local using the Intervac Home Exchange app.
- → Find like-minded seniors to exchange homes with.
- → Use XE Currency to keep track of what you spend in a foreign country.

10

Exploring the World with Your iPad

The iPad makes traveling easier and more enjoyable. Not only can you book your flight from your easy chair, you can plan your itinerary, scope out amazing restaurants and markets, and find key things to do and sights not to be missed so that you take full advantage of your destination. And the great news is that most of the best iPad apps for travel are *free*!

Arranging Travel Using the Kayak App

Kayak has the ideal app to help you find the best way to travel to your next destination. Through Kayak's app, you can book flights and hotels, reserve cars, and maintain your travel details all in one place. Kayak searches the travel options of many airlines and then refers you directly to the airline to make the purchase. A notable exception is Southwest, which doesn't participate in any of these apps. If you want to fly Southwest, you need to use its website to search for flights.

(1) Search the App Store for Kayak. Tap Free and then tap Install to download it. Open Kayak by tapping its icon on your screen.

The Real Deal

One of the great things about being in the senior demographic is the ability to travel "when the spirit moves," rather than at specified times. The opportunity to fly at nonpeak times becomes a reality that can greatly enhance your ability to take advantage of travel deals that others might miss.

(2) The example in this task shows searching for a round-trip flight from New York's JFK airport to San Francisco, departing April 10 and returning May 10. There are several easy ways to modify your search. You can choose different dates, locations, and cabin options.

(3) One option is to choose seating other than economy. Your choices range from economy to first class; tap CABIN line to access other seating options.

(4) After you make all your choices, tap Search to find your outbound flight.

Apps Change Frequently

The images you see here are how these apps appeared at the time this book was written. App developers do occasionally update their apps by changing the way it looks, moving buttons around, or adding new features. You might find that an app looks slightly different from what you see here, but unless the developer has given it a total overhaul, it should function basically the same way it did when these steps were written. So don't let that stop you from trying it out!

5 This search yields round-trip flights starting at $647 (US Airways).

6 The time for the least expensive option to San Francisco is 9 1/2 hours. However, looking at the other results it appears that Delta has a flight with a duration of 6 3/4 hours, at a cost of $661. The $14 additional cost per ticket is well worth the shorter flight.

7 In this example, the second Delta flight, departing JFK at 3:30 p.m. on April 10, was chosen along with the return flight departing San Francisco at 4:00 p.m. on May 10. You can see that each flight is nonstop and travels across the country in the shortest time.

8 The next screen contains a summary of your flight choice. The summary has two options for next steps: You can either tap the upper-right corner to email the information to yourself or fellow travelers, or tap the arrow after Delta to go to the airline website to buy the tickets.

9 For this example, tap the arrow after Delta to buy the tickets. At this point, you leave the Kayak app and go directly to Delta's website. When at the Delta website, you can proceed to buy your tickets, choose seat assignments, complete passenger information, as well as add on other optional items such as baggage fees and other extras.

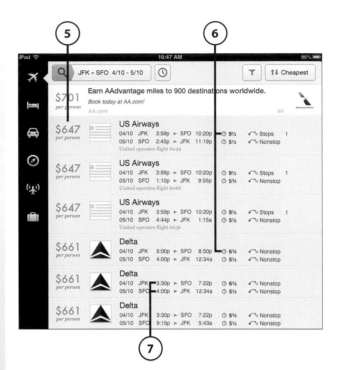

You can use this same process to search for hotels and car rentals to add to your itinerary, or you can book only hotels and a car rental if you don't need flights. Kayak also has a My Trips option that enables you to save your travel itinerary in one place. Time to pick a destination, book your flight, and start exploring!

Using the AARP App

AARP has built an awesome app that provides many interesting insights for seniors. The travel section of the app is useful. It zeroes into several stunning travel ideas, and annotates them individually so that with a tap of your iPad, you can be planning your next trip.

1. Search the App Store for the AARP app. Tap the Free button, and then tap Install to download it. Tap Open to open it. If you are not already a registered user, you must register at the AARP website (www.aarp.org) to access this app.

2. After you register with AARP, you can use the same password and username to access the AARP app. Tap the icon for the AARP app on your iPad, and then sign in with your AARP username and password, or if you choose, tap register to be transferred to the AARP website to register.

Only One Sign In Required

After you open the AARP app and sign in using your AARP username and password the first time, opening the app in the future takes you directly to the home page.

3 The AARP home page contains several interesting options to explore. Health, money, latest, work and retirement, care-giving resources center, life tools, and, of course, travel. Each of these segments is well thought out and contains a number of helpful articles to anyone 55 and over.

4 For this task, explore the Travel section of the app. Tap the AARP travel icon.

5 In the Travel section of this app, you meet the AARP Travel Ambassador, Samantha Brown. Ms. Brown is a well-known travel show host and an excellent choice to represent AARP Travel.

6 You can find several additional pages of options by swiping your finger across your IPad from right to left to move on to the next page. AARP has chosen some enticing travel titles including Captivating Island Getaways, 9 Thrilling Drives Across America, New Air Travel Rules, 5 Must See Rome Sights, and more. There are a total of 70 different articles available at this time.

7 For this task, tap 9 Thrilling Drives Across America.

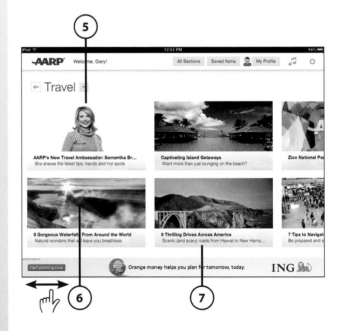

(8) Tap the View Slideshow button to access the article.

(9) The slideshow begins with Mauna Kea Summit Road in Hawaii. Swipe right to left to move along to the Dalton Highway in Alaska, Highway 1 in California, and on to many other breathtaking drives across the United States. This is an enticing app that can certainly stimulate your wanderlust.

Check Out the Website

The AARP website (www.aarp.org) also provides a more extensive look at the prolific offerings this organization provides to the senior community, so take a look at that via your iPad's Safari web browser. For help finding and viewing web pages, see Chapter 7, "Surfing the Web."

AARP's Travel options change continually, so check often to see new and interesting articles.

Finding Your Way Using the iPad Maps App

The Maps app comes installed as part of the iOS operating system for your iPad (similar to Email and other built-in apps). There are many uses for this app, but it is particularly helpful when you travel. You can find your present location, get directions, check traffic, view the map from a satellite perspective, and search the area for various services, such as coffee shops, restaurants, gas stations, and more.

(1) Tap the Maps icon on your iPad.

(2) Tap the arrow at the bottom left of the page to see your present location.

Maps

Location Settings

Location services for Maps must be enabled for the Maps app to find your location automatically. Tap the Settings app on your home screen, and then tap Privacy on the left side. Tap Location Service at the top of the right side of the screen, and then slide the Location Services switch to ON. If you have allowed the Maps app to have access to your location, you should see it in the list below Location Services. Make sure its switch is set to ON. If it is not in the list, after you tap the location arrow in the lower-left corner of the Maps app, it asks to allow the app to have access to Location Services. Tap OK.

(3) Your location is indicated by a blue dot on the map.

(4) To find directions, tap Directions in the upper-left corner.

(5) If you allow Maps access to your location, Current Location is filled in the Start Field for you. If your current location is not your starting location for the directions you need, type in the address you are traveling from in the Start field. Type the address of your destination in the End field. In this example, the directions are for traveling from the current location to Saratoga Springs, NY. Maps fills in possibilities as you type. I tapped Saratoga Springs as my destination.

(6) Maps gives you the option to choose directions for car, walking, or bus.

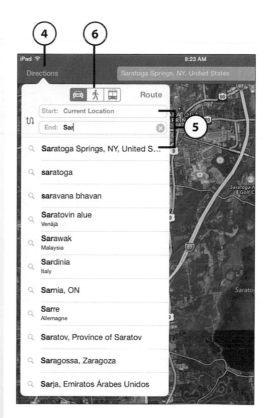

(7) This example chooses to get the best route by car. After you determine how you want to travel and where you are going, and have plugged that information into the start/end boxes, the Maps app automatically shows your potential routes.

(8) Tap the Start button and Maps starts step-by-step directions. Tap End to stop the turn-by-turn directions.

(9) Tap the List icon at the bottom center to get a summary of your directions.

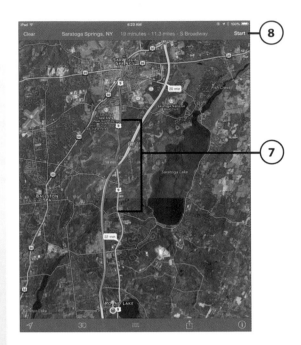

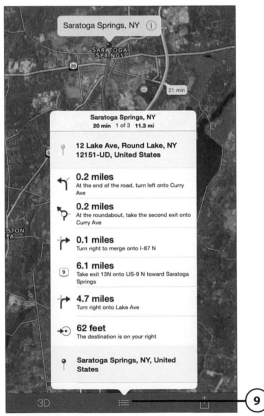

(10) Tap the i at the bottom right to Drop a Pin (which marks a new location point for you), Print Map, Report a Problem, or Show Traffic.

If you have a cellular-enabled iPad, it can also give you turn-by-turn directions. If you travel to an area that you are unfamiliar with, the iPad provides you the perfect way to familiarize yourself with the area from your hotel or apartment.

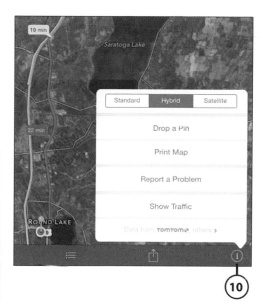

It's Not All Good

Maps Eat Data

Be aware that, although having those turn-by-turn directions as you travel to a destination is convenient and reassuring, it also uses up your monthly data plan quickly. You will receive an email warning you when you are nearing the maximum data allowed by your plan, and offer you the opportunity to pay for more data. It is recommended that you open your Settings app and tap Cellular Data in the list on the left side. On the right side, make sure Data Roaming is set to OFF to avoid any unexpected charges! You can save your data plan by simply planning and reviewing your route while you have access to Wi-Fi and not tap your monthly data plan for this convenience.

SeatGuru by TripAdvisor

Have you ever boarded an airplane, made your way to you seat and settled in, only to find you have chosen the only row on the plane that doesn't tilt back? After you download SeatGuru from the App Store, those days will be over. The idea is to do your research upfront and get to know the aircraft you will be flying on before you buy you tickets and choose a seat. Using SeatGuru you can choose the best possible seat to make your trip as comfortable as possible. Your days of selecting the worst seat on the plane are over!

(1) Search for SeatGuru by TripAdvisor, an iPhone app, in the App Store. Tap Free and then tap Install to download it. Open it by tapping its icon on your home screen. Tap on the Maybe Later link if you see no need to connect using Facebook; otherwise, tap Connect using Facebook for SeatGuru to log you in using your Facebook account and enable you to directly post photos and reviews to your Facebook page.

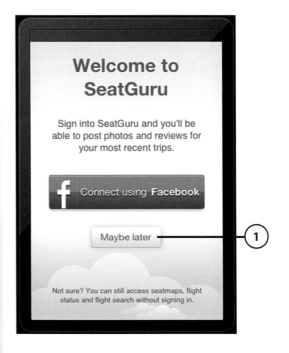

2 Tap the Seat Map Advice option.

3 If you know your flight number or airline, plug those in to find the type of aircraft you will be flying aboard.

4 If you are unaware of the flight number, you can tap the route or airline and search for the flight you are choosing.

5 After your flight info is entered, tap Find aircraft and an illustration of your plane's seat map opens.

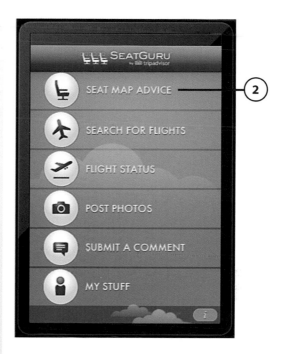

(6) This illustration indicates the great seats (green), lousy seats (red), seats with some draw-backs (yellow) and standard seats (white) available on your flight.

(7) Tap a specific seat number to see a description of the pros and cons of that seat.

(8) In this example, tap seat 26B and the characteristics of this seat are shown. This is great information particularly if you plan a long flight where comfort might be a priority.

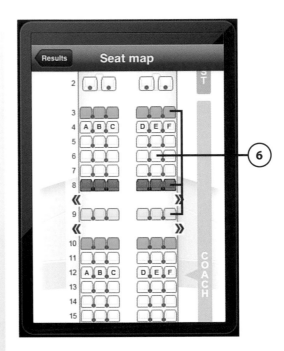

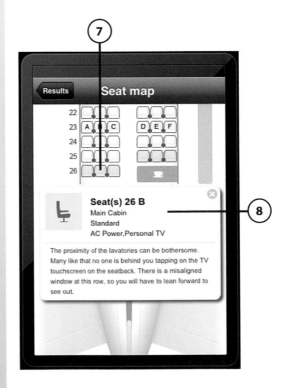

9 The seat map key offers other types of information on seating that can be found using SeatGuru.

Communicating in a Foreign Country Is Easy When You Use Talking Translator

Talking Translator is an amazing App that enables you to speak into a microphone in your native tongue and instantly have the phrase translated into another language. You are allowed five free translations per day, after that you need to purchase further translations. This is a remarkable app that can greatly enhance your ability to communicate in a foreign country.

To try out this app, do the following:

1. In the App Store, search for Talking Translator. Tap Free, and then tap Install to download it. After it is installed, tap the Talking Translator icon on your iPad's home screen to open it.

2. The opening page gives you a few options to review, including Continue, Leave Feedback, Buy, or Activate.

3. For this task, tap Continue, which takes you to the free translations.

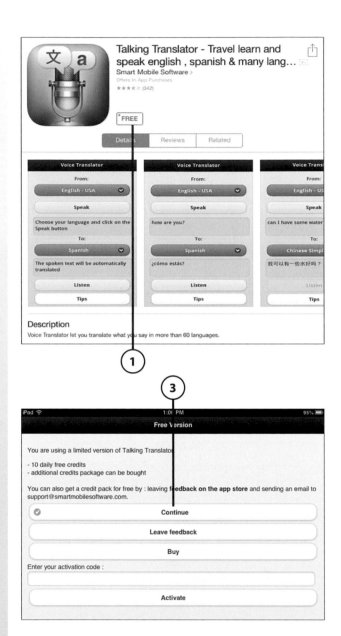

(4) The next page requires you to choose your native tongue. For this task, chose English USA. As you can see, there are many languages to choose from.

(5) Next, choose the language into which you want your phrase translated.

Apps Change Frequently

The images you see here are how these apps appeared at the time this book was written. App developers do occasionally update their apps by changing the way it looks, moving buttons around, or adding new features. You might find that an app looks slightly different from what you see here, but unless the developer has given it a total overhaul, it should function basically the same way it did when these steps were written. So don't let that stop you from trying it out!

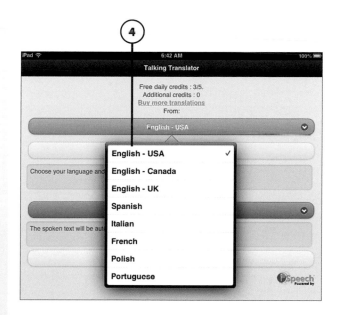

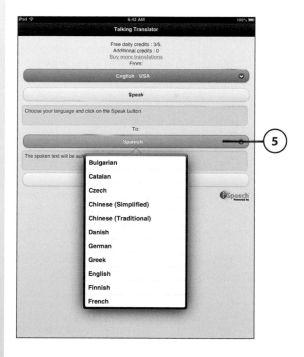

(6) For this task, choose to have English USA translated into French.

(7) Tap Speak and choose a phrase you commonly need to translate when abroad, "Please help me find the nearest bathroom."

(8) To do this, tap the red dot at the bottom of the app. As soon as the dot begins to flash, speak into the microphone. The app writes what it heard you say. It is important to make sure that the app has captured your exact question.

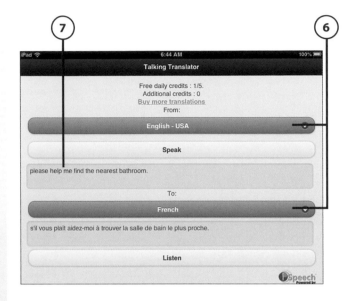

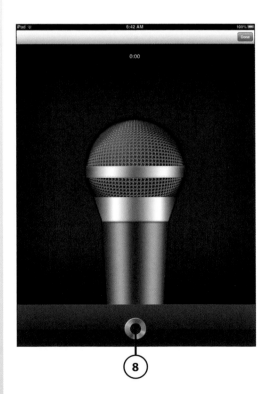

9 Talking Translator shows your phrase written in French.

10 Tap listen to hear your phrase.

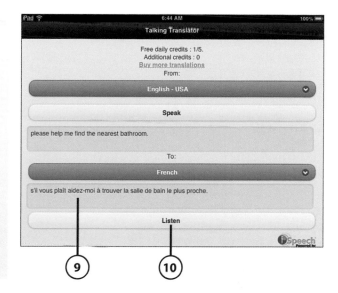

Getting Travel Advice from Others Using TripAdvisor

Whether you travel a few miles or thousands of miles from home, TripAdvisor serves to enhance that experience. With just a few taps, you have access to restaurants, hotels, things to do, and the thoughts of many people who have preceded you at your chosen destination. With TripAdvisor, you also have the ability to save your favorites.

① To start, search the App Store TripAdvisor Hotels Flights Restaurants. Tap Free and then tap Install to download and install the app. Tap the icon for the app on your Home screen to open it.

Opening Apps

There are two ways to open an app. After you download and install an app from the App Store, the button you tapped that said Free, and then changed to Install App changes to read Open after the app is installed. You can tap the Open button right there in the app store to open the app, or you can press the Home button on your iPad and then you will see the new icon on your Home screen for the app you just downloaded. Tap the icon to open the app. If the app already exists on your iPad, such as the built in apps like Maps or iTunes, you simply tap that apps icon. You never need to download or install the apps that are part of the iPad's operating system.

② You can see the options you can explore through TripAdvisor along the top of the screen (hotels, restaurants, things to do, flights, forums, and so on).

③ For this task, choose Find Restaurants to explore in the San Francisco area.

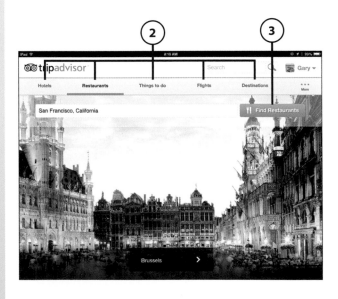

4 The restaurant page now enables you the opportunity to refine your search by cuisine, price range, and locations within the city by tapping the Filter button.

5 In this example, we chose all cuisines, all prices, all neighborhoods, and all dining options.

6 At the time of this search, there were 4657 restaurants listed in San Francisco. The top-rated restaurant, Kokkari Estiatorio, had 681 reviews and a rating of almost a perfect 5. In addition, you can move around the map, zooming to your present location and finding the best restaurants or services near you or where you plan to go.

7 Tap on the Kokkari Estiatorio insert to see further details.

Location Settings

To change your location settings, open the Settings App from your iPad's home screen, and then tap Privacy on the left side. Along the right side, be sure that TripAdvisor is set to ON. This ensures that should you choose Current Location, your iPad can find you.

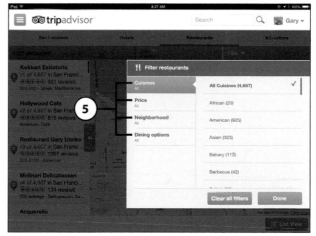

(8) If you find the information interesting, you can tap reviews, photos, or menu to see what others are saying or get even more information.

(9) After you find a restaurant or hotel that you want to check out, tap the Save button to add it to your favorites. To do this it will be necessary to sign in to TripAdvisor.

(10) Finally, tap Reserve with OpenTable to make a reservation.

Exchanging Homes Is a Great Way to See the World

Exchanging homes with like-minded folks around the world is quite possibly the best way to experience a foreign country. Home exchangers can live like a local, shop in local markets, cook as if a local, get to know neighbors and friends of the homeowner, and in many cases, become lifelong friends with the people they exchange with. Although the Senior Home Exchange is a website, not an app, I have included it in this book because it is a great way to initiate travel with like-minded seniors.

Using Intervac Home Exchange

Intervac is the oldest home exchange site, and one that is popular. Although you can search the site to get an idea of what options might be available, to actually initiate an exchange you must join and list your own home as an option for exchange. There is a fee for joining. The amount depends on the type of membership you choose. The following task provides a look at this cool and inexpensive way to see the world.

(1) Search the App Store for Intervac. Tap Free and then tap Install to download and install the app. After it has loaded, locate the Intervac app icon on your iPad, and tap it to start the app.

(2) The email address, button. login, is for existing members to access their accounts.

(3) Tap the View listings button to access the visitors view of the exchange options available. A variety of different options appear.

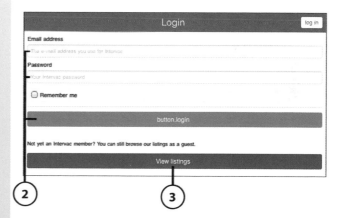

(4) Tap the green Selectcountry bar near the top of the screen to restrict your search to the country you are interested in visiting.

(5) Scroll down the list of countries to make your choice of listings to view by country, and then tap Next. For this task, I chose France.

(6) The France options are listed randomly; I chose to tap the first Paris listing.

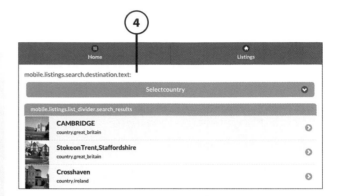

(**7**) The first photo of this apartment in Paris appears. Details about the listing are seen at the bottom of the page. Tap the green View All Photos button to see all the photos for this apartment.

(**8**) The next page includes many photos that the apartment owner has chosen to show. This is a great opportunity to get a feel for this location as a potential exchange.

As a visitor using this, you can get a general feel for the home exchange options available through Intervac. A visit to the website gives you the options to refine your search by date and those who are interested in visiting. I would suggest taking a look at the website prior to signing up—there is a fee involved to be a member.

What About Our Stuff???

Our take on this is it quite similar to a nuclear stand-off. Yes, they are living in your house and using your "stuff" but equally, you are living in their house and using their "stuff." My wife and I have personally participated in many exchanges and never had a problem. As an added bonus, we now have friends throughout the world.

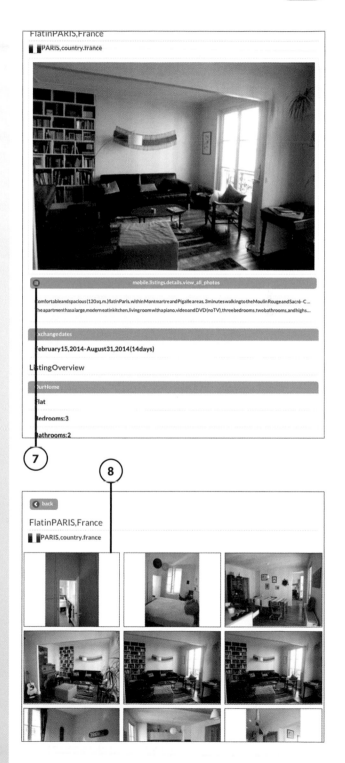

Using Senior Home Exchange Website

The Senior Home Exchange website is designed for 50+ year olds who are interested in exchanging homes. This website caters to those who are adventurous and interested in vacationing by exchanging homes with other seniors.

1 Type **www.seniorshomeexchange.com/** into your Safari web browser, or search for Senior Home Exchange.

2 To have full access to this website you can pay $59 for a 3-year membership or $100 for a lifetime membership. In addition, you will list the characteristics of the home you want to exchange. This photo illustrates the kind of information needed to join the group.

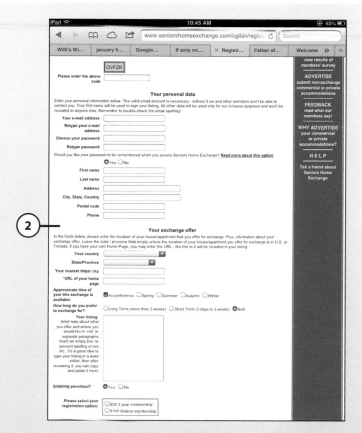

2

3 The option chosen for this example was to access the Visitors directory to see just what might be available to meet your needs.

(4) France is chosen as the country to visit. To narrow the search further, select a city such as Paris. Tap Display

(5) As you can see from the example, 18 records matching the search came up.

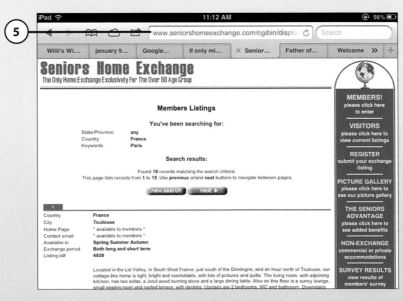

(**6**) In this example, scroll down to find a particularly interesting example—a penthouse apartment in central Paris.

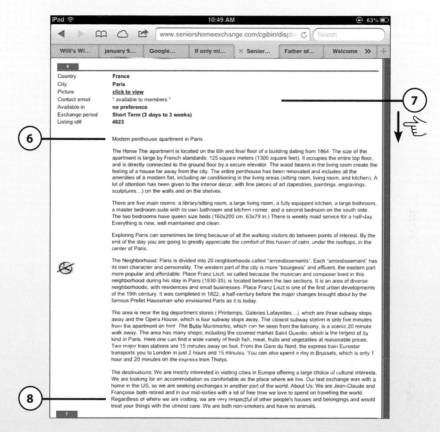

(**7**) There is an eloquent description of the apartment and surrounding area. The description also provides valuable insight into the owners and gives a real sense of who they are as people and individuals that will be staying in your own home.

(**8**) At the end of the description they state, "Regardless of where we are visiting, we are very respectful of other people's houses and belongings and would treat your things with the utmost care." This statement is generally indicative of the kind of people that are interested in exchanging homes. Exchanging homes with others enables you to not only explore the world on a budget, but expand your group of friends worldwide— great fun!

Understanding Foreign Currency Exchange Using XE Currency Converter

When traveling abroad, it is essential to keep track of your spending and to be familiar with the currency in whatever country you are traveling. Understanding the relationship between your own currency, and the currency where you are traveling, ensures that you will not make costly errors when making purchases internationally. The App XE Currency Converter is a very helpful tool when you are in a land with an unfamiliar currency.

(1) Search the App Store for XE Currency. Tap Free and then tap Install to download and install the app. Tap the XE Currency icon on your home screen to open it.

(2) A Getting Started option enables you to become familiar with the app. It provides pop-up notes that describe the different parts of the app. You can find Getting Started by tapping on the **?** at the top.

(3) Choose your "from" currency. This will be the currency you are familiar with. This example uses U.S. dollars.

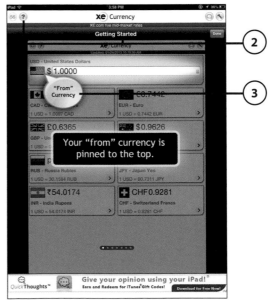

4 Tap any other currency to change your "from" currency.

5 You can now change the amount or activate the calculator to see the relationship between your currency and what you are considering spending in the new currency.

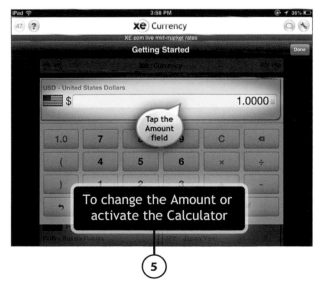

6 Currency rates change continually. XE Currency provides the opportunity to refresh the rates by tapping the Refresh icon or change the settings to have the rates refresh automatically at intervals you choose.

7 Tap Done.

8 After you enter an amount and activated the calculator, the conversion rates you're looking for display on the screen.

There are several other options to add currencies and further refine your use of XE Currency, but the primary objective when traveling is to know the value of the currency you are working with in relation to your home currency.

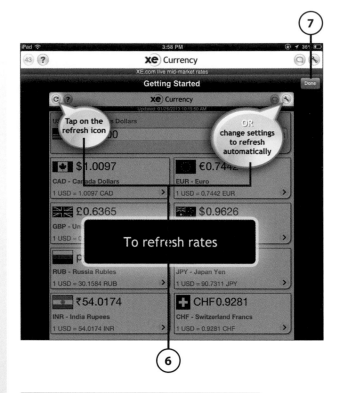

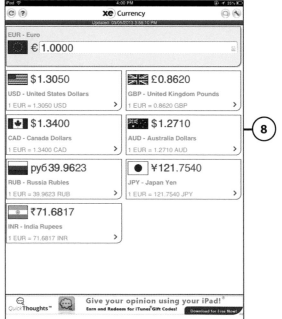

Use Allrecipes Video Cookbook to find great recipes and watch them being created.

Escoffier's Cook Companion offers an encyclopedia of cooking information.

Search for thousands of awesome recipes with Epicurious .

Explore Yelp to find great restaurants and places to shop for food.

In this chapter, you learn to use your iPad and the many apps available to make great meals, find awesome restaurants, and make reservations from your easy chair.

→ Use Yelp to search out a great restaurant wherever you travel.

→ Create and manage restaurant reservations using Open Table.

→ Use Epicurious to match awesome recipes with the food you have at hand.

→ Access thousands of recipes using Allrecipes Video Cookbook.

→ Use The Daily Meal website to find interesting information about all things culinary.

→ Use The Food Channel app to find the ingredients for the recipe you saw that famous chef cooking on television.

Enhancing Your Next Meal with Your iPad

Having the time and opportunity to experience great food is just one of the pluses of moving into the senior demographic. Traveling to far-off lands and experiencing the cultures, finding farmer's markets and the vegetables fresh from the field, or checking out a new recipe in your own kitchen, your iPad can be your best friend. Also, you can explore sites that provide great insight into those who cook and sites that will give you the tools to become a great cook. And the great news is that most of them are FREE!

Choosing a Restaurant Using Yelp

Yelp is an excellent app that enables you to take a look at the restaurants (and many other things for that matter) in an area, see what others have to say about them, and many times link to their websites and menus on line. Each business included in Yelp is given a rating based upon the reviews it has received. You can use Yelp when choosing a place for lunch or dinner, particularly when you are in a place where you have limited familiarity. In addition to finding restaurants, you can use Yelp for any number of purposes because thousands of different businesses are referenced and rated through this app. This is one of the most useful iPad apps.

(1) Search for Yelp in the App Store. Tap Free and then tap Install to download the app. Tap the Yelp icon on your Home screen to open the app.

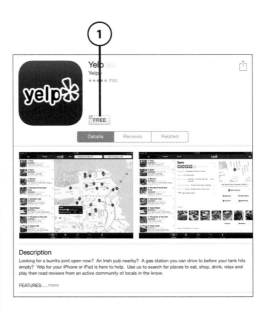

② The list view shown for your current location includes all sorts of different businesses. To narrow the list of possibilities, you must search for something specific—in this case, restaurants.

Different Ways to Search

Depending on your search preference, you can check out Yelp by either using the list, map, or photos feature. You may also filter your choice by distance, rating, cost, or even Open Now.

③ In the upper-right corner, tap in the find box. Popular categories come up automatically, including restaurants. If you have an interest in something more specific, simply type in your topic and Yelp automatically searches for listings that match it.

(4) Our search yielded eight restaurants on the first Yelp page with their locations. You may have more results than can fit on one page. To see the rest, swipe the screen with your finger from bottom to top.

(5) The results include details about the individual restaurants, including a photo, the type of food offered, the address, the received customer ratings, and how expensive they are (the more dollar signs, the more expensive).

Reading Ratings

When considering what restaurant to choose, check out the rating and also the number of reviews. If a place has only five reviews, the results might be considered less accurate than the one with 500.

(6) For this example take a closer look at Rivoli, the 4th restaurant in the search—it has 499 reviews and a rating of 4/5 stars. To do this simply tap Rivoli on the list.

(7) The expanded version for Rivoli provides more information, including a map, a phone number, hours of operation, and the opportunity to make reservations via Open Table. In addition, all 499 reviews can be viewed, and included are photos of Rivoli's food often submitted by reviewers.

(8) With each review you have the opportunity to provide feed-back at the bottom by tapping useful, funny, cool, or comment.

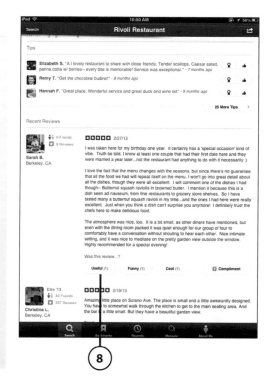

8

Finding Recipes Using Epicurious

Epicurious is a culinary app that will stimulate your creative juices when planning a special meal or simply putting together dinner based upon what remains in your refrigerator. This is my go-to app when in need of a recipe or an idea for a meal.

Apps Change Frequently

The images you see here are how these apps appeared at the time this book was written. App developers do occasionally update their apps by changing the way it looks, moving buttons around, or adding new features. You might find that an app looks slightly different from what you see here, but unless the developer has given it a total overhaul, it should function basically the same way it did when these steps were written. So don't let that stop you from trying it out!

1 Search the App Store for Epicurious Recipes and Shopping list. Tap Free and then tap Install to download the app. Tap the Epi icon on your Home screen to open the app.

2 Tap title page to get to the home page. The Epicurious App goes straight to the Control Panel, an option to help you focus your Epicurious experience.

3 The Control Panel's Featured list has several options including seasonal specials and healthy breakfasts, lunches, and dinners. This list changes frequently, so the options seen in the corresponding figure for this step might be different from what you see in the app when you view it.

4 The box in the upper-right corner enables you to enter keywords to promote a search for recipes containing those specific words, a marvelous resource.

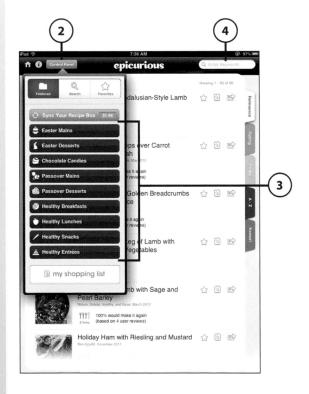

5 There is also a Search button at the top center of the Control Panel. Tapping Search moves you to a screen with a wider variety of search criteria, including Food, Drink, Ingredients, Courses, Cuisine, and more.

6 In addition, Epicurious has the option for you to create a shopping list based on the meal you choose.

7 For this task, begin by adding the words chorizo, lettuce, and chicken broth in the keywords box (upper-right corner).

Guided Search

Epicurious offers a more guided search using the Control Panel. Using that search option, the app makes suggestions on main ingredients, dietary consideration, or cuisines to help you find an appropriate recipe. The dietary consideration is particularly helpful if you want to cook using low sugar or sodium.

8 This search yielded four recipes: Cuban spiced chicken thighs with chorizo and rice, creamy white bean and chorizo soup, chickpea, chorizo, and chicken stew with Mt. Tam cheese, or warm chicken and chorizo salad. This sounds like a tasty list, given the diverse key ingredients you started with.

9 For this task, tap the warm chicken and chorizo salad.

(10) On the recipe's screen, the ingredients list appears with a complete list of what you need to make this recipe.

(11) Tap the body of the recipe to get the directions for making the dish.

(12) After you decide that this is a dish that you want to make, tap the small notepad at the upper-right corner. This enables you to add this recipe to your recipe list, and from there tap to see a shopping list for this recipe.

(13) At the bottom-left corner of the recipe page, there is a Reviews tab to tap to read reviews of this recipe, or tap About to find more about the origins of this recipe. Tap Reviews.

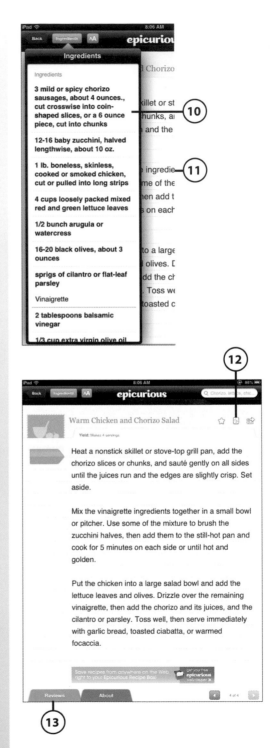

14 The reviews provide some insight into how others viewed the recipe, often a diverse cross section of opinions.

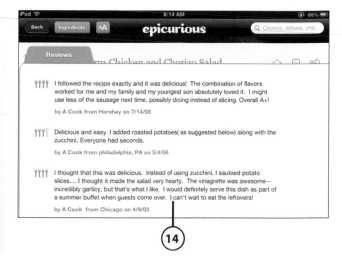

Allrecipes Video Cookbook

1 Search Allrecipes Video Cookbook in the App Store. Tap Free and then tap Install to download the app. Tap Open.

(**2**) The app's opening recipe page includes several video options from which to choose. You can scroll from left to right at the top and down along the bottom to see more recipes.

(**3**) To further explore the options available in this app, tap the 3 lines in the upper-left corner.

(**4**) On this page is an option to search for a recipe or choose to look at any of the many categories of recipes.

(**5**) Tap Main Course to see the 622 videos available there.

Recipe Box for Pros

If you use AllRecipes.com and already have a nice selection of recipes in your recipe box, you might want to consider upgrading to the Pro version of the iPad app. Doing so enables you to sync your AllRecipes.com recipe box with your AllRecipes iPad app. An added benefit is if you have the Pro version of its Dinner Spinner app on your iPhone, it also sends a grocery shopping list to your iPhone for any recipes you choose.

(**3**)

(**2**)

(**4**)

(**5**)

6 You now have the option to scroll down to see all 622 recipes.

7 For this example, I tapped "World's Best Lasagna" to see that recipe and video.

8 With this recipe, you can read the directions along the right side.

9 Tap the arrow to see a high-quality video of the recipe.

10 You also get prep time and cook time estimates as well as nutritional information.

11 Tap Save to create a free account and your own recipe box.

12 Tap Not a member to create an account. You are asked for your email address and to create a username, password, and list your zip code to become a member.

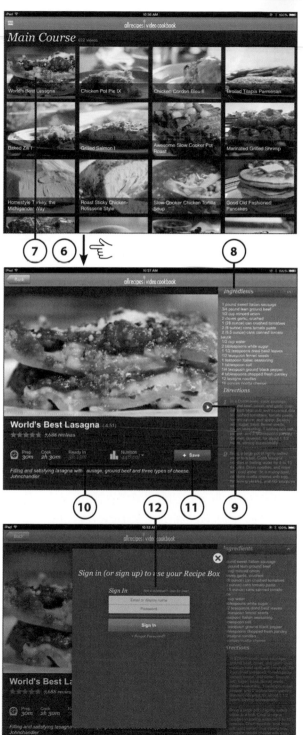

13 After your sign-in is complete, you will receive notification that The World's Best Lasagna has been saved to your own personal recipe box. You can now save any of hundreds of recipes available through the Allrecipes Video Cookbook app.

Reading The Daily Meal to Expand Your Culinary Knowledge

The Daily Meal is not an iPad app, but it is one of my favorite websites to access on my iPad. You can find a huge number of culinary-related topics including cooking, eat/dine, drink, travel, entertain, best recipes, holidays, lists, and community. Within each of these general categories are several subcategories that are sure to peak your imagination for ideas from future travel to just what you are going to cook this evening. The range of interesting articles related to food in this website is staggering. I highly recommend that the foodies among us take a good look at this and plan an afternoon of browsing; it's a great read.

1. Either type **The Daily Meal** in the search field, or type **thedailymeal.com** into the main address field of your Safari web browser.

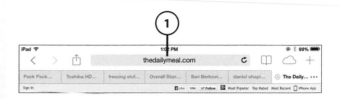

Surfing Safari

For tasks covering how to use your iPad's Safari web browser to search for websites, see Chapter 7, "Surfing the Web."

2. On the day this task was written, the lead story on the website was "The 101 Best Restaurants in America for 2013." One of the best things about this list is that it does not include only the high-end restaurants in the United States, but also some phenomenal inexpensive places. I find nothing better than the thrill of discovering an eatery with awesome food and prices that do not require me to refinance my home.

3 In the menu options along the top of the page, tap Eat/Dine.

4 A pop-up list emerges containing several subcategories, including Restaurants, Chefs & Personalities, Casual Eats, Sandwiches, Products, Food for Thought, and In Your City. This website contains a wide variety of thought-provoking ideas in every category.

5 For this task, you can explore "Chefs & Personalities" by tapping the link.

6 As you can see, there are articles on the first page ranging from "Anthony Bourdain's Dating Turn Ons" discovered in Cosmo to "Obama treating the Republicans to Dinner" and the menu from which the politicians could choose. That's an interesting variety of topics.

7 In an effort to delve more deeply into The Daily Meal's main topics, I chose to tap Drink along the top menu.

8 The subtopics include Wine, Cocktails & Spirits, Where to Drink, Beer, Coffee and Tea, Non-Alcoholic, and In Your City. Each of these subtopics includes a large number of interesting and diverse articles.

9 For this task, I tapped Wine.

10 The wine subtopic provided articles ranging from "7 Women who Rule the Wine World" to "Pinot Noir that sells for $4100 a glass," (I'll no doubt be skipping that one.) By the way, the Pinot Noir article also references a burgundy that sells for $8125/glass, I'll skip that one, too!

We've only touched upon the tip of The Daily Meal iceberg of culinary information. If you like to cook and enjoy food, you'll like this website.

Watching the Pros from The Food Network

Most of us in the senior demographic who are interested in food and cooking are familiar with The Food Network. The Food Network provides an opportunity to see the pros in action and often, we can score a recipe for this evening's dinner. It's just another great thing about being a "senior," having the flexibility to find an interesting recipe and make it for dinner that night. It's a great thing to have thousands of recipes at your fingertips, tested by the pros, and a wonderful tool to help you make great meals based upon what is fresh at the market, or lurking in your fridge. Just plug in the ingredient you want to use, tap that iPad, and away you go! The Food Network also stores thousands of recipes from previous shows that you can access on a whim for a special dinner, or just Tuesday night at home, via your iPad. The iPad app for The Food Network seems to focus primarily on recent shows and what's currently playing. I have found that the best way to access recipes and historical Food Network info is by going directly to the website at www.foodnetwork.com.

1 Search for foodnetwork.com using your iPad's Safari browser, or type **www.foodnetwork.com** into the main address field. This website gives you the opportunity to search by recipes, shows, and chefs. If you remember a specific show that featured a recipe you want to try, just search that show and the recipes contained within the show.

Surfing Safari

For tasks covering how to use your iPad's Safari web browser to search for websites, see Chapter 7, "Surfing the Web."

(2) For this task, I searched for recipes that include beans as an ingredient.

(3) The search yielded 4,155 recipes containing beans, a remarkable number at your fingertips. At this point you can scroll down the recipes for something that suits your fancy or further refine your search by plugging in a specific type of bean.

(4) I tapped the first recipe for green bean casserole.

(5) The green bean casserole recipe was provided by Food Network regular Paula Deen and contains all the information you need to successfully prepare this recipe, as well as the ratings and videos of others who have tried the recipe.

The Food Network has made cooking cool and spawned many other food-related television shows, and even such things as local Iron Chef competitions. Now, using your IPad to access the Food Network website, you can find a huge number of recipes and information on cooking, shows, and the chefs that have made this show so popular.

Using Escoffier Cook's Companion

The Escoffier Cook's Companion is an iPad app that provides support for your cooking projects. It includes easy-to-find sections on ingredients, equipment, a measurement converter, a glossary, and even a timer. What cook could not make use of this?

(1) Search the App Store for Escoffier Cook's Companion. Tap Free, and then tap Install to download the app. Tap the app's icon on your home page to open it.

(2) The opening page provides access to the site content simply by tapping one of the categories encircling Chef Escoffier's head. For this task, tap Ingredients.

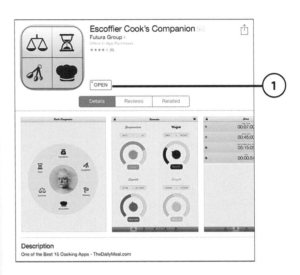

Apps Change Frequently

The images you see here are how these apps appeared when this book was written. App developers do occasionally update their apps by changing the way it looks, moving buttons around, or adding new features. You might find that an app looks slightly different from what you see here, but unless the developer has given it a total overhaul, it should function basically the same way it did when this was written. So don't let that stop you from trying it out!

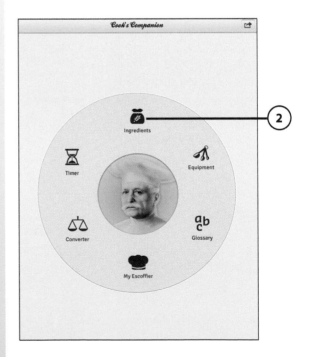

3 This page lists and defines hundreds of ingredients in alphabetical order. I chose Armagnac and tapped it to see the definition.

4 On the right side of the screen, a fairly extensive definition of the French Brandy Armagnac emerges including sections on Overview, Menu Uses, Quality Signs, and Purchase Specs.

5 Tap the Home button at the top left of the screen to return to the home page and check out another category.

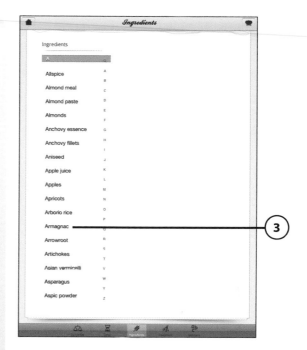

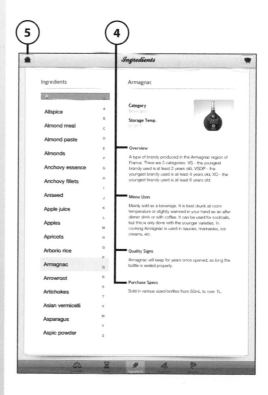

6. Tap Equipment to see the long list of interesting types of cooking equipment. I tapped one I had never heard of, Dariole Moulds. This created not only an excellent description of what a Dariole Mould is and does, but also a photo and information on how to use such a thing.

7. Back again at the home page, check out the Converter by tapping on that symbol. The Converter offers several conversions including temperature, weight, liquids, and length; very handy in the kitchen.

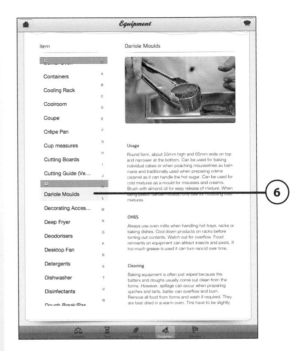

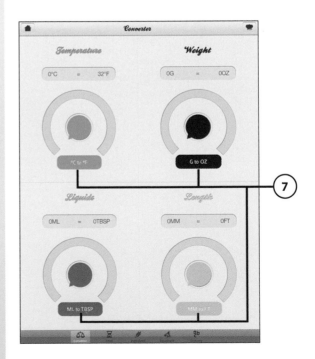

8 Tap the Timer button at the bottom of the screen or on the home screen. Tap the + sign to add a new timer, and then use the scroll wheel to set the amount of time. Hours are set on the left side and minutes on the right. Type a name for the timer in the Name field, and choose the type of alert you want in the Alerts list. Tap Start timer to begin the countdown. Tap the + sign again, and another timer pops up for you to again set the duration of time, type the name, and choose the type of alerts.

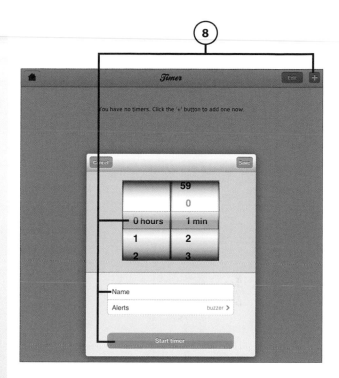

The iPad's Clock App has a Timer

Your iPad's Clock app has built-in world clock, alarm, stopwatch, and timer functions. Simply tap the Clock app's icon on your iPad's home screen. Then, tap the icon at the bottom for the function you want to access. The advantage to the Escoffier app's timer is that you can set multiple timers at once. The iPad's Clock app allows for only one timer; although, you can set up multiple alarms and world clocks.

9 The next screen shows the progress of both timers. If you need to temporarily pause the countdown, tap the little Pause button on the left side of the timer.

10 Tap Edit in the upper-right corner to change the amount of time a timer is set for or to delete a timer completely.

Use these apps to talk with friends and family just like you are in the room with them.

Photo-sharing apps are easy to use and give you options to add effects to your photos.

Find videos of friends and family, as well as how-to videos and much more.

Facebook is one of the most popular ways to keep up with the daily lives of friends and family.

Share and view photos and short videos.

In this chapter, you learn to use iPad apps to stay in touch with family and friends, as well as share photos and videos.

→ Use email to correspond—no stamp required.

→ FaceTime and Skpe offer the ability to be there when you aren't.

→ Facebook's iPad integration helps you share with friends and family with just a quick tap.

→ Instagram and Vine are social media apps that the younger generations use daily—and you should, too.

→ Share and view photos quickly and easily using Shutterfly and Flickr.

→ Post or view videos on YouTube for an easy way to share life's moments.

Communicating with Your Loved Ones Using Your iPad

There may be no more important activity than communicating with those you love. Sharing your lives with the lives of your children and grandchildren is a source of incredible happiness. You no longer have to wait to receive the photograph of some great event through the mail. You can now receive that communication almost as fast as it happens. Thanks to your amazing iPad, you have the opportunity to become much more involved in your loved ones' lives, even if they live thousands of miles away. This chapter explores some of the ways to make this happen.

Using Email to Stay in Touch

Unfortunately the handwritten letter and the postcard—that personal touch in communication—though not dead, are certainly on life support thanks to email. Email is free, easy to use, and there is absolutely no excuse not to have your own email account. Everyone who has an iPad has access to an email account. Even if you do not have one with an outside service, you have access to an iCloud email account.

Email is often your first line of communication with the outside world. Your children, grandchildren, and friends can easily communicate with you via your email account, no matter where you (or they) are. They can send you photographs, video, and updates on their current activities with you using mail. Additional options for instant communication are texting and iMessage, discussed in detail in Chapter 8, "Communicating with Email, Messaging, and Twitter."

If you've not already done so, create an email account. If you aren't sure how to set up email accounts on your iPad, return to Chapter 8 for the information. Email is a lifeline that you can't do without in this day and age.

Communicating (Almost) Face to Face with FaceTime and Skype

You may remember as a kid, hearing futurists speak of the video phone—a telephone where you could actually see the person you were speaking with! Do you remember the comments? First, "That would be so cool," and then right after, "Oh my, I'll have to comb my hair, put on my makeup, and make sure I'm dressed before answering the phone." Well folks, it's here! Thanks to your amazing iPad and the FaceTime and Skype apps, you can make calls and see the person you are talking to up close and in living color.

Think about all the great opportunities you could avoid missing out on by using just these two apps. Can't attend the family reunion? Have someone take her iPad and open up a Skype call or FaceTime connection with you. Spend the winters in Florida while the rest of your family is back in the cold? Skype and FaceTime can help you feel like you are there, while you are still enjoying the warm weather.

FaceTime

On his 90th birthday I handed my dad my iPad so that he could see *and* talk to his granddaughter in California. (He was in New York.) He looked at her with amazement and wondered just how that thing worked with no wires or anything. Your iPad and FaceTime can open up a whole new world of communicating with family and friends.

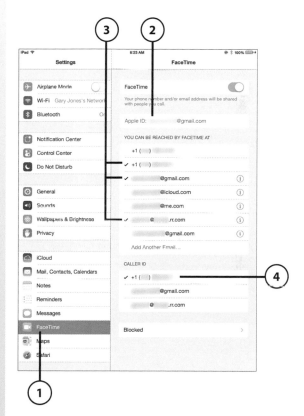

(**1**) Prior to using FaceTime a bit of set up is required. Tap your Settings app to open it, and then tap FaceTime on the left.

(**2**) Enter your Apple ID and Password if it isn't already entered.

(**3**) In the list of phone numbers and addresses that can be used to reach you using FaceTime, tap to check the ones you prefer to use. (My personal contact information is blurred out in the associated image intentionally.) Your list will contain any contact information you have previously entered into your iPad. Tap Add Another Email to enter new contact information that you want to use with FaceTime.

(**4**) The last piece is the caller ID; just like the caller ID on a phone, it lets the person you are contacting with FaceTime know who is calling. You can now close the Settings app by pressing the Home button.

FaceTime Is Limited

FaceTime is an Apple product that works only with other Apple products (iPhones, iPads, and so on). You can still have a video conversation using Skype on your iPad to anyone else who has Skype on any device or computer.

(**5**) Tap the icon for the FaceTime app on your iPad to start it.

(**6**) The FaceTime app opens, and you see yourself via the front-facing camera on your iPad. At the bottom, tap the Contacts button to choose the person you want to FaceTime with.

FaceTime

7 In this example, I chose to FaceTime my wife, Susan. I tapped her name in my Contact list and her information comes up opposite my image.

8 I tapped her phone number to activate the FaceTime call to her iPhone.

9 After the contact number or email is tapped, FaceTime responds with a message, such as FaceTime with Susan Jones. If the person you are trying to FaceTime with accepts your "call," FaceTime shows a Connecting message.

10 Either party can end the call at any time by tapping End at the bottom of the screen.

11 After the connection is made, the person you are calling can be seen on your iPad.

12 Your image appears at the upper-right corner of your screen, and the person you are calling sees you on their full screen with their own image in the upper right. (You can drag that image to other locations on your screen if you want.)

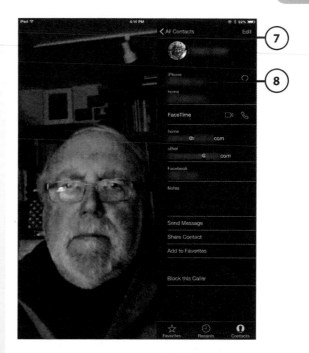

(13) By tapping the rotate camera symbol, you can see what the rear-facing camera sees. This is a great feature if you are trying to show your surroundings to the person you are talking with. To end the call, tap End.

Muting a Call

There may be times when you don't want to end the call, but you also do not want the person on the other end to hear what is going on around you. To mute the call, tap the Mute button (the microphone with the slash through it). To turn mute off, just tap the Mute button again.

>>>Go Further

UNIQUE USES FOR FACETIME

It's a Saturday afternoon and all is well. Then your cell phone rings. It's your daughter from her apartment in New Jersey asking the question, "Dad, what can I do, I have no hot water?" You try to solve this problem via the telephone asking questions about the hot water heater, is it gas or electric, who pays the gas bill, are you sure it's turned on, did a circuit breaker trip?? You appear to be asking your questions in some language that your beautiful child cannot understand. Somehow, while she was growing up at your house, she missed the course in hot water heaters!

Finally, it occurs to you that you might be able to facilitate the solution to this problem with your iPad. Could FaceTime actually allow you to see and diagnose the problem? Go to the hot water heater and call me back on your iPad using FaceTime I suggested.

I notice that the control was set to pilot, not to the on position. I asked if she had been doing anything around the water heater, she said that they were cleaning in the area of the water heater. "Oh, maybe we did bump the heater...?"

"Turn the knob from pilot to on," I suggested. "Will it explode?" she responded. Finally she turned the knob and schwoosh, the heater lit. There was a scream in the background, but the water was now heating.

My girl was happy once again. Thank you iPad and FaceTime, another mystery solved!

Since the hot water heater incident, we have had several instances where we could solve problems using FaceTime. This app and my iPad have become an invaluable tool.

Skype for iPad

Skype and FaceTime do some similar things. With either one you can make video calls with your friends and loved ones far away. One advantage with Skype is that anyone with a computer, laptop, other Internet device and a web camera can use it. FaceTime, on the other hand, is only available to Apple products, like your iPad, iPhone, and so on.

One other great aspect of Skype is the ability to make phone calls using Skype. It's a free call to any other Skype users' computer, and for a small fee you can make calls worldwide using your iPad. Whenever traveling to a foreign country that might not be compatible with your cell phones, you can add the extra Skype service to your account so that you can contact your family in the United States. As long as there's a good wireless signal, it works just great.

(1) Search for Skype in the App Store. Make sure you look for the iPad app, not the iPhone/iPod touch app of the same name. Tap FREE to download and install it.

2 When you run the Skype app, you need to enter your ID and password and then sign in. After you do this the first time, you can skip this screen.

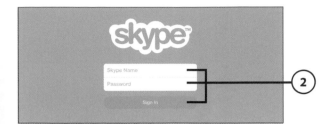

Get a Skype Account

You need a Skype account to use the Skype app. You can get a free one at www.skype.com/. If you find the service useful, you might want to upgrade to a paid account, which lets you call land lines and other phones. The free account lets you call only other Skype users.

3 Use the on-screen keypad to enter a phone number. You need a country code, too, which means using a 1 for U.S. calls. It should be there by default.

4 Tap Call.

5 While placing a call, you see the status, and eventually the elapsed time.

6 Additional buttons are available across the bottom for things like mute, volume, voice call, recent chats, and accessing your profile.

7 Tap the end call button to hang up.

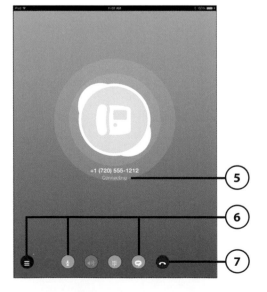

How Do You Hold Your iPad to Talk?

The microphone is at the top of your iPad. The speaker is at the bottom on the back. The best way may be to just put the iPad in front of you and ignore the locations of both. Or, you can get a set of iPhone EarPods, which include the speakers and the microphone.

How About Skype Video?

You can also make video calls with Skype using your iPad's cameras. But you must be connected to another Skype user who also has a video camera connected to their computer, or perhaps they are using an iPad as well.

Sharing Photos, Videos, and Other Information

Facebook is one of the most widely used apps to keep in touch with friends and family. It is also integrated into many of your iPad's default apps, such as the camera, Safari, and even Siri. With the tap of a button on your iPad, you can share a comment, photo, or video with your Facebook friends. When your grandchildren do something that is just too cute, you can capture it with your iPad camera and share it within seconds. It is a great way to stay connected with those you care about. Other apps that your grandchildren (or even your older children or other family members) are most likely using to share their daily lives with others are Instagram, Vine, and YouTube. The following tasks explore some of the ways to use these apps to stay in touch.

Facebook

Some people actively post on Facebook (everything from what they had for lunch to how many loads of laundry they got done that day), and others choose to stay in the background, simply viewing the posts of their friends and family and not actually saying anything themselves. When we travel, my wife posts a photo a day of something interesting she has seen. That way we can share our trip and our family knows that all is well with us in some far-off land. To start using Facebook, follow these steps.

(**1**) Search the App Store for the Facebook app. Tap FREE to download and install it.

(**2**) Enter the email address and password you use to log into Facebook.

(**3**) Tap Log In.

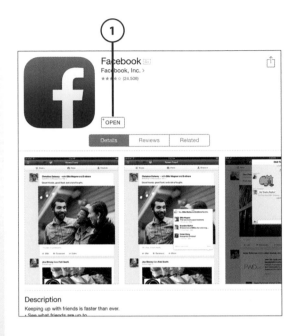

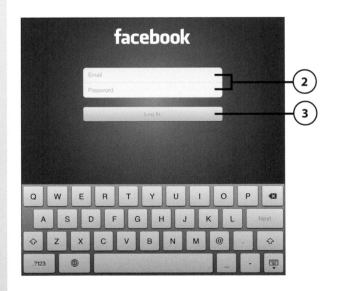

4 Scroll up and down to view your News Feed.

5 You can Like posts just as you would on the Facebook website.

6 You can also tap Comment to add a comment to a post.

7 View and handle friend requests.

8 View direct messages and send messages to friends.

9 See your list of Facebook notifications.

10 Tap the menu button or swipe left to right to bring up the sidebar.

11 Tap your name to examine your own wall and edit your profile.

12 Tap the gear button next to News Feed to switch between only showing top posts or all recent items.

13 See a list of your friends and view their information and their wall.

14 You can also post to walls of Facebook pages that you manage.

15 Tap Status to update your Facebook status, adding a post to your wall.

(16) Type the text of your update.

(17) Add friends who are with you to the update.

(18) Add a photo from your Photos library, or take a new photo using your iPad's cameras.

(19) Choose groups you want to allow to see your update.

(20) Post the update to Facebook.

It All Looks Different

If there is one consistent thing about Facebook, it is change. Facebook loves to change how its website and apps look. So if the Facebook app looks different from what you see here, it could simply be that Facebook has, once again, decided to redesign the interface.

Post from Outside

You don't need to use the Facebook app to post pictures. You can do it right from the Photos app and other image-handling apps. But you first need to go to the Settings app, then the Facebook section, and enter your email and password again. This gives iOS permission to use your Facebook account for posting. Then you can do things like post pictures from the Photos app, post links from Safari, and ask Siri to "update my Facebook status."

Instagram

Another social media app that your grandchildren are apt to tell you about is Instagram. It is a photo-sharing site that is popular among the younger segments of the population. You need to learn how to use apps like this one to effectively communicate with your grandchildren.

1. Search the App Store for Instagram. Instagram is an iPhone app that works fine on your iPad. Tap Free and then Install App to install it; tap Open to open it.

2. You have the option to Register or Sign In. If you do not have an Instagram account, tap Register.

(**3**) An easy way to register is to use your Facebook profile.

Forget Facebook

You can also just create an account with Instagram if you prefer not to use your Facebook account to sign in. However, you need to go to your Instagram profile settings and manually choose to have your Instagram photos posted on Facebook. It will not happen automatically if you go this route.

(**4**) Enter a Username and Password to use when you sign into Instagram.

(**5**) I signed in using my Facebook profile, so I was able to find my Facebook friends that also use Instagram. Tap the Follow button for any friends that you want to follow on Instagram. I tapped Follow on one friend to see photos of my nephew.

6 I can now see photos of my nephew playing baseball. I can choose to tap the Like or Comment button if I want to express my thoughts on these photos.

Hashtags

If you use Twitter, you already know what a hashtag is. A hashtag always starts with a pound sign (#) and can consist of any word, series of letters, or phrase that you want to use to describe a photo (or a tweet, in Twitter). If it is a phrase, you type the words all together without punctuation or spaces. A hashtag can then be used to search for similar photos (or topics, in Twitter). The photo shown with step 6 might have a hashtag of #baseball. If someone searches Instagram for #baseball, this photo will appear (unless the owner has marked it as private).

7 To post a photo of my own I tapped the camera icon in the row of icons at the bottom.

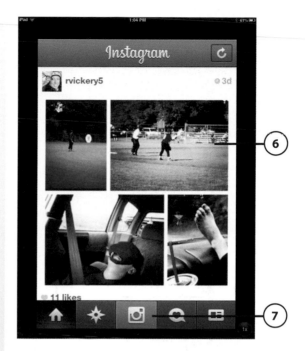

(8) There are three options. Tap
the image on the bottom left
to choose an existing photo,
tap the camera in the center to
take a photo, or tap the video
camera image on the right to
take a short video. For this task, I
selected a photo from my iPad's
camera roll to post.

Editing Photos

If you choose to take a new photo
within Instagram, you then have the
option of making a variety of edits
to the photo before you post it. You
can add filters to give it a different
look, such as turning it into a black-
and-white photo. You can adjust the
brightness and contrast, and can even
add a frame. There are other apps
out there as well, such as InstaFrame
that give you the ability to make even
more edits to your photos before you
post them.

(9) The photo shown for this step
is of a house we are considering renovating. After the photo
is posted, my Instagram friends
can see the photo and choose
to Like or Comment on it.
Instagram is a great way to stay
connected. For the moment, it is
the photo-sharing app of choice
for your grandchildren; therefore, it is a must to learn how to
use it. You don't want to miss a
precious moment!

Vine

If you want to know what apps are
hot and what apps you might want to
take a look at, just ask your grandchildren. They generally know far more
about new technology than you do
and can show you just how to make
all those great apps work. One example is Vine, which is another social
media app. It enables you to video
record whatever you are doing and
leave a short (6 second) clip online to
share with all your friends and family.
It is a lot of fun!

1. Search for Vine at the App Store.
   Tap Free and then Install App.
   After it downloads, tap Open to
   open it.

2. The opening page appears small
   because this still just an iPhone
   app. Tap the 2X button in the
   bottom-right corner to make it
   full screen.

3. You can tap Sign in with Twitter
   or Sign up with Email. I chose to
   sign up using email.

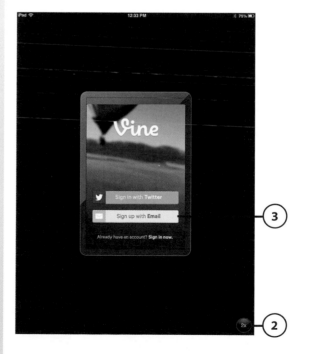

(4) Tap the @ button to use your Address Book to search for your contacts who might also be on Vine. You do have to give Vine permission to access your Address Book to use this search method.

(5) Search Vine using your friends' Twitter names by tapping the Twitter logo.

(6) Tap the magnifying glass to search for people you know by entering their Vine username, or real name, in the search field.

Getting Back to Search

On your profile page, tap the button in the top-right corner that looks like the outline of two people to return to the search options. Tap the left-facing arrow in the top-left corner to return the page you were viewing previously. The left corner now becomes a menu that lets you switch between Home, Explore, Activity, and Profile pages in Vine.

(7) For this task, I tried searching for my friend Emily and found several people with similar names, but sure enough, there she was. I tapped her image to see her Vine page.

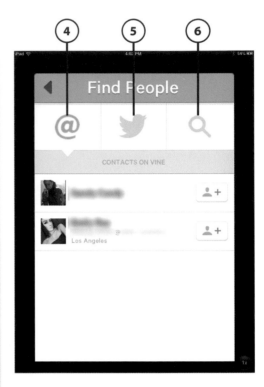

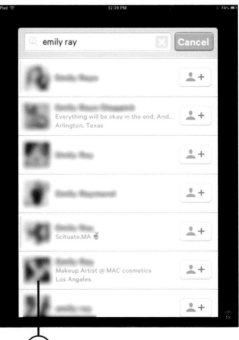

8 Emily's profile showed several 6-second videos of her life at home and her pal, Bam Bam the cat.

9 When you post a video for the first time, Vine has a tutorial that helps you start. From the Vine home screen or your profile page, tap the camera icon in the top-right corner. Tap OK to proceed with the tutorial, or tap Skip the tutorial if you already know what to do.

Tap here to return to the search options.

Tap here to access options to block this person or to share their profile.

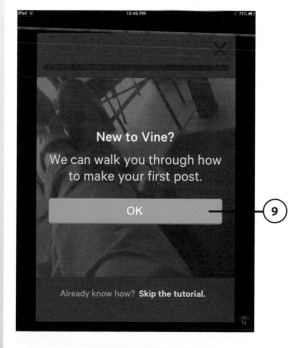

(10) Using Vine is incredibly easy. Point your iPad's (or iPhone's) camera at what you want to record and touch the screen. It records! Release and the recording stops. So that's it, tap and hold your finger down to record. Lift your finger to stop. But remember, you have only 6 seconds of video, and then you're done.

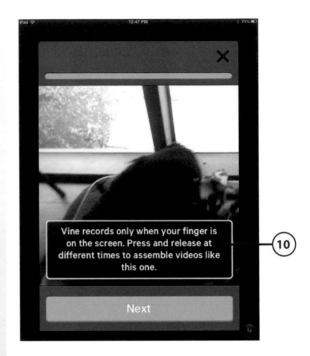

(10) Vine records only when your finger is on the screen. Press and release at different times to assemble videos like this one.

(11) For my first video I touched the screen and scanned around the room where I was sitting and then stopped. Then I tapped to scan my dog in his dog bed. One other quick scan and I was done. At this point you can add a caption and location and choose to also post on Twitter or Facebook. My first Vine video is produced!

There are many more features to explore in Vine than are covered here. Just ask your grandkids!

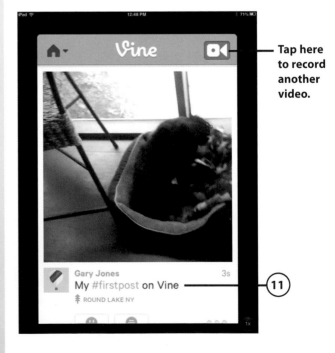

Tap here to record another video.

Gary Jones   3s
My #firstpost on Vine
ROUND LAKE NY

(11)

It's Not All Good

It's Not ALL Good

Vine presently has NO privacy options; anyone can see whatever you post. You have the ability to block others from following, you but that's it.

Using Photo Sharing, Storage, and Managment Apps

Posting pictures on Facebook or Instagram is great because they are immediately viewable by anyone you are friends with. However, you cannot order prints or other photo products, so your pictures just stay in the virtual world. You cannot put one in a frame or create a photo calendar to hang on the wall. Sites like Shutterfly.com offer the ability to not only share and organize your photos, but also to order products or prints of those photos—or of photos someone shares with you. Shutterfly also offers an iPad app so that you can easily post the pictures you take on your iPad (or iPhone) to an existing album, or create a new one.

Flickr gives you an opportunity to upload and share your photos as well as the opportunity to see the photos of others. One of the activities you might enjoy with Flickr is searching others' photos for travel destinations. The results are inspiring, and can give you an opportunity to see a location through the eyes of others.

Sharing with Shutterfly for iPad

Shutterfly is a free photo storing and sharing site and is connected to the Shutterfly app. After you upload your photos to Shutterfly, it's easy to share them with family and friends. The days of film developing are clearly over.

1. Search the App store for the Shutterfly app. Tap Free and then tap Install to download. Depending on how you have your security set up, you might also have to enter your Apple ID and /or password.

2. The first Shutterfly screen asks for your email and password if you are a member, or tap "Not a member" to create an account.

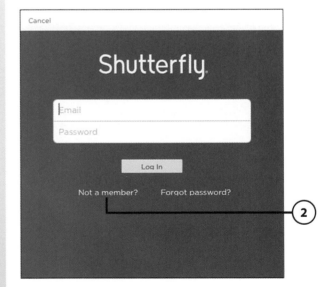

3 Creating a Shutterfly account is easy. Simply enter your name and email address in the appropriate fields, create a password, and tap Next on your keyboard.

4 You need to accept the Terms of Use for Shutterfly to then create your account. Tap Accept.

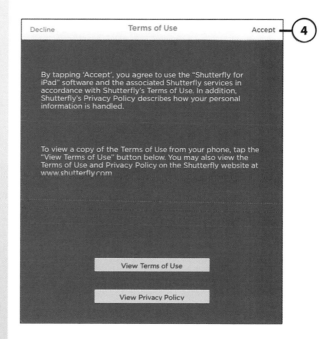

5 Shutterfly asks you to "Allow Photo Access" after you agree to allow access to your photos. You will see your iPad photos on the next screen.

6 Tap an album that contains the photos you want to upload to Shutterfly. For this task I chose Prospect/kitchen, and the entire album of photos came up on the next screen.

7 Tap Order Prints to choose photos to print through Shutterfly

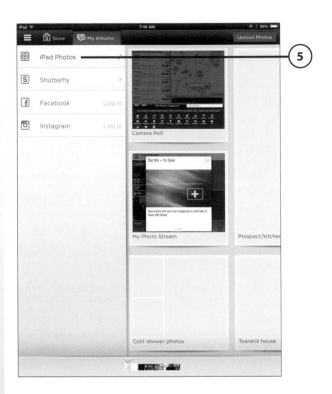

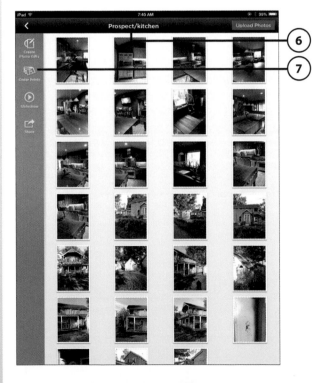

8 Tap the size prints you are interested in ordering; we chose 4x6.

9 Tap the photos to be printed; they will be collected at the bottom right of your screen.

10 Tap the collected photos, and they can be added to your cart.

11 When you reach your cart, add your shipping address, shipping method, and payment option.

12 Tap Place Order and follow the directions from there.

Much More to Do

There is a lot more you can do with the Shutterfly app, including accessing social medial sites like Facebook and sharing your photos there. Shutterfly can also store a large number of photos for you to access, share with loved ones, and print at your leisure.

Flickr by Yahoo

Flickr is an app designed for the iPhone that works just fine on your iPad with no ill effects, other than that the image size will be a bit reduced.

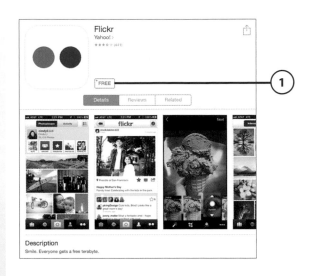

1. Search the App Store for Flickr by Yahoo. (Be sure you tap the iPhone Apps button at the top of the screen.) Tap FREE and then Install to download the app. Tap the Flickr icon on your Home screen to open it.

2. Flickr opens with two options to choose from. You can sign up with Facebook or sign in using an existing Yahoo! account.

Signing In

To access Flickr, you must sign in using your Facebook or Google account, or create a Yahoo! ID and password. Doing so is easy and free from the Yahoo.com website.

(3) For this task, I am signing in using an existing Yahoo! ID and password. Tap Sign In after you type your ID and password.

(4) There are two ways to add photos to Flickr. The first way is to tap on the camera button. Doing so turns on your iPad's camera. You can now take a photo of whatever you are looking at and load that to Flickr.

Sharing Privacy

Through the Flickr settings you can add layers of privacy to your photos ranging from Public, to Friends and or family, to totally private (only you). Security settings are something to be considered if you are at all sensitive about who sees your photos.

(5) Another option is to tap the photo at the bottom-left corner to access all the photos on your iPad. A list of your albums will appear. Tap the album of your choice, and the photos in that album will come up. In this example, I tapped the Prospect/ kitchen album.

(6) For this task I selected a photo of my new kitchen; note the check mark indicating that this is the chosen photo. Tap next in the upper-right corner when you finish selecting photos to upload.

(7) After you have chosen your photo, Flickr gives you several options on the filter page to alter or improve your photo. Tap a filter at the bottom of the screen to see how it changes your photo. You can always tap Original to remove any effect of a filter if you don't like it.

(8) Tap Next to begin the upload process.

9 Flickr requests that you add some relevant information about your photo so that others may find it in their searches. In the example image, I added the title, Kitchen.

10 The next screen shows your new photo added to your photo-stream for the world to see.

(11) In addition to uploading your masterpieces, you have an opportunity to make contacts and join groups that have similar interests. I joined a group that includes nearly a thousand photos of wood-fired ovens.

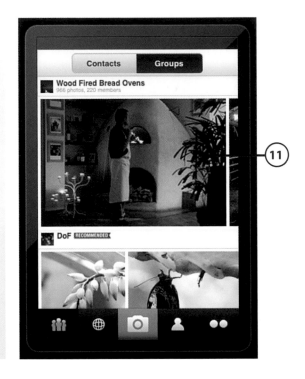

OTHER FLICKR OPTIONS

There are many other options and ways to enjoy and use Flickr. If you are planning a trip, you can search for photos of your destination to see all the photos others have taken. This is a great way to get your creative juices flowing and prepare for a great adventure. Other options available in Flickr include

- Create favorites.

- Separate out photos of yourself.

- Join others whose photos you admire by making them contacts.

- Join any number of groups taking photos that interest you.

- Search all Flickr photos, all people, or groups. You can also do a search specific to your photos or groups.

There is a great deal of flexibility using Flickr, and it's fun to see what others are photographing. Flickr is filled with photographs posted by talented people.

>>>Go Further

YouTube

YouTube is an app that enables you to save and share video moments that are meaningful to you. In addition, you can view the videos of family and friends and keep in touch with those you love. YouTube provides a nearly endless supply of entertainment viewing the videos of others, as well as those of friends and family. In addition to many entertainment videos, there is a plethora of do-it-yourself videos to help you with some of those home projects.

Often you see a YouTube video linked to a friend's Facebook page, indicating something that they would like to share. YouTube is great fun and a must for any iPad user.

(1) Search for the YouTube app in the App Store. Tap Free, and then tap Install to install the app.

(2) Tap Open to open the app.

(3) In this task, YouTube opened to the Popular category of videos.

(4) Tap the Sign In button.

(5) Setting up your YouTube account is easy, even for seniors! After you tap the Sign In button, you see two options. Enter your login information and tap Sign In if you already have an account, or tap Sign Up to create an account. For this task, I am going to tap Sign Up.

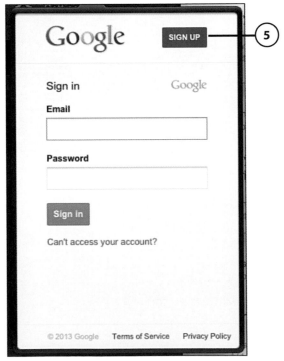

(6) You will be asked to create a
Google account. (Hint: Google
owns YouTube.) This is not a big
deal but you will be required
to provide your name, create a
username and password, and
give some personal information. You then enter the letters
shown in the captcha (they ask
you to interpret some misshap-
en text to prove you are not a
robot), give your location, and
then agree to Google's terms.

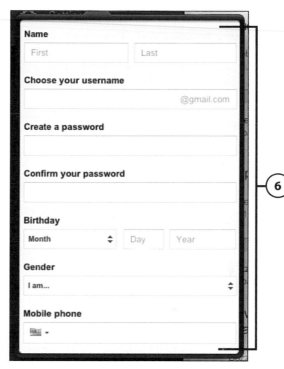

Information Overload

Providing all this information can be
annoying and might even make you
feel uneasy. It is all worthwhile when
you can see videos of your grandchildren in plays, in dance classes, or
playing soccer. In addition, you can
share your own videos with family and
friends.

(7) Now that you have your official
YouTube account, its time to
upload a video. First, choose the
video you would like to share
with your loved ones. For this
task, I searched the photos on
my iPad and tapped the video
I wanted to share on YouTube. I
chose to share a short video of
my new kitchen. Tap the symbol
at the bottom-left corner (box
with an arrow pointing up).

8 As you can see, I now have several options including sending the video as part of a message or email. For this task, I am tapping the YouTube button.

9 YouTube's Publish Video screen is your next challenge. You are required to complete several boxes that describe your video for others. Options that need to be entered include title, description, tags, category, and privacy determinations. (These settings determine how public or private your video is.)

10 Tap the blue Publish button in the upper-right corner and off it goes!

8

10

9

(11) The example video was named
"Kitchen" Published. After a
video is published to YouTube,
you have a couple of final
options. You can view it on
YouTube, tell a friend, or close
the notice.

Searching YouTube

At any time while viewing videos in
YouTube, you can type keywords in
the search box and find the YouTube
videos related to the words. I use
YouTube to search for everything from
learning how to install a dishwasher to
finding my favorite Paul Simon videos.

Listen to your favorite
music using Pandora and
Tunein Radio.

See and hear all
that NPR has to
offer through the
NPR News app.

Check out the
latest movies
and even buy
your tickets
using Fandango.

Experience a
world filled
with great ideas
through Podcasts
and the TED app.

Visit world-class
museums from
your armchair.

Use your iPad
to play some of
the best games
around.

In this chapter, you learn some other wonderful ways your iPad can enhance your entertainment options:

→ Listening to music using Tune in Radio and Pandora Radio
→ Listening to new and stimulating ideas using Podcasts, the NPR app and TED Talks
→ Checking out movies in your area and buying tickets using the Fandango app.
→ Visiting virtual museums through the Museum Guide
→ Passing the time playing fun games with Solitaire, Blackjack, and Words with Friends

Finding and Using Apps for Entertainment

Finding a great radio station to listen to "your music" as you sip coffee on a Saturday morning might be one of your quests in life. Watching that great movie that stays with you long after the final credits have run; listening to a song that transports you to a wonderful memory; reading a great book; visiting a world-class museum; listening to international or local news and ideas/discussions; or simply playing a game of solitaire are all activities that you can experience using your iPad. The tasks in this chapter give you clear, easy-to-follow steps to accomplish all of this—and more!

Accessing Music Through iTunes

Apple has changed the music world in remarkable ways. You can quickly and easily search for, purchase, and download your favorite songs and albums using only your iPad. Within seconds after purchasing, you can have that favorite song loaded on your iPad and listen to it.

You can use the iTunes app to purchase and download music, and you can simply add more music to your iTunes collection on your computer and then sync those songs to your iPad. You can also use iTunes Radio to listen to streaming music. See Chapter 4, "Playing Music and Video," for instructions on how to use iTunes and iTunes Radio to access your favorite music.

Tuning in to Music Through TuneIn Radio

Another great radio app is TuneIn Radio. I discovered TuneIn while riding on BART, the Bay Area Rapid Transit, heading into San Francisco. On the wall of the subway was a poster for TuneIn. I made a note and later that day discovered a wonderful entertainment app. You never know where you will discover your next great app.

(1) Search the App Store for TuneIn. Tap the Free button and then Install to download and install it. Tap its icon on your Home screen to open it.

(**2**) Along the left side of the opening page are four general categories to facilitate your search: Live, Browse, Favorites, and Search. Tap Browse to find many interesting types of content available through TuneIn.

(**3**) Tap Music in the center of the screen.

(**4**) A long list of several pages (swipe the page up to see more) of items are available in the music category.

(**5**) Tap the 60's.

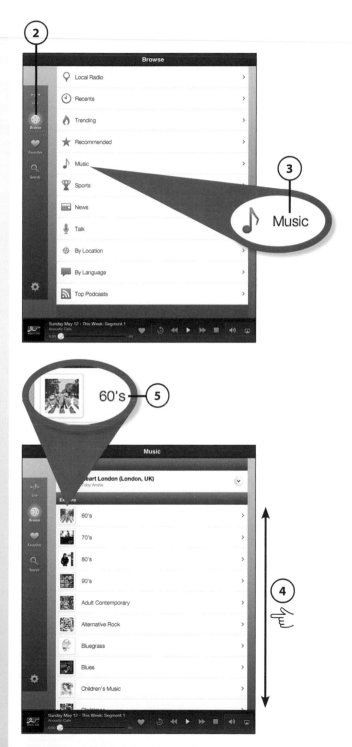

(6) The 60's search turned up many stations, several shows, and a category labeled Explore 60's that appears by swiping up on the page to scroll down the list. I chose to tap 1.FM-50s & 60s (Switzerland). Where else can I listen to a Swiss station here in the United States? Sure enough, 60s rock music played on my iPad from Switzerland!

(7) Tap Live.

(8) The next screen shows an ever-changing group of photos that you can tap to go to the music genre of your choice.

(9) Until you tap a new choice, your former choice continues to play. In this task, I am still hearing Bobby Rydell's "The Wild One" (played from Switzerland).

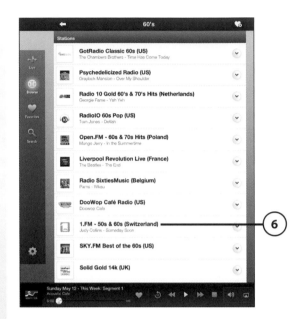

10 Now try the search feature. Type the stations, shows, songs, or artists in the search field. For this task, enter **Paul Simon**. A huge number of Paul Simon related options display. This is exciting for a dyed-in-the-wool Paul Simon fan.

11 After you find a station you like, tap the heart button at the bottom of the screen and save it as a favorite. Then, if you tap the heart button along the left side, any stations you saved as favorites appear in the list.

Listening to Music Through Pandora Radio

Pandora Radio is a popular app that enables you to choose your favorite musical artist and then creates a radio station that plays only music similar to that of your favorite artist. One of the nice things about Pandora is that you can hear and learn about artists you might never have known. It provides a biography and other interesting information about artists while their songs play.

1 In the App Store, type **Pandora Radio** in the search field. Tap the Free button and then tap Install to download it. Tap the Pandora icon on your Home screen to open it.

2 When Pandora opens for the first time, the sign in screen is shown. Type your email address and password for your Pandora account. If you do not have one yet, tap Register for Free and sign up for one.

Opening Apps

If you have already downloaded an app, you no longer see the Free or Buy button when you search for that app in the App Store. Instead, you see an Open button that enables you to open the app on your iPad from within the App Store. If you downloaded the app on another device, you might see a cloud button with an arrow in it. This means the app is in iCloud but not on your device. Tap the cloud button to download and install the app. You can always open an installed app by tapping its icon on your iPad's screen.

3 The opening page shows along the left side all the Pandora radio stations that I have already created.

4 One nice thing is that you can create a station for almost anything, including a special event. For example, we were having a pizza party and someone asked for some traditional Italian music. Simple! Create a Pandora station and you are transported musically to Italy.

5 Each time a song plays, biographical information on the artist shows on the right side of your screen often enhancing your knowledge of the artist or group.

6 Tap the gear symbol to access the settings for Pandora.

7 To create a new station, simply type your favorite artist, song, or genre's name in the search box at the upper left. As you can see, Pandora makes suggestions based upon what you type. Tap Return on the keyboard to keep what you typed, or tap one of the listed suggestions, and poof, you have a new radio station!

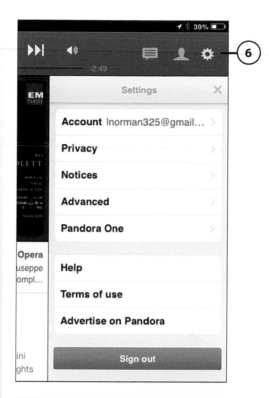

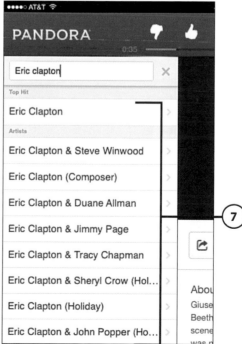

8 On occasion, Pandora asks if you would like to upgrade to Pandora One for $3.99/month to receive your music ad-free.

Continue to Use Pandora for Free

You do not have to pay anything to continue using the version that includes ads. Just ignore that ad and it will go away and return to playing your station. That goes for any other ad that is played. Just wait a few seconds and the music returns.

9 Tap … to bookmark the song or the artist track you are listening to.

10 At any point during a song, you can tap thumbs up or thumbs down to communicate to Pandora your approval or disapproval of its choice. Tapping thumbs down doesn't necessarily mean you won't hear that song again.

11 To skip to the next song, tap the fast forward button. You can tap this only a certain number of times before Pandora tells you it can't skip the current song. After a period of time, you can again tap to skip the current song. In the Pandora One version, you can skip as many songs as you like.

12 Tap Shuffle to have Pandora play randomly from all your saved stations. Tap again to remove the Shuffle option and return to playing just the selected station.

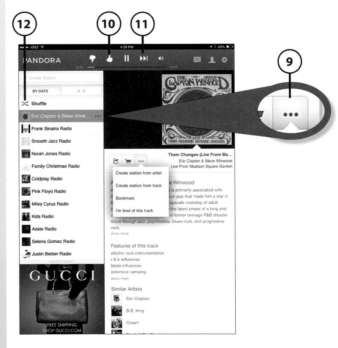

National Public Radio (NPR) for iPad

NPR for IPad offers any number of interesting articles, both written and broadcast, on a variety of topics. In addition, you can listen to updated Hourly News any time you feel the need to catch up. You can search for your favorite station to listen to, whether it is one from far away or the NPR station in your hometown, and listen anytime you want on your IPad!

1 In the App Store, search for the NPR for IPad app. Tap Free and then tap Install to download it. Tap its icon on your screen to open it.

2 The opening page shows many articles that you can choose to listen to in three main categories: News, Arts and Life, and Music.

3 You can swipe each category from right to left to see more offerings.

(**4**) For this task, swipe the music column to find a show involving the violin virtuosos, Joshua Bell and Jeremy Denk, discussing a topic they call "Song Travels."

(**5**) You have two options. You can listen to the program right now by tapping the speaker symbol, or you can tap the + Playlist to save it for later.

(**6**) Also along the bottom of the screen are a number of options to further diversify your listening experience.

(**7**) You can find your Playlist by tapping the menu button.

(**8**) Tap on Hourly News to get a news update any time you want.

(**9**) Tap programs. A page consisting of many, if not all, the NPR offerings displays.

(**10**) Tap Stations at the bottom, and you can choose to listen to any of the NPR stations across the country. For this task, I chose to find my local station by tapping find nearest. You could also choose to type a ZIP code, city name, state, or a station's call letters in the search field to find a specific station.

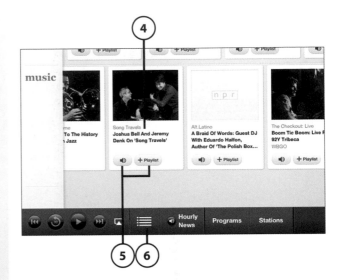

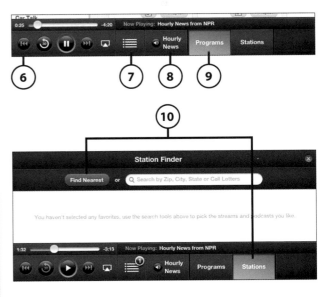

Finding and Listening to Podcasts

By listening to Podcasts on your iPad, you can learn new things and experience many delightfully entertaining and stimulating hours learning about subjects that are appealing. Simply put, it is just one more remarkable way to use this device.

That said, this whole podcast business can be a bit overwhelming (but worth it). There are hundreds of thousands of podcasts. That alone can be a bit daunting. This task gets you started and encourages you to explore further and experience this remarkable world of information.

(1) Search the App Store for the Podcasts app. Tap Free, and then tap Install to download the app. Tap its icon on your iPad's screen to open.

Apps Change Frequently

The images you see here are how these apps appeared at the time this book was written. App developers do occasionally update their apps by changing the way it looks, moving buttons around, or adding new features. You might find that an app looks slightly different from what you see here, but unless the developer has given it a total overhaul, it should function basically the same way it did when these steps were written. So don't let that stop you from trying it out!

(**2**) You are asked if you would like to "Turn on Auto Downloads" and if you would like to "Sync your Podcasts between Devices." Answer no to each in this example, and you come to the main Podcasts page where you tap Featured. This page shows a large number of featured apps that can be swiped from right to left.

(**3**) Tap All Categories to see a list of Podcast categories you might be interested in.

(**4**) The Top Charts page lists the most downloaded podcasts in the audio and video categories.

(**5**) The Top Podcasts are divided into two columns: Top Audio Podcasts and Top Video Podcasts.

(**6**) Tap This American Life to open. Tap Subscribe to see all the podcasts available.

7 You can also tap an episode at the bottom to hear a podcast before subscribing—just tap on any of the shows listed that you find interesting. For this task, I chose #508: Superpowers 2013.

Storytelling Podcast

If you like This American Life, take a look at The Moth. It is live storytelling in front of an audience and an entertaining podcast.

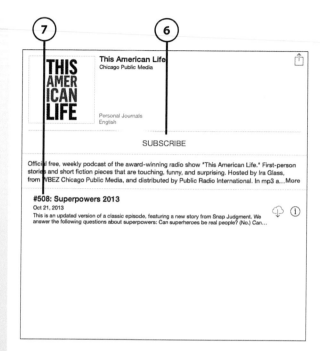

8 Tap the play arrow to move back to the Podcast app screen and listen to the podcast.

9 Tap the sleep timer to turn the podcast off after a certain amount of time.

10 To make the podcast play faster or slower, tap the 1x button at the top. If you keep tapping the button, the speed increases to 1.5x, and then to 2x. If you tap again, it goes to .5x which is the slowest speed. Continue tapping to return to 1x.

11 After you finish listening to the podcast, tap the arrow at the upper left to return to the Main This American Life page in the Top Charts category of the store.

(12) At this point, you have experienced a podcast. To find other podcasts that you might enjoy listening to or watching, tap Categories or Search.

(13) You can also choose to revisit Top Charts or Featured along the bottom of the page. These are all ways to explore the voluminous world of podcasts.

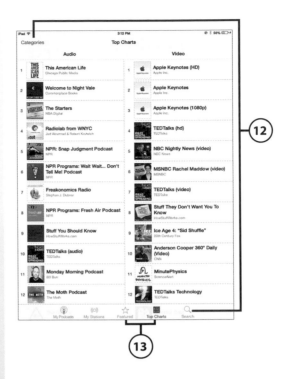

TED Talks

The TED app can provide hours of stimulating discussion and interesting viewing. Periodically, the TED organization gathers many great thinkers and creative people and puts them on stage to talk about topics that they find of interest. These recordings are available through the TED app.

(1) Search the App Store for TED (TED Conferences), a free app. Tap Free and then tap Install to download the app. Tap its icon on your iPad's screen to open it, or tap the Open button on the App Store page.

2 The opening TED page shows links to the TED Talks that are trending currently.

3 For this task, I chose to tap Inspire Me from the options along the bottom.

4 The Inspire Me tab takes you to another page. Tap Inspire Me again, and then choose a topic to be inspired by. I chose Beautiful.

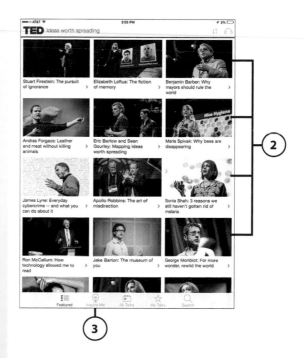

5 A part of becoming inspired is just how much time you have available. I chose the default time of 20 minutes and then tapped Continue.

6 TED chose to inspire me with a 19-minute piece on mistakes doctors make and encourages doctors to talk about being wrong.

7 You have the option to Watch Now or Watch Later. I chose to Watch Later so that I could find another talk to watch.

8 Tap Cancel.

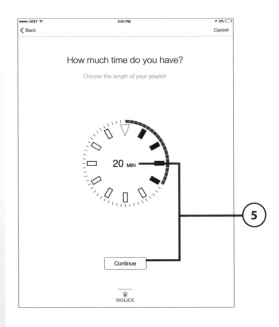

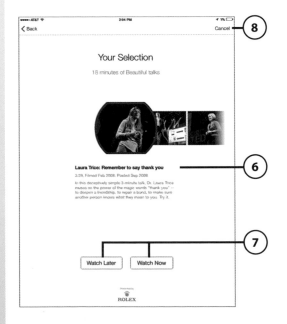

9 Tap the Search button.

10 Type **Virtual Choir** in the search box, and tap Search. (Your keyboard's Return button now says Search.)

11 Two choices come up; tap Eric Whitacre: A Virtual Choir 2,000 Voices Strong and prepare to be blown away!

12 A description of the TED Talk as well as a photo of Mr. Whitacre appears. Tap the play button to watch the video. This video shows you how, with the power of the Internet, Eric Whitacre incorporated 2,000 voices to sing one of his compositions, a beautiful experience to be sure.

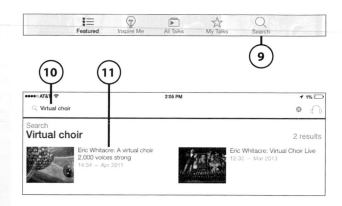

Getting Times and Tickets Using the Fandango Movies App

Your iPad can not only give you access to the movies playing at a "theater near you," but using the Fandango app, you can also see trailers, read reviews, find out where and when your favorite movie will be playing—and even buy your tickets! Not quite the same as standing in line in the rain to get into the latest blockbuster.

(1) Search the App Store for the Fandango app. Tap Free and then tap Install to download it. Tap the icon for the app on your iPad's screen to open it, or tap Open on the App Store page.

(2) The opening page shows cover photos of all the movies now playing. To view movies in your region, you must allow Fandango to access your location. To do this, go to settings-privacy-Fandango and slide the location button to the right, which turns on location services.

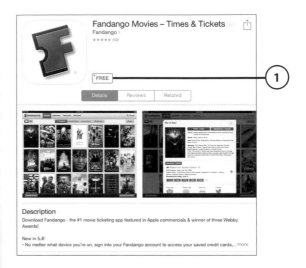

3 You can tap a movie to get more information, or there are several ways to alter your search. Tap the filters button. Now you can filter by genre or MPAA rating.

4 You can also tap the Coming Soon button to plan future movie ticket purchases.

5 I chose to tap The Great Gatsby to get further information.

6 The resulting page gives access to the movie's trailer and clips.

7 You can also find show times and tickets at your local theater if you have manually set a location or given Fandango permission to access your location. If no theaters show up here, you have not yet set the location.

8 Tap a time to find ticket availability. To change to another day, tap the blue arrow, select the day and time you want.

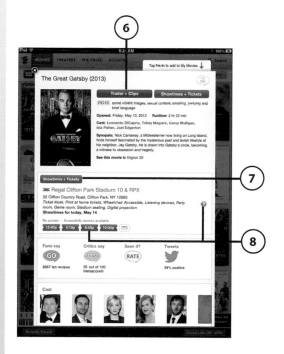

9 Tap the number of tickets you want to purchase, and then tap Next to make payment.

10 You now have two purchasing options: Guest Checkout or Fandango sign in. Because you haven't yet established a Fandango account, tap Guest Checkout. You need to add your email address to receive your receipt.

11 Tap Next to go to the payment screen.

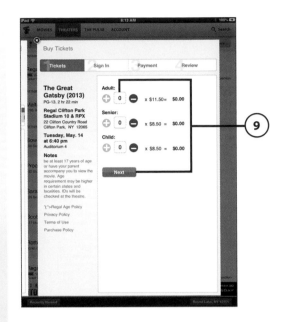

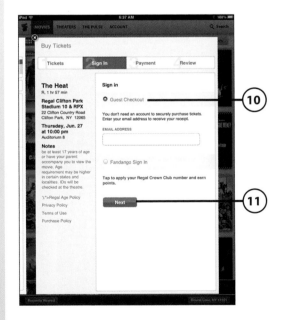

12 You have three choices for payment: Fandango code (for account holders); credit card (Visa, MasterCard, American Express, Discover); or PayPal. We tapped the middle one to use our Visa card. Then tap Next.

13 On the next screen, fill in your credit card information, and tap Next to complete your purchase.

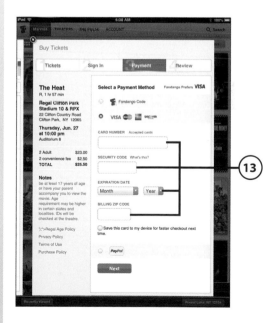

iTunes Movies

Using your iPad, you have the ability to buy and download movies. You can find a movie you loved as a child or browse through recently released movies. You should never have another, "There's nothing on TV I want to watch" evening.

1. Tap the iTunes icon on your iPad.

2. The iTunes screen opens to whatever category of content you were viewing the last time it was opened. Tap Movies along the bottom to go to the movie category.

3. Recently added movies scroll across the top of the page. You can tap one to go directly to its information page, or you can type the name of a movie into the search field.

iTunes Store

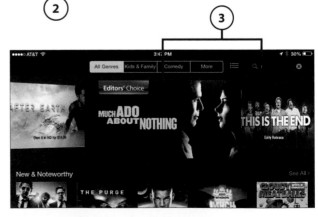

(**4**) In addition, you can select from a number of movie categories by tapping the More button. A list of many different genres of movies appears.

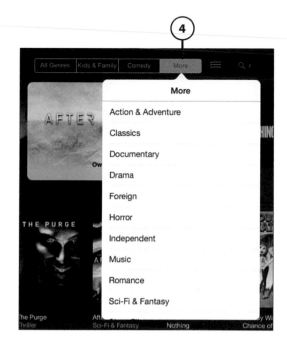

Rules for Renting Movies in iTunes

- You have 30 days to start watching after download.
- The movie must be watched within 24 hours after you start it.
- The movie expires 24 hours after you start watching or 30 days after download.
- You can move the rental between devices but watch on only one device at a time.

(**5**) For this task, I searched for one of my all-time favorites, "Doctor Zhivago."

My search produced several options in addition to the movie. There were songs, albums, ringtones, books, audio books, and podcast episodes.

(**6**) I chose to tap "Doctor Zhivago," the movie.

(7) The page for "Doctor Zhivago" includes a trailer, plot summary, cast and crew, as well as other information.

(8) Tap $17.99 BUY to buy the movie for $17.99.

(9) Tap $3.99 RENT to rent the movie for $3.99.

(10) After you tap Buy, you have the option to download the movie now or download it later. If you rent, you must start watching within 30 days, and the movie expires 24 hours after you start watching.

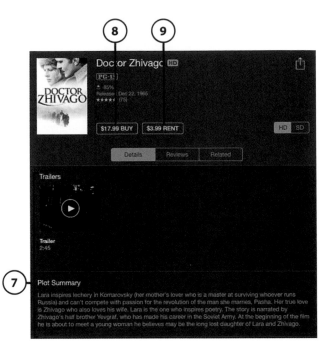

Using the New York Museum Guide

New York City has a huge number of fine museums, some certainly world class. The New York City Museum Guide is certainly a help when planning your museum visits in New York. In addition, your iPad, through this App, enables you to visit these great museums vicariously. You can see what they are showing, find their location, be transported to the museum websites for a first-hand look at their displays, and even give them a call. This is a must for any art or museum lover.

1. Search the App Store for the New York Museum Guide app. Tap Free and then tap Install to download the app. Tap the icon for the app on your iPad's screen to open it.

2. The opening page provides an overview of the museum guide's offerings. As you can see, NYC has a widely diverse cross-section of museum topics, from Art to Culture and design.

3. For this task, I tapped Art to view New York's 58 art museums.

Apps Change Frequently

The images you see here are how these apps appeared at the time this book was written. App developers do occasionally update their apps by changing the way it looks, moving buttons around, or adding new features. You might find that an app looks slightly different from what you see here, but unless the developer has given it a total overhaul, it should function basically the same way it did when these steps were written. So don't let that stop you from trying it out!

4 As you can see, the list is remarkable with all sorts of interesting art-related subjects. I chose to scroll down (swipe the screen from bottom to top) to the Metropolitan Museum of Art and tapped that listing.

5 The opening page for The Met provides essential information, such as locations, hours of operation, cost, mission, as well as a map.

6 You can tap the symbols just below the title to add this listing to your Favorites (heart icon), see the Wikipedia listing (W icon), go to the website (chain link icon), and access the phone number (telephone icon).

7 I tapped the chain link icon to see what the website had to offer.

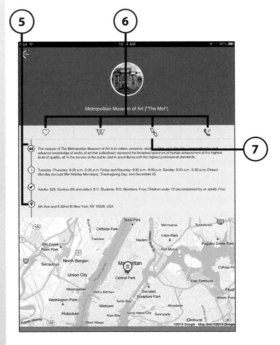

8 The Metropolitan Museum of Art website shows events occurring in the next 7 days, as well as exhibitions showing now. The Met has an ever-changing number of exhibits, so check back often to see what's "playing."

9 To return to the New York Museum app, tap close to return to the previous illustration. Then tap the arrow in the upper-left corner.

Finding and Reading Books in iBooks

iBooks offers a great read experience to seniors. Many people are fond of having an actual book in their hands, turning the pages, and enjoying all that reading a book entails. Your iPad and the iBooks app represent a new frontier in reading that I encourage you to try. With the iPad, you can download and read almost any title you can think of. You can also browse best sellers, read a sample of your favorite author's most recent book, and if you choose, purchase it on the spot. Your iPad is, in reality, a library and bookstore at your fingertips! See Chapter 5, "Reading Books," for details.

Playing Games on the iPad

Many of you enjoy playing games; card games, board games, and games of chance are some of the favorites. There are apps that re-create the game environment and enable you to have similar, if not the same, experience as you did playing the games at home. Games is a huge segment of the iPad App Store and worth exploring further than the one reviewed here. Take a look; chances are that you will find a digital version of a game you have always loved.

Playing Solitaire

Games on your iPad can range from simple to incredibly complex, This section discusses the iPad version of a few classic games: Solitaire, Blackjack, and Words with Friends. Playing these games on your iPad is a fine way to spend some time and in at least one case, have a little friendly competition with friends and family.

1. Search the App Store for Solitaire. (I chose the Mobilityware version.) Tap Free and then tap Install to download it. Tap Open (or tap the app's icon on your iPad's screen).

2. Using the free version of this app, you do have to deal with some annoying ads that pop up between games. You have to watch them, at least briefly, and then tap an X or cancel to close.

3 After you get past the ads, you have access to the game. Tap Play to start.

4 You have two options: New Game or Multi Player. I chose New Game.

5 The solitaire card game we all played as kids (or maybe even adults) appears on the screen. To play the cards simply tap them. In this example, I have no plays on the board so I tapped the deck to see the next card. We chose to play draw 3 solitaire (see step 10 for choosing the game type).

6 As the game progresses, make plays by tapping cards that reflect the next play. You can either tap a card and it automatically moves to the correct place, or you can tap, hold, and drag the card to where you want it placed.

7 If you are stumped, tap Hint and the cards automatically move to show what you missed, or you see a "No useful moves detected" message.

8 Tap Undo to go back to the previous play.

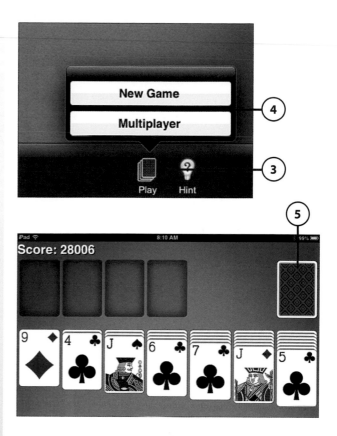

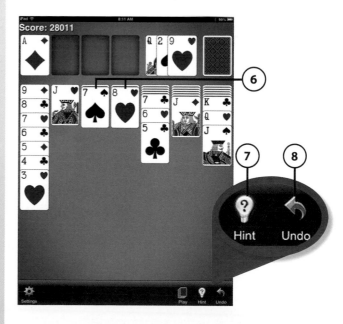

9 After you have clearly made all the moves required to win the game, a sign emerges, Auto Complete to Win. You can tap that and your iPad finishes the game for you, or you can ignore it and finish the game yourself.

Finishing the Game

There is some on-screen "celebration" when you win, and then a screen displays that calculates how well you did compared to your other games. You are also given an opportunity to tell your friends via Facebook or email.

10 Tap Settings to access other ways to adjust the game to your liking.

11 You can also choose to tap the Hate ads banner at the top to buy the gold edition and avoid the annoyance. Tap Done to close the Settings window.

Blackjack

Whether you actually partake in Blackjack at a casino, or simply enjoy pretending to be a big spender, Blackjack on your iPad is a fun way to enjoy the game and sharpen your skills.

(1) Search for Blackjack in the App Store. You have several good options. For this task, I chose Blackjack Free. Tap Free and then tap Install to download it. Tap the app's icon on your iPad's screen to open it.

(2) In this Blackjack game, the casino fronts you $500 to play with. Also, should you run out of money, the casino refills your $500 stash—you are like Bill Gates playing Blackjack.

(3) To start the game, tap the chips to choose your bet. For example, tap the $100 chip twice to bet $200.

(4) After you place your bet, tap Deal to deal the cards.

(5) The dealer's cards are at the top.

(6) Your hand is at the bottom.

(7) Your possible plays are at the bottom. You can double your bet, hit, or stand. If you tap Double to double your bet, you can take only one card.

(8) I tapped to Hit (get a card) on my original 14. I caught a 3 giving me 17. The dealer showed a face card but it was too risky to hit 17, so I tapped Stand to end my play.

(9) As soon as I chose to stand, the dealer's cards were turned over and that hand was played. In this example game, the dealer showed two face cards, (20) and I lost with my 17.

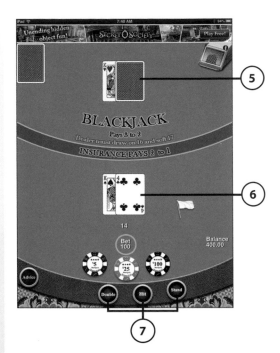

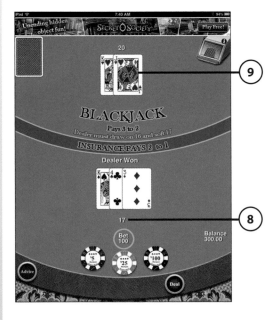

10 If at any point you are unsure of whether to hit or stand, you can always tap the Advice button. The advice I received for the hand I was playing in the example was "I suggest you Stand."

11 Finally, you can change several aspects of the game to suit your preferences by tapping the i button in the upper-right corner. You can change the rules, sounds, decks, and many other things.

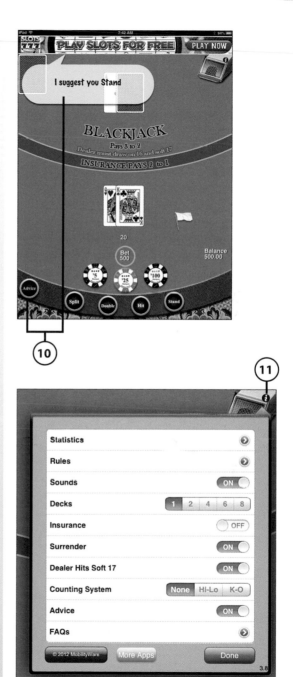

Words with Friends

Words with Friends is a wildly popular Scrabble-like game. You can play games with any number of people, and you can play any number of games at one time. The "board" is set up like a Scrabble board with each letter assigned a value and certain spots on the board earning bonus points. Playing Words with Friends keeps your mind sharp and your competitive spirit alive; it's a great game.

(1) Search the App Store for Words with Friends HD Free. Tap Free, and then tap Install to download it. After it downloads, tap Open in the App Store to open it.

(2) As shown in the examples on the left side of the screen, I have four games playing simultaneously.

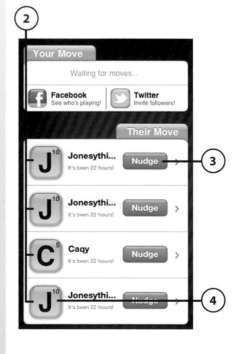

(3) Each of my competitors have been a bit slow in playing their turn, so Words with Friends has an annoying Nudge option that can remind them to play. I prefer to just wait for them to take a turn.

(4) I can tap on any of the games to view our progress.

5 This example represents a new game where I have made the first move, playing the word sleek.

6 For the word, sleek, I earned 20 points. From here we go back and forth, playing our words and getting new letters, just as one would in the Scrabble board game.

7 The number next to the score represents the number of letters remaining.

8 The box in the upper-right corner enables you to chat with your competitor. Just tap it, and then type your comment. A green bubble with a number that represents the number of unread chats you have appears when someone else has left you a comment.

9 In this case, Jonesy13 is my daughter, and I trash talk her all the time. She consistently beats me.

10 To begin a new game, tap Start at the top.

11 Choose a Facebook friend or someone in your Contacts list to play against. You can also tap Random Opponent to be paired with another Words with Friends player.

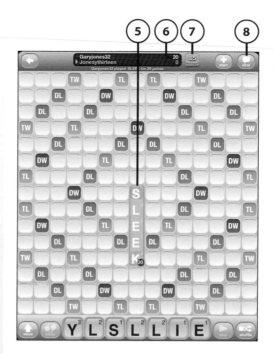

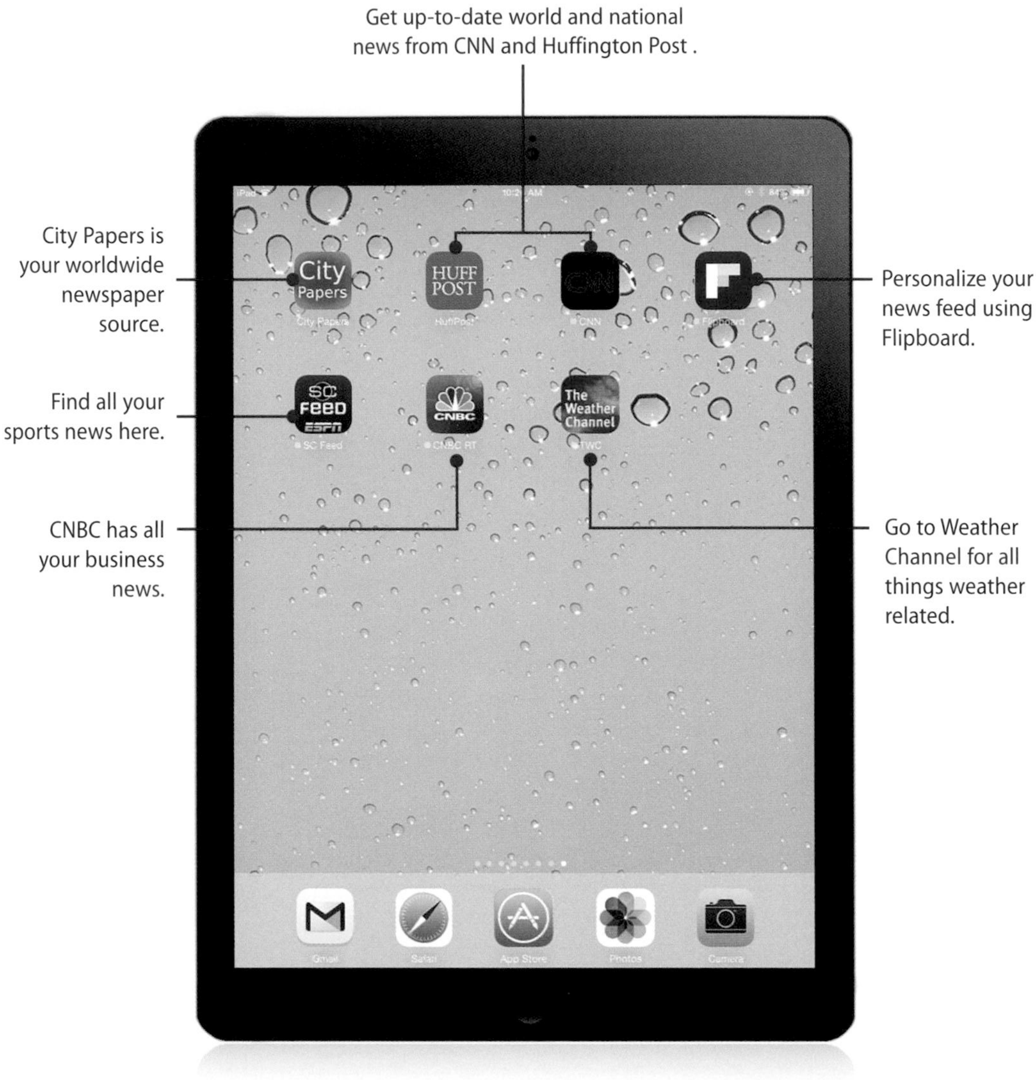

Get up-to-date world and national
news from CNN and Huffington Post .

City Papers is
your worldwide
newspaper
source.

Personalize your
news feed using
Flipboard.

Find all your
sports news here.

CNBC has all
your business
news.

Go to Weather
Channel for all
things weather
related.

In this chapter, you look at apps that help you keep up with the latest in news, sports, finance, and weather.

→ Using the City Papers app to get local news throughout the world.

→ Keeping up to date with news, entertainment, and media using the Huffington Post app.

→ Keeping up with breaking news around the world with the CNN for iPad App.

→ Customizing your news sources using Flipboard.

→ Following all your favorite sports news with the ESPN app.

→ Staying current with financial news using the CNBC Real-Time for iPad APP.

→ Using the Weather Channel app to check the forecast anywhere in the world.

Keeping Informed Using News and Weather Apps

Whether your interests are finding out what is happening in your hometown, following the world and national news, checking out your favorite team or your stock portfolio, or simply finding out the local or international weather forecast, a tap of your iPad screen can meet those needs.

Getting Local and Global News Using City Papers

City Papers is an app that gives you up-to-date access to hundreds of newspapers worldwide. Browse the papers that are set up by state, then by city in the United States, or internationally by continent and then by country. Take the time to take a good look at these offerings, such fascinating access to news.

1. Search the App Store for **City Paper**. This app does cost a little ($.99), but it's worth the investment.

2. Tap the price button and then tap Install to download the app. Tap Open.

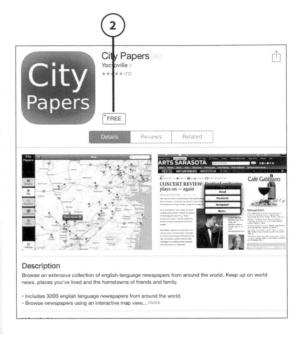

DOWNLOAD TIPS

If you've read earlier chapters in this book, you'll remember that when you tap the button to download and install an app (the button is sometimes labeled FREE and sometimes shows a price, if the app is not free), you might be asked for your Apple ID password. If this occurs, it means you've enabled the setting in the Restrictions that requires your Apple ID password to be entered every time you download an app (whether or not it costs money). This is a good security feature to have enabled, especially if others use your iPad (such as grandkids who might not understand in-app purchases). If you prefer not to have to enter the password, or if you want to change the frequency that it has to be entered when downloading apps or content from iTunes, go to the Settings app and tap General, Restrictions. If you've already enabled Restrictions, you'll be asked to enter the four-digit password that you would have created when you set up the restrictions initially. Swipe from bottom to top until you see the Allowed Content section. At the bottom you should see Require Password. Tap the Require Password setting, and you can choose Immediately, which requires your password be entered for every download regardless of how long it's been since the last time you entered the password. Or you can choose 15 minutes, which allows you to download content or apps for 15 minutes before being asked for the password again.

>>>Go Further

Tap the Restrictions button at the top of the screen to return to the list of settings. You also see In-App Purchases in the list of Restrictions settings. If it is set to OFF you cannot make In-App Purchases without entering a password. This is a useful security feature that prevents someone from accidentally downloading paid content within a game or other app without realizing it. If you set it to ON, In-App Purchases will be made immediately without requiring the password.

(**3**) The opening page shows the regions represented and the newspapers you can browse. For this task, tap the United States.

(**4**) Another option is to search by Map.

(**5**) You can save searches by Favorite, Quick Lists, or History.

(**6**) Searching in the United States yields a scrollable list of all the States. Scroll down and tap California.

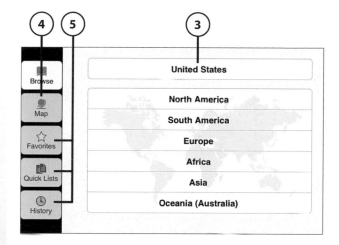

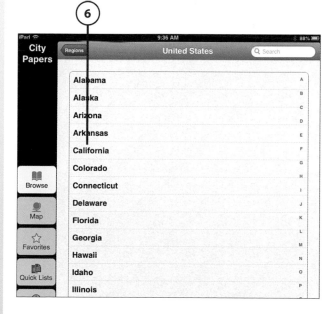

7 The California search lists literally hundreds of newspapers throughout the State of California. One of my favorite newspapers, in one of my favorite cities, is the *San Francisco Chronicle*. Scroll down and tap the Chronicle.

8 Today's issue appears, live and in living color.

9 If you like the food section of this newspaper, tap the Food link at the top to check it out.

10 Sure enough, the Food section of the *San Francisco Chronicle* emerges. It is so exciting to get a look at this from your home in another state.

11 After scanning this paper, tap Done in the upper-right corner to return to the states list to browse further.

12 You can look at local papers to get a sense of how thorough the City Papers app is. To do so, tap New York. Albany is the first listing. Included in the Albany listing is the largest local paper, *The Times Union*, and a weekly, *Metroland*.

13 Tap *Metroland* to again check out the quality of this app, which is outstanding. You can view the latest issue of this weekly in its entirety. City Papers may just be the best $.99 you will spend this year. Not only can you find local news, but also local news throughout the world. This is great fun!

12

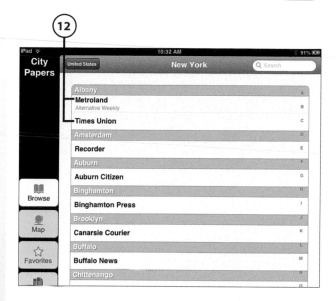

13

Finding New and Entertainment Information Using *The Huffington Post*

There are many news apps available for your iPad. *The Huffington Post* is a well-known purveyor of world and national news and it is a good place to get an overview of news you may be interested in. *The Huffington Post* does a nice job of covering a wide variety of news stories, as well as entertainment and other stories that might be of interest. It's worth a look.

(1) Open the App Store by tapping its icon, and then type **The Huffington Post** in the Search field. There are several other iterations of this app, so look for the one with the green HUFF POST symbol. Tap FREE and then tap Install to download the app.

2 The lead story today is a piece with a somewhat sensationalize title about a sheriff in Arizona. To read that story tap on the photo.

3 To move on to other news, swipe up and down to scroll through the page.

4 The *Huffington* has headlines for a number of news- and not-so-news-related stories. Tap any one to read or see the associated video.

5 In addition, you can refine your search to topics that interest you by tapping the H symbol in the upper-left corner.

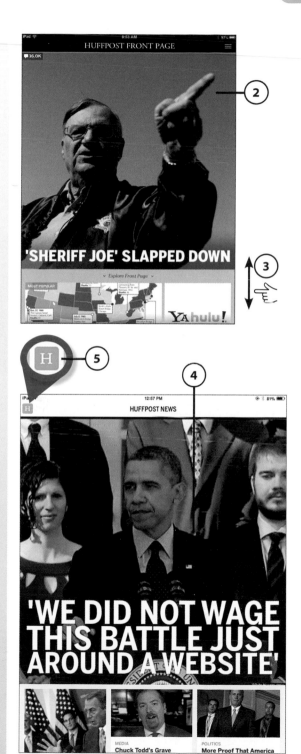

6 At this point you have two options: scroll from left to right along the top to view different categories, or tap the + button at the bottom to see a list of topics.

7 The list of topics can be viewed as Alphabetical, Categories, or Favorites you have earlier identified.

8 I chose to go back and tap the article on bridge collapses to see if anything in our area might be at risk. The complete article appears on screen.

Staying Informed Using CNN for iPad

It seems that anytime there is a breaking national or international news story, the place I end up watching it on television is CNN. The Cable News Network is a 24-hour news program that is often right smack in the middle of the action. Now, you can join it using your iPad.

(1) Open the App Store and type **CNN App for iPad** in the Search field. Tap FREE and then Install to download the app. Tap OPEN.

(2) The opening CNN page shows a CNN Live TV option that enables you to watch live TV. This feature is limited to certain cable providers. Tap OK to see if you have the live capability. Even if your cable provider does not support this option, there are plenty of videos stored on the CNN site to access.

3 The Top Stories features page has a lined symbol at the top left. Tap to get a list of sections and all the other top stories you might be interested in.

4 Tap any article on the home page to go to the newscast or written story.

5 Should you have the live TV option, tap Watch CNN to see the options.

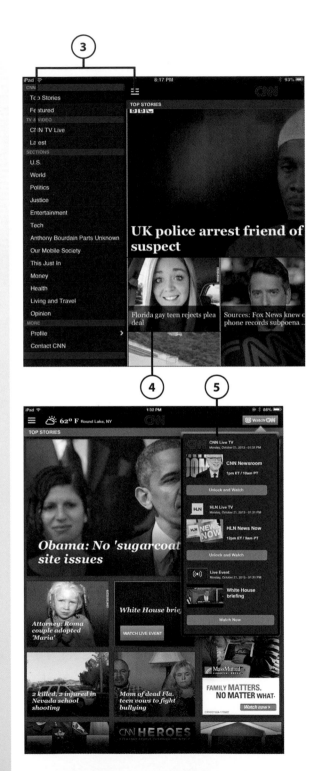

6 Tap a story of interest and move through the list of photos by swiping from right to left. It displays as either a photograph or a video.

7 For a video, tap the play button.

Customizing Your News Sources Using Flipboard

Flipboard is one of the oldest and best news apps on the iPad. In spite of being around since nearly the beginning, Flipboard has evolved and provides the capability to create your own individualized source of news. Flipboard does a remarkable job of accumulating news from many different sources and storing them on its app so that you can access any story you want with a tap. This is clearly one of the most useful news apps.

(1) Search the App Store for **Flipboard: Your Social News Magazine**. Tap FREE and then tap Install to download the app. Tap OPEN.

(2) Your first trip into Flipboard results in several "welcome" pages as well as a brief tutorial on how to use Flipboard. In the future, whenever you enter Flipboard you go directly to "my Flipboard," your personalized news source. Tap the FLIP button to move on.

3 To begin, create your personalized Flipboard page. This page
gives you the opportunity to
choose from many general content areas. To start, tap some
areas of interest. For this task,
tap News, Technology, Travel,
Food, and Music.

4 After you choose some areas of
interest, it makes sense to create
a Flipboard account so that your
preferences can be saved and
accessed whenever you sign
back in. Tap Create and complete the required information
to create your own Flipboard
account.

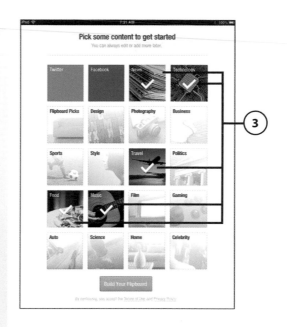

5 Now that you have your own account, you can explore the news.

6 Tap one of your content areas. For this task, tap News.

7 You can find stories of national and international news, as well as many other interesting topics. For instance, I found a story that was quite close to home. It seems that 34 inches of snow fell on Whiteface Mountain in New York's Adirondack Mountains. I knew it had been a chilly Memorial Day weekend but had no idea that this had occurred. Now I do—thanks to Flipboard!

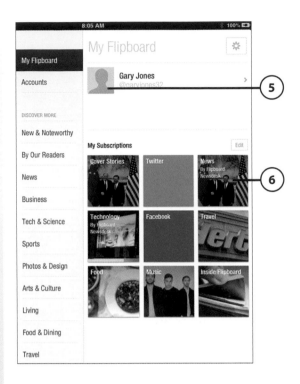

Following Your Favorite Team Using the ESPN App

The sports channel ESPN has several apps available in the App Store. Some require a specific Internet provider, whereas others can be viewed on any connected iPad. Take a look at the ESPN SportsCenter Feed app, which is available to everyone.

1 Open the App Store and type **ESPN SportsCenter Feed** in the Search field. Tap FREE and then tap Install to download it. Tap OPEN.

2 The ESPN SportsCenter Feed opens with an option to Sign In, or Sign In with Facebook. Because it's not required to sign in to use the app, tap Not Now. If you tap Sign In, you need to provide the username and password you use for the ESPN SportsCenter website. Tap Register if you want to create an ESPN SportsCenter account.

(3) The ESPN Feed opens with a list of articles along the left side. Swipe the list up or down to find the article that interests you.

(4) For this task, tap NBA Grizzles Back Off.

(5) The article emerges on the right with an accompanying ESPN video. Tap the play button to view the video.

(6) Tap the menu icon at the upper left to view more options.

(7) Several options show up along the left side, including Top Stories, Most Popular, Video, and so on, which give you more control over the type of content you can view. Tap More Sports.

8 This yields a list of options that enable you to focus your search to ensure that you can keep up with your favorite sport. Tap any of the topics to see related content.

There is much to explore in this app. If you create an account or sign in as an ESPN SportsCenter user, more options become available. The options range from football to golf, basketball to tennis, and most any other sport you can think of.

Getting Financial News Using CNBC Real-Time for iPad

These days, you should keep current with the changing financial times. It is particularly important if you are retired or nearing retirement. CNBC Real-Time for iPad is an App that provides all the necessary tools to make wise financial decisions. In addition to finding up-to-date information on stocks that you might follow, CNBC has a huge amount of information on currencies, bonds, and a number of other financially related items. This is a key app for anyone who dabbles in the stock market.

(1) Open the App Store and type **CNBC** in the Search field. Tap FREE and then tap Install to download the app. Tap OPEN.

(2) The opening page shows an overview of all the financial indexes that you need to be aware of. You can see individual stocks on the ticker at the bottom, and the activity on the individual indexes in the middle.

(3) When you are ready to find more information, tap one of the icons along the top of the screen. I Tap News.

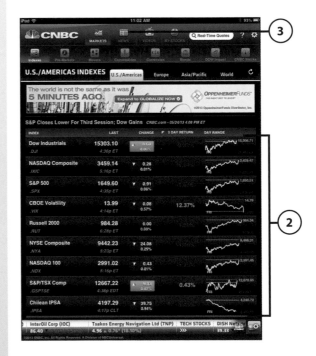

(4) The News button produced a single lead story. Tap the Top Stories button to see a list of all the top stories.

(5) Tap My Stocks to view a list of the stocks that you watch.

(6) Each stock you watch has information on the last sale price, the change on the day in dollars and percentage, the 52-week high and low, and the range for the day.

(4)

(5)

(6)

7 Tap the text box in the upper-right corner to get stock quotes. A list of recently viewed items displays.

8 You have the option to get a quote or add any one of these stocks to your My Stocks list by tapping the relevant button for each stock. If you tap Add to List, the stock is added to you're My Stocks list (see step 5).

As with most of these content-rich applications, there is more to explore than covered here. Tap different buttons to find more information or to narrow the type of content shown.

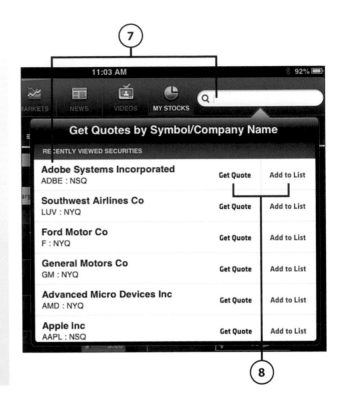

Using the Weather Channel for iPad

Paul Simon said it best when he sang, "I get the news I need from the weather report. I can gather all the news I need from the weather report…." Well, now, you can get all the weather reports you need on your iPad. The Weather Channel is clearly the standard to finding out what's currently happening with the weather, and what future weather conditions will be, for just about anywhere.

1. Open the App Store and type **The Weather Channel for iPad** in the search field. Tap FREE and then tap Install to download the app. Tap OPEN.

2. After tapping on The Weather Channel home page, you are transported to your own favorites page (if you haven't used the app before, you set a "home" location at this point) providing weather information on the location of your choice.

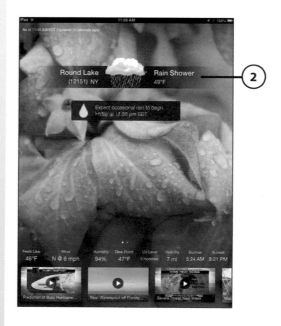

(**3**) Tap the personalized home page, and a more detailed forecast appears. In this page you can scroll along to see the forecast up to 10 days out.

(**4**) You can change your favorites page by tapping the search symbol at the bottom right.

(**5**) This example shows two favorites: Round Lake, NY and El Cerrito, CA. You can add more favorites by tapping the text box and adding another location. You will instantly be transported to a page that shows the weather in that location. This is a great resource for planning a trip and figuring what clothes to bring.

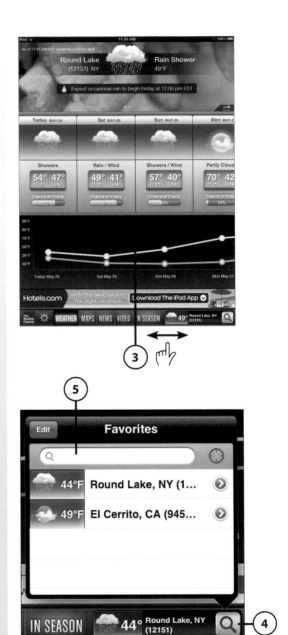

6 Tap the In Season button on the bottom to view the weather with seasonal information.

7 Tap the Flu or Pollen button at the top to get seasonal information concerning things such as pollen count and the spread of the flu.

8 Tap Radar at the bottom to get a look at the radar showing the weather that is coming your way.

The Weather Channel for iPad is an awesome resource to keep you up to date on the weather at home, wherever your loved ones are, or just a location you are interested in. With this easy-to-use, free app, your iPad is like having your own personal weatherman at your side at all times.

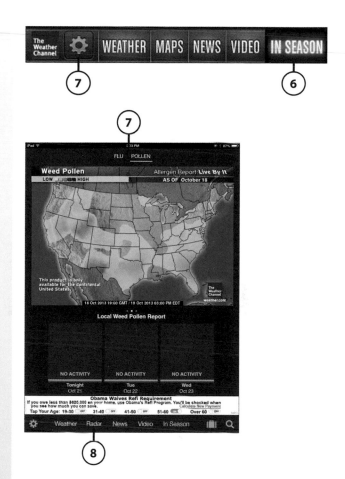

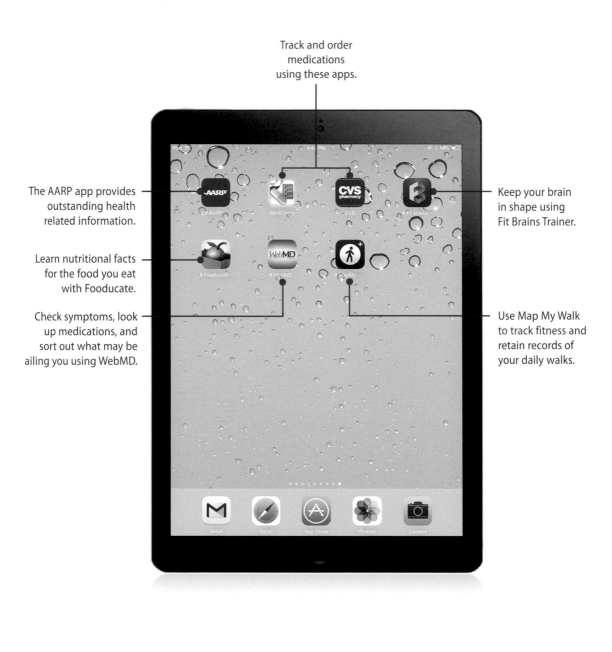

Track and order
medications
using these apps.

The AARP app provides
outstanding health
related information.

Keep your brain
in shape using
Fit Brains Trainer.

Learn nutritional facts
for the food you eat
with Fooducate.

Check symptoms, look
up medications, and
sort out what may be
ailing you using WebMD.

Use Map My Walk
to track fitness and
retain records of
your daily walks.

In this chapter you explore ways to take control of your health and well-being.

→ Use the AARP App to gain insight into a wide variety of topics that help keep you healthy

→ Store all your medical and prescription information in one easily accessible place using the Medcoach Medication Reminder App.

→ Use a pharmacy app to fill prescriptions and even print photos.

→ Exercise your brain to stay mentally sharp using the Fit Brain Trainer.

→ Use the Fooducate App to positively affect your food choices.

→ Use WebMD to check out bothersome medical symptoms.

→ Track your exercise using the Map My Walk App.

Using Apps That Help You Stay Healthy and Fit

Check out several apps that help track your physical and mental exercise, track your medications, navigate the pharmacy, and learn to approach your daily life in a healthful way.

Finding Health-Related Information Using the AARP App

The AARP app was covered previously in this book in the travel chapter (Chapter 10, "Exploring the World with Your iPad"). The reality is that this app does a fine job of finding and relating many different kinds of important information that your "demographic" finds interesting. Health and fitness is another one of those areas in which the AARP app can provide tips and information that is helpful to all seniors, whether you have issues with your health or want to avoid them.

(1) If you didn't already download and install the AARP app, open the App Store and type **AARP** into the Search field. Tap FREE and then tap Install to download the app. Tap OPEN.

(2) The AARP App opens in landscape format and the topics it covers appear on the Home screen. Tap Health.

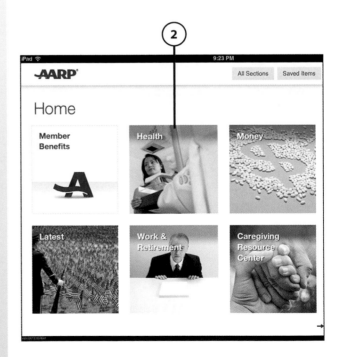

3 Swipe from right to left to view the many topics that this app covers on healthcare. At the time this task was written, there were tips to keep your brain healthy, a list of surgeries to avoid, and information on insomnia-inducing medications. Tap Insomnia-Inducing Medications.

4 The resulting article is a well-researched piece, *10 Types of Meds That Can Cause Insomnia,* written by Dr. Armon B. Neel, Jr. The article discusses insomnia and conditions that can contribute to insomnia. It then talks about the drugs that contribute to insomnia. You can routinely find well-thought-out, informative articles such as this one using the AARP app.

5 Tap the arrow to return to the list of topics within the Health category.

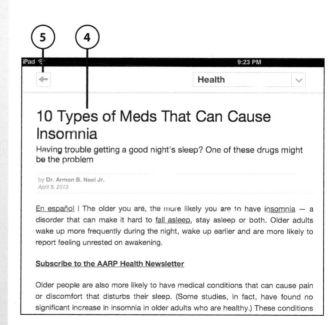

6 To look a bit further and find an interesting piece on 6 Fabulous Foods to Fight High Blood Pressure, I tap it to read further.

7 This article gets straight to the point describing six great foods that can fight high blood pressure. Who knew that the dark chocolate that you love so much can contribute to keep you healthy.

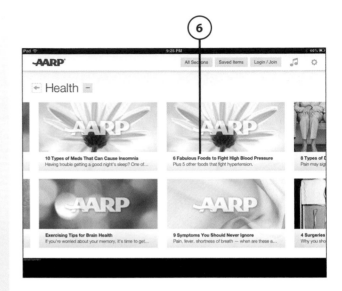

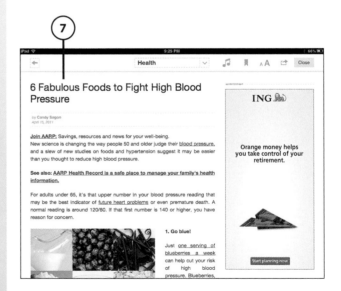

Staying on Track with the MedCoach Medication Reminder App

MedCoach Medication Reminder is an app that not only helps you keep track of your medications, but it also acts as a storage device for prescriptions, your doctor's contact info, and a reminder for when you need to reorder your medications. MedCoach is an app that provides help you might need to be sure you follow your doctor's orders and stay on track with your medication.

(1) Open the App Store and type **MedCoach Medication Reminder**, an iPhone app, in the Search field. Tap FREE and then tap Install to download the app. Tap OPEN.

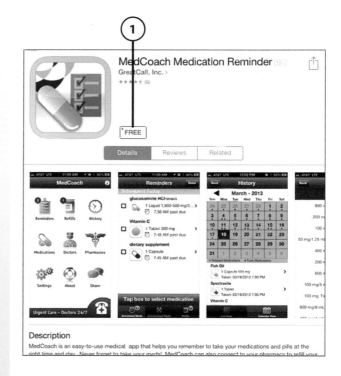

(**2**) The opening page shows a help bubble. Tap it to get information on how this app works.

(**3**) The help page illustrates how serious this app is in making sure that you get the help you need to make this a useful tool for your healthcare.

(**4**) The app is actually an iPhone app. Tap the 2x button in the bottom-right corner to make the image full screen on the iPad.

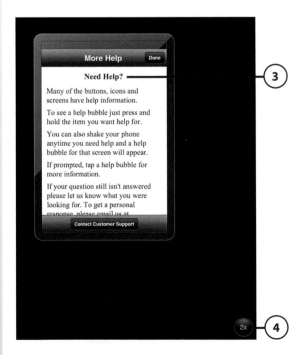

(5) Tap Get Started, and the primary MedCoach page opens. You are urged to start with the medications sections. Tap Medications.

(6) I have asthma and use an inhaler daily. I decided to add that medication by tapping Lookup Medication.

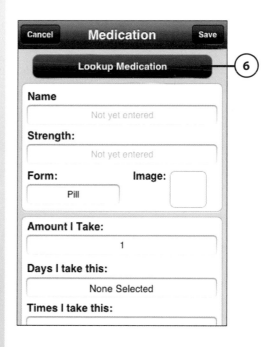

(7) To begin, start typing the name of your medication. I typed in **Advair**. I no sooner typed adv and Advair came up as an option in the results list. Tap your medication name in the results list.

(8) I tapped Advair Discus and a dosage chart appeared. I tapped my dosage, 250/50.

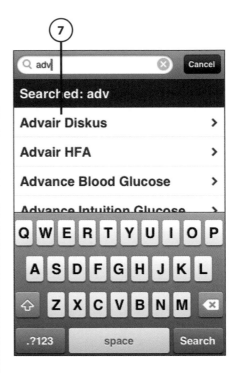

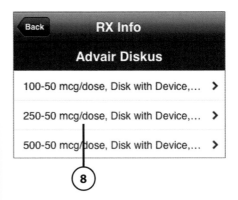

9 The next screen shows the added the medication and the dosage.

10 Several other items of information are now clearly displayed that need to be tapped and completed, including amount, days, and times I take this medication, and an image of the medication to help ensure I did choose the right one.

11 After completing all the fields, I also took a photo of my Advair Diskus with my iPad and posted that so I would be sure to know which med I was referring to.

Take Your iPad Along

It is handy to have all your medication and physician information in one place. Whether you are talking to a new doctor, specialist, or pharmacist, you won't have to worry that you've forgotten to mention one of your medications. I will be bringing my iPad to the office the next time I see a doctor!

12 Tap Reminders. As you can see, I missed my 8 a.m. dose and MedCoach noted that for me. Reminders are handy if you have trouble remembering to take your medication, or if you have multiple medications to take throughout the day at different times.

9

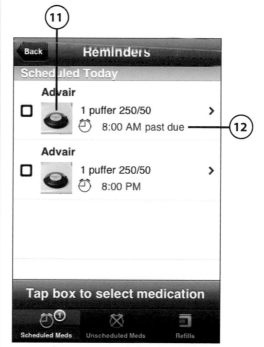

11

12

(13) I went about my business and while sipping a beverage that evening on my back porch, my iPad made a strange noise. I picked it up to see a message from MedCoach that I had missed my evening dose of medicine. This is obviously the kind of help I need.

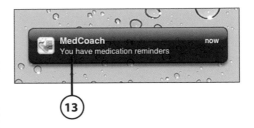

(13)

Using a Pharmacy App to Refill Prescriptions

The App Store contains many apps specific to businesses you might deal with, such as pharmacies. As the choice of app depends on the pharmacy you work with, your app may differ somewhat from the one shown in this task, but most of the concepts should be similar. I've chosen to take a look at the CVS Pharmacy app.

(1) Open the App Store and type **CVS Pharmacy** in the Search field. Tap FREE and then tap Install to download the app. Tap OPEN.

(2) The opening page for the CVS app indicates that the App would like to use my current location. In this case I tapped OK. My rationale was that the app would provide more location-specific info if I included this.

(3) The opening page shows many options for consideration including Prescriptions, Photo, Shop, MinuteClinic, and Extracare. Each of these can be tapped to explore further. For this task, tap RX to take a look at managing prescriptions.

(4) To access the CVS prescription option, you first need an account. If you don't already have a CVS online account, tap Create an Account, and fill in the requested information, including an email address and creating a password.

(5) You can now sign in by simply typing the email address and password you entered when you created your account.

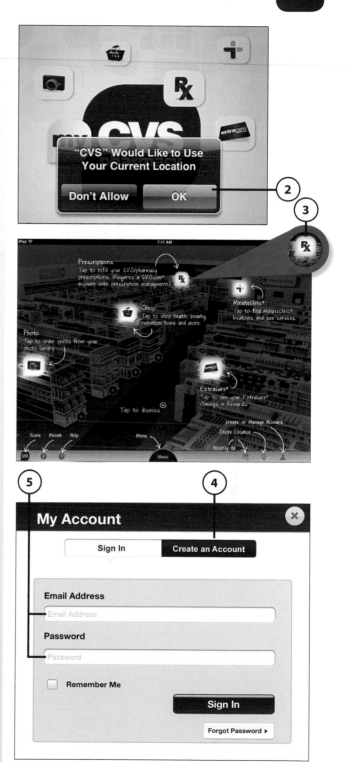

(6) You can refill your prescriptions using a number of different approaches. You can tap Prescription Center to see the prescriptions you currently have with CVS, Refill by Label to enter information off your prescription bottle label, or Refill by Scan to use your iPad's camera to scan the label's barcode.

(7) CVS communicates the status of your prescriptions in the Ready for Refill, Ready for Pickup, or Requires Renewal areas.

(8) Tap Menu to go to another section of the app, or tap Sign Out to prevent anyone else who uses your iPad from accessing your information.

(9) Tap the Ad button to see the CVS weekly ad.

Many major pharmacies offer the convenience of ordering prescriptions and maintaining information on prescriptions via their iPad app. It sure beats standing in line at the pharmacy, handing off the prescription, and then waiting 45 minutes to get your medication.

Exercising Your Brain Using Fit Brains Trainer

There's a rumor afloat that as we get older our brains tend to not work so well. My significant other would certainly attest to that being true. Of course, via the iPad we can delay the deterioration and possibly—with some serious training—reverse it. I checked out Fit Brains Trainer, an app that operates like a gym for your brain. At the time of this writing, Fit Brains Trainer had 4,276 people that had rated it highly. That's a large contingent of supporters, so it seems to be worth a look.

Push Notifications

When you open games and other applications for the first time, such as Fit Brains Trainer, you see a box asking if the app can send you Push Notifications. You have the option to allow this. If you do allow it, the app can send you notifications about different things, such as reminding you to play. If you prefer not to get these notifications, tap Don't Allow. If you accidentally allow those notifications, you can turn them off by opening the Settings app and tapping Notifications. Swipe up until you see the app that is sending notifications. Tap the name of the app, and then slide all the switches from ON to OFF. You will no longer receive those annoying notifications from that app.

(1) Open the App Store and type Fit Brains Trainer in the Search field. Tap FREE and then tap Install to download the app. Tap OPEN.

(2) Fit Brains Trainer opens with an overview of the approach it takes to getting your brain fit. Tap Continue.

(3) Enter your email address. Tap Mail, and disable the reminder.

(4) Tap Get Started.

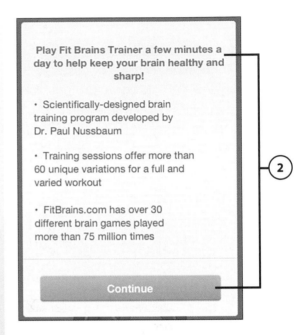

Play Fit Brains Trainer a few minutes a day to help keep your brain healthy and sharp!

• Scientifically-designed brain training program developed by Dr. Paul Nussbaum

• Training sessions offer more than 60 unique variations for a full and varied workout

• FitBrains.com has over 30 different brain games played more than 75 million times

Continue

(2)

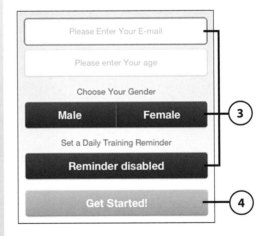

Please Enter Your E-mail

Please enter Your age

Choose Your Gender

Male   Female

(3)

Set a Daily Training Reminder

Reminder disabled

Get Started!   (4)

5 The first training session relates to brain speed. The object is to tap the number that represents the number of blocks in a pattern. Tap Start Training to dive right in.

Ready, Set, Go!

Be sure you read and understand the purpose of the task prior to diving in. There's no time to figure out what you should be doing…only time to do it! Don't worry if you make mistakes. You can always repeat the game or task to improve your score.

6 The games begin with a countdown, 5-4-3-2-1…immediately increasing my anxiety. (It was so quick that I couldn't capture the image to show you.) Then, the training begins. It's a timed training, so the more you do get right within the time limit, the better your score. For the first game, you count the blocks and tap the correct number at the bottom. I counted 3 and tapped 3. BING, I get a check mark for being correct!

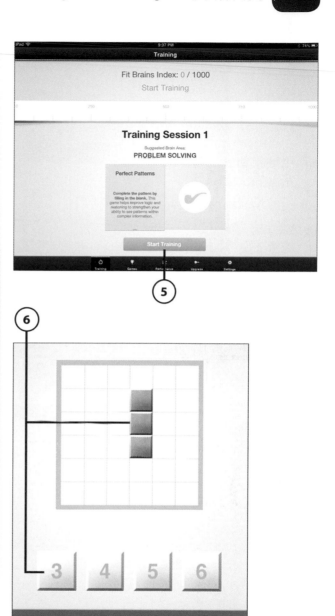

7 Immediately more blocks come up with more numbers; only now the numbers are in a different order. This goes on for probably a minute, and at the end there is the sound of a clock ticking that indicates I am running out of time.

8 After the session is complete, you get instant feedback on how you did relating to time and accuracy. So, the faster and the more accurate you are, the more fit your brain is. It's not enough to be accurate or fast, you need to be accurate AND fast!

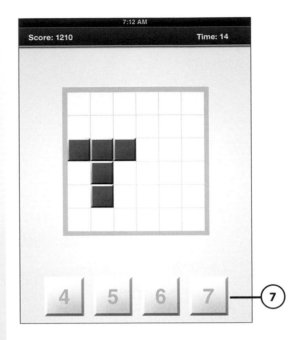

(9) After I trained for a while in a number of different areas, I was provided a summary of my progress in the areas of concentration, problem solving, memory, visual, and speed.

(10) Then the Fit Brain Trainer gave me a Fit Brain Index of 147/1000; oops, maybe not quite as fit as I thought?

I found the Fit Brain Trainer an interesting App that will surely enhance my brain fitness as I work on the challenges. It's actually fun and enables you to track your progress daily. There are options to upgrade to a paid version that may be of interest as I continue my training. It is clearly worth a look. Remember, it's not where you start that counts, it's where you end up.

Using the Fooducate - Diet Tracker & Healthy Food Nutrition Scanner

With the huge variety of food items available at your local grocery store and some, presumably, that would not be so good for you, an app like Fooducate is essential. Using this App, you can determine a great deal of information about what you put in your mouth. Simply point your iPad's camera at the bar code to get nutritional and other information about the product. The Fooducate app is a great way to get up to speed with ways to positively affect your well-being through the food choices you make.

1 Open the App Store and type **Fooducate - Diet Tracker & Healthy Food Nutrition Scanner**. Make sure you have iPhone apps tapped at the top of the App Store screen because this app does not have an iPad version. Tap FREE and then tap Install to download the app. Tap OPEN. Tap the 2X button in the lower-right corner to make the app iPad size.

2 Tap the I agree to the terms of use box, and then tap Agree.

3 Tap Create an Account. Fill in the required fields. (Your ZIP code isn't required.) Fooducate sends an email confirming the successful account creation and a link to click to activate the new account. This email link is valid for only 7 days, so if you do not use it before it expires, you have to return to this page and create an account again.

4 After completing the preliminary information, tap Let's get started to provide more goal-specific details and begin to track your progress.

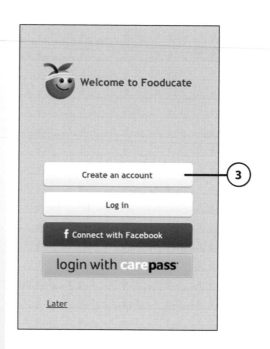

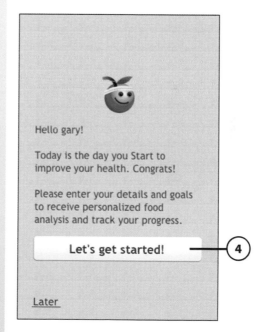

5 There are seven steps to complete the personal profile. Tap Next at the top right of the screen to proceed to the next step in the process.

6 After you complete the personal profile, a screen appears that tracks your progress. The screen has three options: a built in scanner, a place to track your progress, and a section to browse a wide variety of food categories and specific items. (The developers of this app have clearly done their homework.)

7 For this task, I tapped Scan.

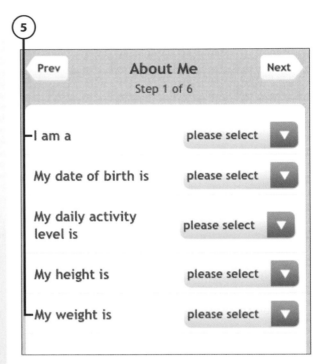

5

Prev	About Me	Next
	Step 1 of 6	

I am a — please select ▼

My date of birth is — please select ▼

My daily activity level is — please select ▼

My height is — please select ▼

My weight is — please select ▼

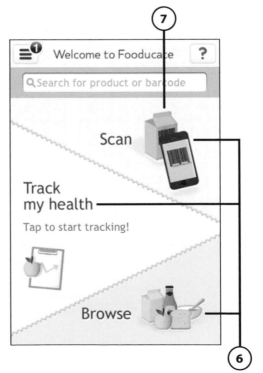

7

≡ Welcome to Fooducate   ?

🔍 Search for product or barcode

Scan

Track my health

Tap to start tracking!

Browse

6

(8) I went to the fridge with my trusty iPad and pulled out a container of Chobani pineapple yogurt (my favorite). After I got the barcode centered between the lines of the camera screen, almost like magic all the information about my yogurt came on the screen.

(9) My Chobani yogurt rates a B+ in my personalized grade, not bad.

(10) Each container has 160 calories.

(11) The positives for the item are listed including low cholesterol, low sodium and heart healthy.

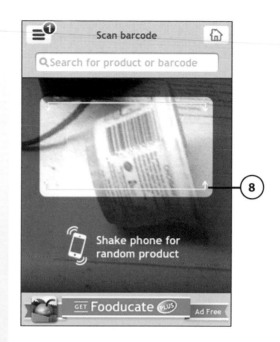

Well, that's where the good news ended. My pineapple yogurt appears to contain 4.5 teaspoons of sugar per serving. I can no longer delude myself into thinking it was totally healthy. Great information to know the next time I go to the fridge looking for a snack!

The app goes on to track several different forms of exercise and calculates the calorie burn of each, subtracting that from your accumulated calories for each day. This enables you to be far more involved with what you put in your body and how it affects your goals for better health.

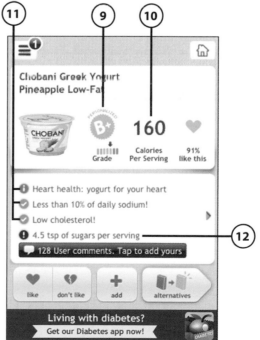

Getting Medical Information from WebMD for iPad

There are thousands of medical related apps that you can access via your iPad. For this task, I chose to take a look at WebMD for iPad. At the time of this writing, there were more than 1,700 users who rated it 4/5 stars. (I always check the feedback from other users before installing an app and certainly prior to buying one.) This app has a great deal of information and it's free!

1. Open the App Store and type **WebMD for iPad** in the Search field. Tap FREE and then tap Install to download the app. Tap OPEN.

2. The first time you open the app, you see a notice about the privacy policy. Review this information, and then tap OK.

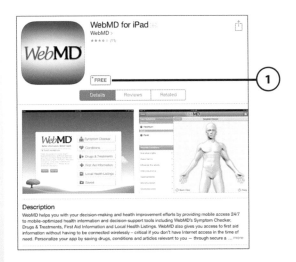

(3) The Home Page offers several options to explore, from Symptom Checker to Local Health Listings, to items you choose to save after you sign up and create a profile. Yes, you can individualize WebMD to meet your needs.

(4) Tap Symptom Checker.

(5) The first time you use the app, you see a How to Get Started screen. Review the instructions, and then click OK.

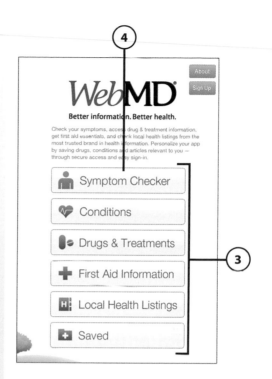

WebMD
Better information. Better health.

Check your symptoms, access drug & treatment information, get first aid essentials, and check local health listings from the most trusted brand in health information. Personalize your app by saving drugs, conditions and articles relevant to you — through secure access and easy sign-in.

- Symptom Checker
- Conditions
- Drugs & Treatments
- First Aid Information
- Local Health Listings
- Saved

How to Get Started

1. **Profile:** Click Profile to set or edit your personal information.

2. **Symptoms:** Click the Body where you have symptoms. Pinch/spread to zoom in & out.

3. **Conditions:** Possible conditions automatically appear to the left. Click one to learn more.

4. **List View:** Click List View to quickly access general & skin related symptoms.

OK

6 The next screen is a drawing of the front view of a body that can be tapped anywhere you might have a medical issue you want to explore.

7 Tap a body part. I tapped the head. A long list of issues with the head popped up. You can swipe up and down in the list to see more of the list. You can also be more specific by tapping the cheek, the jaw and other specific parts of the head to narrow the results.

8 Tap Back View to find issues related to that part of the body.

9 Tap List View to search the lists for your ailment. Each general category leads to a more specific place, such as nose or sternum. After you pin down the specific area, a list of potential symptoms appears. You can tap the symptom to further narrow your search until you receive a potential diagnosis.

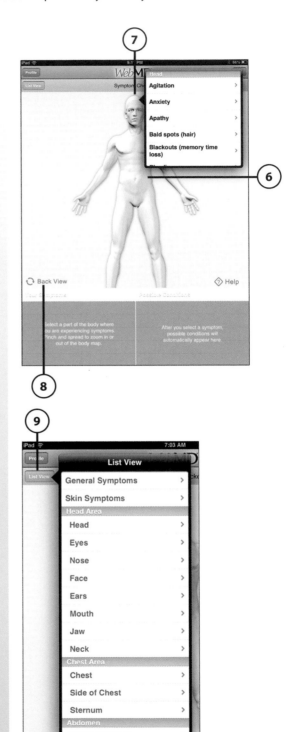

10 You can take the same approach for Conditions, Drugs & Treatments, First Aid Information, and Local Health Listings. Tap the home icon in the upper-right corner (image of a house), and then tap First Aid. A notice to call 911 if you are having an emergency is shown along with another How to Get Started List. Tap First Aid List in the upper-left corner. A long, scrollable list containing the top searches in First Aid opens.

11 Tap View All to see all the First Aid topics. Clearly this is an extensive list.

12 Tap the home icon again, and then tap Local Health Listings. If you have not allowed the WebMD app to use your location (by typing your ZIP code into your Profile) you are asked to allow it now. Tap OK to allow.

13 The Local Health Listings page enables you to search for a doctor, a hospital, or a pharmacy in your area. Tap Hospital to see stick pins indicating hospitals within a 25 mile area of where you are. Pinch the map to zoom into a location and narrow your search.

14 Tap Physician or Pharmacy for similar results.

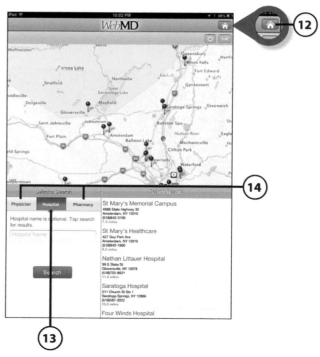

(15) In addition, you can tap Conditions or Drugs and Treatment to search some fairly in-depth information in those areas. First, you see the Get Started screen with directions on how to proceed.

(16) In the upper-left corner tap the Conditions list to see a scrollable list of conditions that can be researched. The same process can be followed for Drugs and Treatments

Walking with Map My Walk - GPS Pedometer for Walking or Jogging

I've always enjoyed the thought of taking a leisurely stroll through a wooded park with my favorite book in hand, stopping at a park bench to relax and read a few pages and listen to the birds chirping. Well, now through the magic of your iPad, you can not only carry your book, but you also can track your walk and calculate the distance, the time, and the positive effects on your health. In addition, you can load "walk specific" music via this app. Remarkable indeed!

(1) Open the App Store and type **Walk with Map my Walk-GPS Pedometer for Walking, Jogging** into the Search Store field. This one is also an iPhone app, so be sure you have tapped iPhone apps at the top of the Store screen or you won't find the app. Tap FREE and then tap Install to download the app. Tap OPEN.

Free Versus Paid

Some apps, such as this one, offer both a free version and one that costs money. This is a common practice among app developers. They offer you some basic features of their app with the hope that you will like it so much you will be willing to pay later for additional features as an "upgrade" to a plus or pro version of the app. Be sure you choose the Free version for any apps you aren't sure you want to keep. It's a great way to test an app before paying for it.

(2) The opening screen requires you to sign up for Map my Walk. My personal preference is to sign up manually, so tap that. The sign-up is easy, asking only for an email address, a name, a birth date, a gender, and a password, which you create.

(3) After signing up, you are transported to a tour of the app. This
is helpful to learn all the aspects
of this app. Tap Skip the tour if
you aren't interested in going
through it.

(4) Tap the 2x button in the lower-
right corner to resize the screen
to fit your iPad.

(5) I chose to go directly to the app
after reviewing the tour by tapping Get Started at the bottom
of the last page of the tour. The
other option, Go MVP, takes you
to an ad page for other, more
advanced apps.

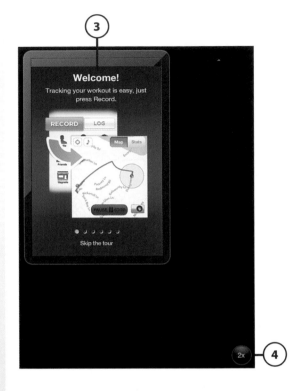

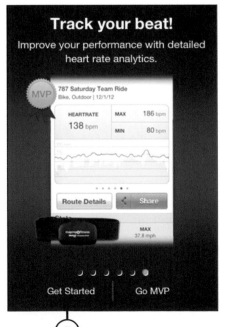

6 After establishing a profile, the app saves your routes and workouts.

7 You can also track your calorie consumption.

8 I decided to give this a try by taking our dog Bubba for a walk. I tapped Record to get started.

9 The workout start provides many choices of activities from walk to sprints, touring bike, and many more. I chose Walk, and this was a new route, so I left the route category as New.

10 The Coaching and Live Tracking (allowing friends to track us "live") options I chose to leave off because they require the advanced, paid app. However, tapping the music option enables you to choose songs from your iTunes library to listen to during your walk.

11 I also chose not to post my walk to Facebook or Twitter. That's a little too much information sharing for my taste at this time. If you like to share that kind of information on Facebook or Twitter, turn them on.

12 Tap Start.

(13) My walk consisted of a treat for Bubba, and then a stop and start stroll around a street near our house. Bubba insists on a treat prior to every walk.

(14) Upon completion of my walk, I tapped End Walk and looked at my progress.

(15) As you can see, we took several side jaunts as Bubba had to sniff everything in sight.

(16) I walked for 7:16 minutes, a distance of .76 miles at a pace of 9.32 minutes/mile. In addition, the stats indicated that I burned 185 calories.

Map My Walk is a great App to maintain a log of your workouts even if it seems like all you are doing is walking your dog. This is definitely worth checking out.

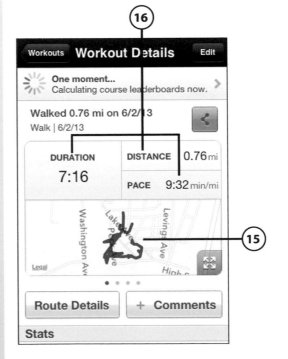

Search your area or the world for great bargains.

Use Ebay to find most anything you might be looking for.

Use Amazon Mobile to make purchases on your iPad.

Access thousands of coupons using the Coupons app.

The YP (Yellow Pages) help you find the best price for gas and other things in your area.

In this chapter you look at apps that can enhance your daily living experiences. These apps include

→ Using Amazon, Craigslist, and eBay to enhance online purchasing opportunities
→ Utilizing the coupons app to save money
→ Using an app to find the best prices on gasoline within your area

16

Using Apps to Enhance Your Life

There are hundreds of thousands of apps. It seems that there are apps for almost everything. When I was considering buying my iPad, I went to my local Apple store early one morning to look around, ask questions, and try out this amazing machine. Standing next to me was a 70ish man in overalls with large, calloused hands. He was holding an iPad, looking it over carefully and obviously pondering something.

I asked him how he planned to use his iPad. He looked at me and said, "I've been a farmer for 50 years. My neighbor feeds his chickens using one of these. I'm going to get one and feed my chickens from my living room!" Well, needless to say, a whole new world of uses for the iPad came to mind that day. Although I've never found the chicken-feeding app, I'm sure that there are apps that can make this farmer's life a bit easier.

Shopping on the iPad Using Amazon Mobile

Although I am definitely an advocate of supporting local merchants, there is also something beneficial about the concept of smart shopping. Amazon has changed the face of shopping forever. You can now buy almost anything from the comfort of your living room and, in most cases, have it shipped for free. So, before you run out to make that big purchase, it makes sense to take a look at Amazon Mobile, if for no other reason than to see what the competition charges. It's also nice to have whatever you purchase delivered to your door. This can also be a huge help to those who find it difficult to leave their homes to shop.

(1) Open the App Store, and type **Amazon Mobile** in the Search field. Tap FREE and then tap install to download the app. Tap OPEN.

(**2**) The ever-changing Amazon home page comes up with items that might peak your interest. It does a good job suggesting products, and I often tap an item to take a closer look.

(**3**) Tap Sign in.

(**4**) Enter your Amazon login info, or tap Create Account if you do not have an account already.

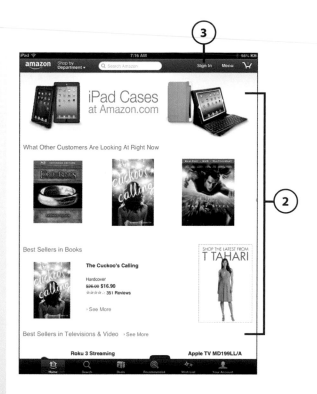

5 Tap in the Search field and type the name or description of the item you are searching for.

6 Tap the Search button on the keyboard.

7 The Search Suggestions list enables you to refine your search, if you choose.

8 Along the left side of the screen, you see a long, scrollable list of items that match your search criteria. Tap an item you are interested in.

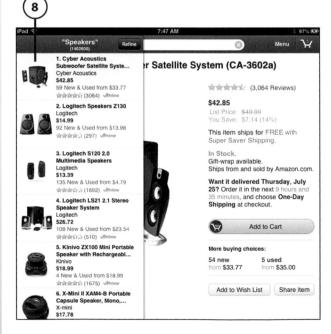

9 The details of that item are shown, including the reviews, rating, price, and whether it is currently in stock. There are other options that you can use if you are logged in to your Amazon.com account, including Add to Wish List and Share Item.

10 Making purchases on Amazon Mobile is almost too easy. Simply tap Add to Cart, and immediately the item is added to your shopping cart. You can proceed to check out or continue shopping.

11 Tap Deals to see Amazon's Deals of the Day.

12 You can swipe the Lightening Deals and Best Deals sections to see more, or tap See More to expand those sections.

13 Tap Your Account.

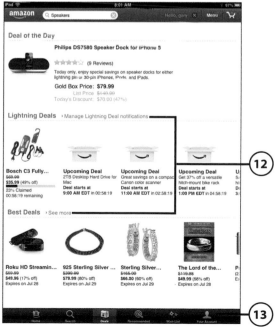

(14) The Your Account button brings up a page that enables you to track your orders or personalize a number of account settings.

(15) Recommended is determined by searching/buying patterns, and Wish List shows anything you've saved to a Wish List on your account (whether on a mobile or browser version).

(16) Tap Cart

(17) You can now either alter your purchase by saving it for later or deleting it.

(18) You can also choose to make the purchase by tapping Checkout.

(19) You can log out by tapping the x next to your name.

The Amazon app is easy to use—not many bells and whistles, just thousands of products for you to search, learn about, and in many cases, buy. This is a must-have app for any online shopper.

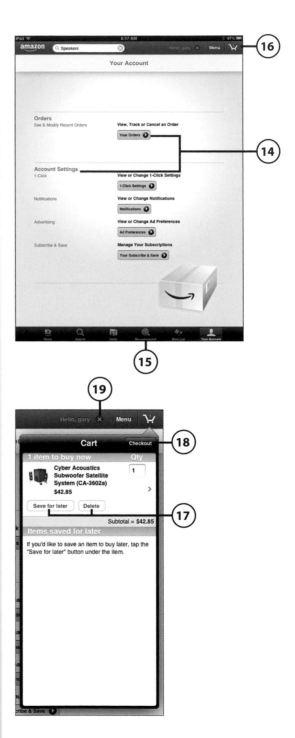

Finding Deals Using the Craigslist App

A Guy named Craig Newmark created Craigslist in 1995 as an email distribution list among friends in the San Francisco Bay area. Since then, it has evolved to cover 50 countries worldwide. Craigslist is a forum where you can buy, sell, trade, find a job, find a relationship, have a discussion, post a personal message—just about anything you can find in a traditional classified ad, only far more. For anyone looking for almost anything, Craigslist is the place to go, and it's free!

(1) Open the App Store and type Craigslist for iPad in the Search field. Tap FREE and then tap Install to download the app. Tap OPEN. You are asked permission for Craigslist to use your present location; tap OK to see the Craigslist offerings in your area.

Choosing Locations Manually

If you prefer not to let this app know your location automatically, tap Don't Allow when you are asked about your location. After you open the app, tap Choose Locations, and you can set some specific locations for which you want to see listings. That way, the app doesn't "follow" your location wherever you roam.

(2) When the app opens, you see the listings for your current location (or nearby). You can add other locations by tapping the arrow next to the location name and then tapping the plus sign. As you can see, you can use Craigslist worldwide.

(3) Listings are broken into categories that you can tap to yield advertisements within those categories. Swipe up and down the list to see additional categories. For this task, I swiped down the list and decided to tap education under the Jobs category.

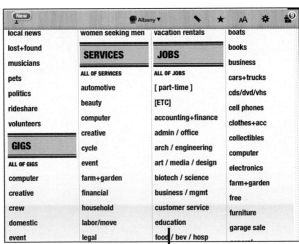

(4) When you find an ad you want to remember, simply draw a circle around it using your finger. (This takes a little practice.) This puts the ad into your favorite list, which you can access by tapping the star icon. When I saw a listing for a Roller Hocker Instructor I had to find out what that was, so I circled it. Then, to delve further, I tapped the ad.

(5) It turns out that this ad is looking for a Roller Hockey instructor for a summer program located in Starlight, PA.

(6) Tap the A**A** symbol to make the text on the screen bigger.

(7) Tap the little printer at the upper left to print the ad (if you have an AirPrint compatible printer).

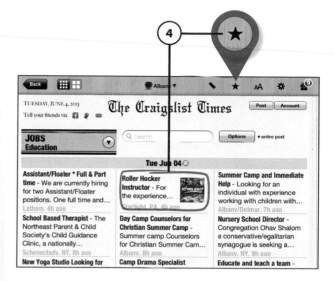

Printing from an iPad

You can print to a wireless printer as long as the printer is AirPrint-compatible. The documentation that came with your printer should tell you if it has this capability, or you can go to your printer manufacturer's website to find this information. You can also go to sites such as About.com and find lists of all kinds of AirPrint compatible printers.

---

(8) Tap the folding map symbol to see the exact location for the person or business who posted the ad.

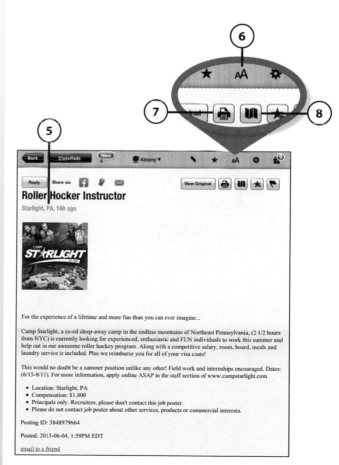

9 Tap the Reply button to send a response to the advertiser via email.

10 Tap Back to return to the previous page of listings.

11 Craigslist also provides a system for users to self-monitor the content found on the list. Tap the flag in the upper-right corner to provide options to flag an item as miscategorized, prohibited, spam/overpost, or Best of Craigslist. This system enlists the entire Craigslist community in making sure that inappropriate items are not posted or that great items are recognized.

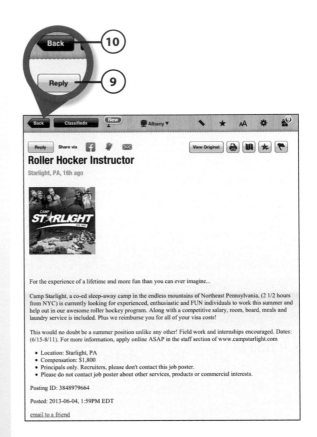

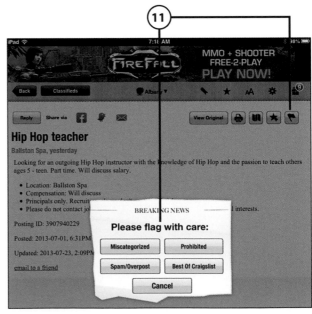

It's Not All Good

Play It Safe

Over the years scammers have learned how to use this amazing resource to take advantage of people. For example, if you find an apartment or house to rent that appears just too good to be true, it probably is. Scammers typically ask for a deposit upfront from several people to be considered as a potential renter and then take their money and run. Others have bought cars with bogus certified checks; the seller goes to cash the check, and it bounces, but the car is gone! It's clearly a buyer-beware situation; though the vast majority of Craigslist users are honest and simply use this service as they would a classified ad.

Bidding on eBay for iPad

In 1995, a software engineer created an auction website and listed a broken laser pointer for sale. Much to his surprise, the laser pointer sold for $14.83. He told the prospective buyer that is a BROKEN laser pointer and was told, "I collect broken laser pointers." That was the beginning of eBay, the Internet auction site where you can buy and sell almost anything.

(1) Open the App Store and type **eBay for iPad** into the Search field. Tap FREE and then tap Install to download the app. Tap OPEN.

(2) The first time you use the app, the opening screen asks you to agree to its Privacy and Terms of Use policies. Tap Agree to continue.

(3) If you have an eBay account, tap Sign In, and enter your user ID and password. If you do not have an account and you want to create one, skip to step 4.

(4) If you don't have an account and just want to browse the items that are listed, tap Not Now. You can browse items, but to bid on something, you need to have an account.

5) To create an eBay account and a handle (the name that you will be known by on eBay), tap Sign In, and then tap Create Account. A Registration page opens where you can fill in your relevant information and then create your eBay username and create your account.

6) The first time you open the eBay app, you see a screen showing some tips for how to navigate the different parts of the app. Tap it to continue.

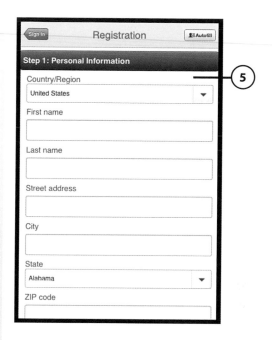

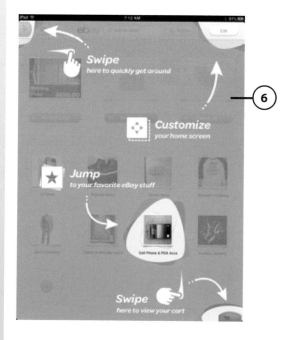

7 The eBay home page contains three main categories: Watching, Buying, and Selling. If you find an item you are interested in, you can watch it to see the price it brings at auction. If you are bidding on something, the Buying link shows those items, and if you are selling, you can track the bidding on the item you are selling via the Selling link. These sections of the site are only available if you are signed in. If not, you can only browse the listings.

8 Tap in the Search eBay field at the top of the screen.

9 If you are signed in, the app remembers previous searches as well as sellers that you have chosen to save. They are listed giving you the option to tap one to return to that search.

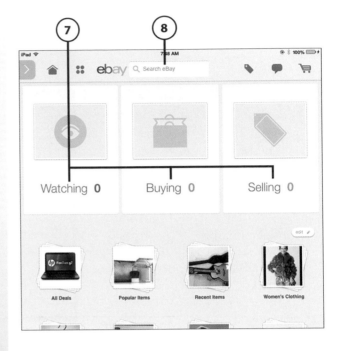

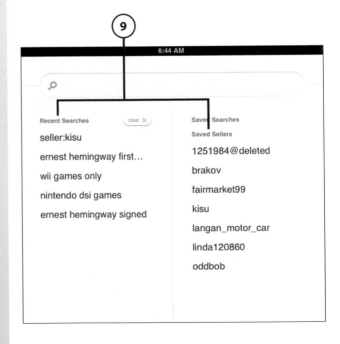

10 For this task, I typed **acoustic guitars** in the search field.

11 At the time of my search for acoustic guitars, there were 44,347 guitars for sale.

12 To find more information on any of the individual items, tap the photo. I tapped a Guild guitar to look further into the listing.

13 In addition to a description, see that the bidding is up to $380.

14 There are four bids thus far, and six hours and 24 minutes remaining in the auction.

15 In this case, shipping options are only in the United States.

16 To place a bid, tap Place Bid.

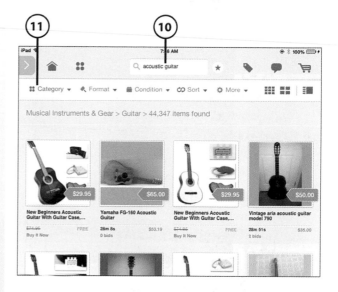

17 A bidding screen opens for you to enter your maximum bid. This means that you are willing to pay up to that amount. In reality, you may get the item for much less if everyone stops bidding against you. There is often a flurry of bidding in the last few seconds of an auction.

18 After you have entered your maximum bid, tap Place Bid. You are now obligated to buy this item if you are the winning bidder. There's no changing your mind at this point.

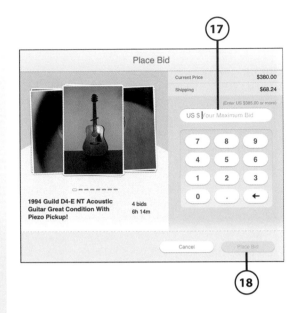

After winning an auction on eBay, you are given the seller's contact information, and the seller is given yours. You will contact the seller and make payment arrangements, and the seller will ship the item to you. Be sure to leave feedback for the seller after you receive your item.

The Coupons App

Collecting coupons has been a way of saving money for as long as I can remember. My mother used to have a handful of carefully clipped coupons with her every time she went to the grocery store. She would announce with great pride that she had saved $3.26 on this week's grocery bill by virtue of her careful couponing. Now, with your iPad, you can collect coupons much more easily. My Mom would be thrilled!

(**1**) Open the App Store, and type **The Coupons App** in the Search field; Tap FREE and then tap Install to download the app. Tap OPEN.

(**2**) To see coupons in your local area tap OK to allow the app access to your current location.

(**3**) Tap No Thanks or Sign Up on the opening page offering deals from "partner" companies. I tapped No thanks to avoid unsolicited emails.

4 The first set of coupons listed was from a number of chain stores such as KFC and Bath and Body Works.

5 Tap Show ALL Coupons.

6 The All Coupons page brought up a long list of couponing opportunities. I tapped a coupon for Old Navy.

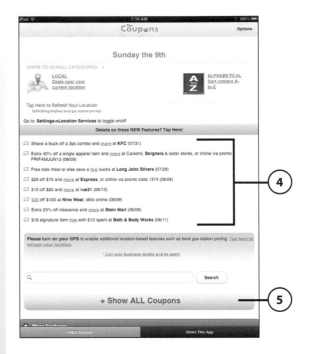

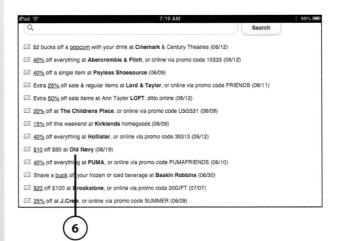

7 The Old Navy coupon is an in-store standard coupon that you can scan from your iPad or iPhone. No more scissors and trying to organize all those little pieces of paper.

8 Tap the X to return to the all coupons page.

9 Swipe right to left in the categories area at the top of the screen to see other ways to filter the coupons to see just what you want. For example, you can see coupons by expiration date or only coupons for food items. You have to unlock these features first by tapping the FREE Unlock! button at the bottom of the screen.

10 Tap the Options button in the upper-right corner to open the More Features area.

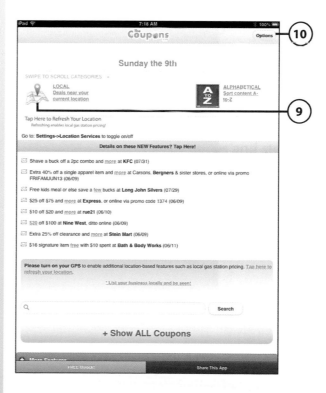

(11) At the bottom, tap Barcode Scanner Price Check to enable a barcode scanner that uses your iPad's camera.

After you focus on the product's barcode in the window, a listing appears showing you the best price found for that product and where you can get it.

(12) I scanned the copy of My iPad and found it on sale through Amazon.

Accessing More Features

This app offers some additional features (such as the alphabetical listing of coupons) that can be accessed only by tapping the FREE Unlock! button at the bottom of the screen. This opens a "sponsored" area in which you can see ads and other offers from various entities.

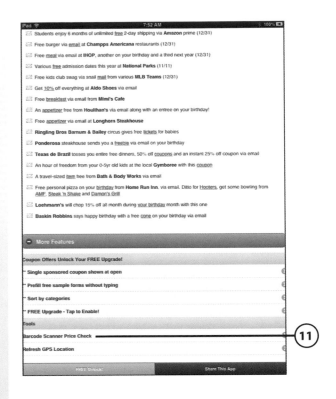

YP Local Search and Gas Prices for iPad

It seems that Apps tend to spring up whenever there is a need. As gasoline prices skyrocket, you now have a need to save as much as possible to operate your car. Many apps can help you search locally for gasoline at the best price. This task takes a look at Yellow Pages Search & Gas Prices. It is free and seems to do the job quite well.

(**1**) Open the App Store and type **YP Local Search and Gas Prices for iPad** in the Search field. Tap FREE and then tap Install to download the app. Tap OPEN.

(**2**) Tap Accept on the license agreement. For YP to search gas prices in your area, it needs to know your current location. Tap OK to allow access to your GPS location, or tap Don't Allow and you can manually enter your location in the app if you prefer.

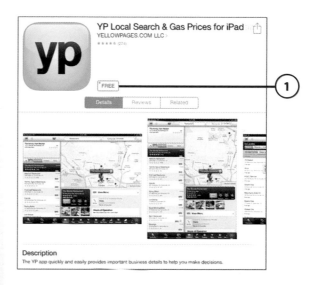

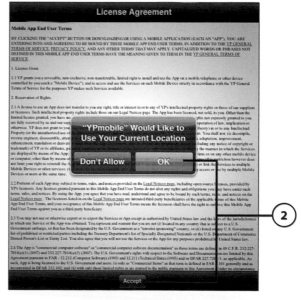

3 Tap Businesses or Deals to find offers in your area.

4 You can swipe through a list of subcategories to find a specific type of deal or business.

5 Tap Gas Prices to check out current local gas prices.

6 As you can see, the list along the left shows gasoline prices for all of the stations near your present location. With a 21-cent difference per gallon, it's clear where you should buy your gas. (My car holds 15 gallons of gas; that's $3.15 in my pocket and not the oil company's.)

7 The map area to the right shows the location of each station. Tap a price in the column on the left, or on the map itself, to see the address for that station.

8 To zoom in on that location, double-tap that price on the map, or you can unpinch your figures on the screen. To zoom back out, pinch your fingers together on the screen.

9 To add other subcategories to your search bar, tap the Edit button at the lower right.

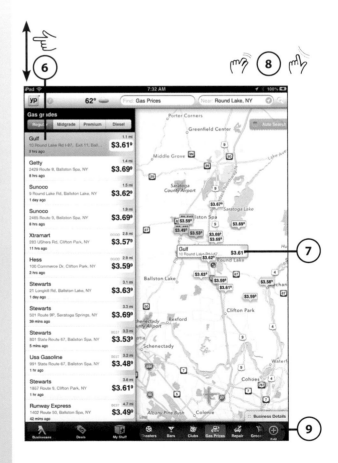

(10) Tap or drag the categories to or from the bar to customize the type of information you can search for in this app. Tap Done when you finish.

FIND MORE USEFUL APPS

>>>Go Further

Given the huge number of Apps and the fact that new ones are added daily, it is impossible to stay current with all of them. The goal in this chapter is to give you a peek at how to use apps to enhance your life. The following list suggests a few you might enjoy:

- **Hangouts**—A free app that enables you to video chat with more than one person at a time.

- **Maglight**—A free app that enables you to use your iPad camera as a magnifying glass.

- **Groupon**—A free app that offers you deals on goods and services in your area.

- **Wikipedia Mobile**—An encyclopedia app where you can find information on almost any question you have.

- **IMBd**—A database with show times, trailers, and filmographies for your favorite actors and actresses.

- **Mint**—An app from Intuit, the makers of Quicken and Turbo Tax that enables you to budget, track, and manage all your finances in one app.

- **Trulia and Zillow**—Real estate apps you should considering if you are moving to another location. These apps show houses for sale, homes recently sold, and estimates of property values.

- **Jumbo Calculator**—Your iPad does not arrive with a built-in calculator. This free app solves that problem.

- **Catalog Spree**—An app that enables you to view your favorite catalog, find what you want, and order it all without cluttering up your mailbox or having to recycle all that paper.

Index

D

E

F

P

U-V

X-Y-Z